Athlete-centred Coaching

Second Edition

For Lynn: To Izzy, welcome to the world!!

For Ben: To my assistant coaches, Angela, John and Susan who continue to support and inspire me.

Athlete-centred Coaching

Developing Decision Makers

Edited by Lynn Kidman and Bennett J. Lombardo

With guest authors Gareth Jones, Paul Cooper, Ian Renshaw,
Christian Edwards, Rick Humm

Second Edition

PRINT RESOURCES

First Published in 2005 by Innovative Print Communications Ltd

This edition published 2010 by
IPC Print Resources
(Formerly Innovative Print Communications Ltd)

29 Bevington Court
Crossley Road
Worcester, WR5 3GF UK

Website: www.ipcltd.com
Email: info@ipcltd.com

ISBN: 978-0-9565065-0-4

Editor: Tanya Tremewan

Printer: Prontaprint, Worcester

Cover design: Regina Morrison

Table of Contents

Preface

Athlete-centred Coaching: Developing decision makers is the second edition to *Athlete-centred Coaching: Developing inspired and inspiring people* (2005) and integrates the work of Ben Lombardo's *Humanistic Coaching* published in 1987. Our intention in combining our work is to offer further insight on how to enhance athlete learning and development through sport. We are extremely pleased to be adding the work of several more authors who have contributed to the essence of humanistic, athlete-centred coaching.

The book includes stories of successful coaches who hold athlete-centred philosophies. Some of these stories (Lyn Gunson, prior England and New Zealand netball coach; Mark Norton with the Riccarton High School Senior Boys' Volleyball team; and Don Tricker, coach of the New Zealand men's softball team, the Black Sox) featured in the first edition of *Athlete-centred Coaching*. For the second edition we have also included Mike Ruddock (Worcester Warriors rugby coach), Guy Evans (developing basketball coach at the University of Worcester), Greg Chappell (Centre for Excellence, Cricket Australia and Australian Institute of Sport) and Matt Powell (rugby player, turned coach). Although from a variety of backgrounds, all of the coaches featured in this book share similar goals in regard to long-term athlete learning and a quality team environment. All the coaches believe in sharing power with their athletes, enabling athletes to be effective decision makers through focusing on their motivation to participate to the best of their ability. As this book demonstrates, coaches who use such an athlete-centred approach inspire their athletes and enable a focus on athlete decision making in the competitions and about their team.

With an athlete-centred, humanistic approach, athletes take ownership of their learning, thus increasing their opportunities and strengthening their abilities to retain important skills and ideas. This learning also develops athletes' ability to make informed decisions during competitions, an important element in successful performance at any sporting level. It helps athletes to take a leadership role and ownership in enhancing the team culture.

Developing the material for this book involved an exciting project of interviewing and observing the range of coaches whose stories are told in the chapters that follow. In addition, we were excited and honoured to obtain for publication in this edition the stories of Mike Ruddock, Lyn Gunson, Don Tricker and Mark Norton. Another exciting addition is Christian Edwards' report on his action research project that followed and analysed Guy Evans in his efforts to move towards an athlete-centred approach to coaching. Matt Powell, who has just taken up a coaching role, provides additional helpful insights based on his experiences as a player in the senior leagues in England with a range of coaches over the years. All coaches and athletes quoted in this book graciously provide insights into their experiences of and perspectives on coaching.

The first chapter of this book defines athlete-centred, humanistic approaches to coaching, which have proved innovative and successful, and provides a brief synopsis of current coaching practices. It discusses athlete development (holistically), the educational intent of sport and the influence of adult-structured sports on athletes. The chapter also compares athlete-centred approaches with their polar opposite—coach-centred approaches—and discusses why coaches should consider using the former. Questioning, Teaching Games for Understanding (TGfU) and team culture are introduced as aspects that are important to enabling athletes to own and take responsibility for their learning. How to develop athlete-centred philosophies is discussed as well. The case studies of the coaches have a commonality that all want to develop athletes as people, not just as sport jocks.

In Chapter Two, we present a critical analysis of the athlete-centred approach. Issues and possible problems, along with contextual and personal–social constraints, are examined with the aim of presenting an objective, balanced view of our thesis. Our intent here is to alert readers to the possible roadblocks and negativity that may arise in relation to an athlete-centred approach, and to encourage them to persist in their efforts to transform the sport experience. In addition, we believe we provide convincing arguments for the viability of this approach to sport leadership.

Chapter Three encapsulates Mike Ruddock's coaching wisdom drawn from his many different experiences. Mike was coaching the Welsh rugby team when it won the Six Nations Grand Slam title for the first time in 27 years, and is now working with the Worcester Warriors. The athlete-centred approach is a notable feature of Mike's coaching approach, in which he focuses on enhancing the decision-making abilities of his players.

With a focus on Lyn Gunson, Chapter Four provides insight into many aspects of coaching as a complex, multi-dimensional role. It has been carried over from the first edition due to its insightfulness and analysis of athlete-centred coaching. After finishing her role as coach of the English netball team, Lyn has moved back to New Zealand to be a netball director and is doing some coaching work with the current national netball team. An athlete-centred coach, she believes that a group within a sports team is a community and develops a team culture based on the notion of community. Given her history of coaching of two national netball teams (New Zealand and England), she has a wealth of experience and knowledge to share.

The athlete-centred, humanistic approach needs some analysis from its athletes and Chapter Five provides Matt Powell's story. Matt shares his reflections on playing under a variety of coaches and on his initial experiences as a coach with the Worcester Warriors now that he has retired from playing.

Gareth Jones from the University of Worcester has authored Chapter Six on team culture. Currently completing a PhD on social loafing, he offers understanding of the importance of team culture in ensuring athletes work together towards a common goal. His seven steps to success introduce some key factors in the process of establishing a quality team culture.

In Chapter Seven, Paul Cooper reviews the current state of play as it relates to sport and coaching. As he sees it, society is now two or three generations removed from the true play experience. Specifically children from subsequent generations have developed into adults without truly knowing what it is to play without adult supervision and/or direction. Children have become so accustomed to being directed, supervised and told how, where and what to play that athlete decision making in sport has disappeared from the landscape. Paul's poignant analysis directs the reader to the game approach, which can encourage exploration, decision-making and self-discovery. He makes a case for an athlete-centred approach as an extension of the exploratory play paradigm and concludes that the games approach can nurture a more holistic and well-rounded approach to children's sport.

Chapter Eight features an innovative approach to skill acquisition as presented by Ian Renshaw of the Queensland University of Technology, with particular reference to his work with Greg Chappell from the Centre of Excellence. The constraints-led approach highlights the complex interplay of skill learning. To develop skill athletes require self-organisaiton using constraints as an aid. The approach also underpins TGfU, which facilitates an athlete's learning process by providing realistic sport situations in which to develop decision makers.

In Chapter Nine, Christian Edwards follows young basketball coach Guy Evans for a season while he learned more about leadership and athlete-centred basketball coaching. Together Christian and Guy highlight many of the challenges that face coaches who try to adopt an athlete-centred, humanistic approach with a group that has been socially constructed by the traditional, autocratic sporting environment. Christian's action research project provides some critique and insight while reflecting on Guy's coaching and efforts to change.

An action research project involving a case study of the Riccarton High School Senior Boys' Volleyball team is presented in Chapter Ten. Originally told in the first edition, Mark Norton's story has proven popular amongst readers. Mark focused on creating a quality team culture for the season in 2003–2004, accompanied by co-editor

Lynn acting as a player manager. The chapter recalls the story of the season and how focusing on team culture helped the team to meet its goals.

Don Tricker discusses his former coaching with the Black Sox and shares his philosophies in Chapter Eleven, another chapter reproduced from the first edition due to popular demand. Don is a legend for aiding the Black Sox to become three-peat world champions in men's softball. As an in-depth analyser of people and sport, he offers great insight for coaches to gain an understanding of how to be athlete-centred. His interesting chapter demonstrates how coaches need to be open to change and how the individuals in the team make the team work. Drawing from his business background, Don uses many analogies to demonstrate how people influence an organisation or team. He is now really enjoying his role as he coaches coaches for the New Zealand Academy of Sport.

In Chapter Twelve, guest author Rick Humm asks, 'How's your coaching?' He uses this question to analyse many aspects of coaching that we tend not to highlight in our coach education programmes—namely, emotional intelligence, self-awareness, self-management and self-reflection for coaches. Coming from a strong, traditional, directive coaching society like the USA, he encourages coaches to think about how they might change to suit the needs of the athletes. Using the athlete-centred, humanistic coaching approach, he challenges coaches to consider the more humanistic side to the development of both the athletes and themselves as coaches.

Earlier versions of Chapters Thirteen have appeared in both *Developing Decision Makers* and the first edition of *Athlete-centred Coaching*. One of the key components of an athlete-centred approach, including the strategy of TGfU, is that coaches ask questions that encourage athletes to be self-aware and learn about tactics and skills. Chapter Thirteen gives practical guidelines for planning and asking meaningful questions. The technique of questioning is addressed as well as the art of asking meaningful questions.

Lastly Chapter Fourteen summarises the key ideas discussed in this book for coaches who are interested in putting an athlete-centred approach into practice. Team culture is further discussed in relation to how coaches can explicitly work on establishing a great team environment. Part of implementation is self-reflective analysis, a tool that coaches can use to monitor their ongoing coaching. The purpose of the chapter, building on the momentum of the chapters before it, is to encourage coaches to start to use an athlete-centred approach, reflect on how they use it and continue to improve. At the end of this chapter, considerations for the future of athletes and coaching are posed for further reflection.

Acknowledgements

There are many people we would like to thank for their various contributions to *Athlete-centred Coaching: Developing decision makers*. This book would have been impossible without the constant critical discussion with the coaching students, both professionally and at the tertiary level. We thank them for their inquisitive minds and the challenges that enable coaches to be the best they can be.

We would like to express a special thanks to the coaches and athletes who feature in this book—namely Mike Ruddock, Lyn Gunson, Matt Powell, Guy Evans, Greg Chappell, Mark Norton and Don Tricker—who selflessly gave up their time to relate stories and share expertise about their coaching, competing and thinking. It is great to have a group of people whose mission is to return athletes to the real values that sport has to offer.

To Simon Kidman and Luke Russell, who drew on their experience with school sport: good luck with your future endeavours. As coaches, we need to listen to athletes better.

We want to acknowledge all the authors who contributed: Gareth Jones, Paul Cooper, Ian Renshaw, Christian Edwards and Rick Humm. We learned so much from their various understandings and knowledge.

To the University of Worcester and Rhode Island College, we thank you for supporting us, which enabled us to observe and interview the coaches and athletes and meet with each other.

Of course, this couldn't have been done without the editor Tanya Tremewan. She continues to amaze us in her ability to say things that make sense and make for enjoyable reading. Thanks Tanya for having such a great talent. You make it seem so easy.

For Lynn—to my husband Bobby, for his, the greatest support of them all.

For Ben—to Angela my devoted wife, and first team coach!

If I had one wish for my children, it would be that
each of them would reach for goals that have meaning
for them as individuals. - Lillian Carter, US nurse, first mother

People with character will find a way to win, those
without character will find a way to lose - Ashley Jones

Chapter One

Being Athlete-centred: the Humanistic Coach

Now that the term *athlete-centred* has become well-known in the work of coaching, it is timely to revisit the rationale enabling athletes to have ownership and responsibility for their sporting environment. Before beginning the main part of our story, however, we will identify some general features of the sporting environment that why we think help to justify the aim of moving further toward a humanistic approach to coaching sport.

First, most sport is not professional; it tends to be voluntary in nature and the experiences that athletes get as volunteers can make or break their experience in continuing sport for life. Because it is voluntary, most participants come to the sport of their own choosing. Yes, there are people who join because a significant other has coerced them, but generally they want to be there. By the same token, participants usually leave an experience of their own free will. There is much attention on research concerned with keeping athletes in sport, but the bottom line is that if the experience is not to their satisfaction, athletes will leave and find something else that is. Unfortunately leaving is just what the adult-structured sport of today's society encourages: athletes are leaving sport experiences in masses because of unpleasant experiences, or an experience that does not meet their needs (Roberts and Treasure, 1995).

Second, athletes participate for many reasons. Although the majority of the reasons relate to enjoyment and satisfaction, each athlete has multiple motives of which coaches need to be aware (Weinberg and Gould, 2007).

Building on these observations and in response to the concerns about athletes leaving sport, we propose that certain aspects in sport appeal intrinsically to athletes and will keep them in sport. Someone who leaves one particular sport to join another sport or activity is not a drop-out. To the contrary, if they are staying in sport it is fantastic. What we are afraid of is losing people from lifelong activity of any kind.

Third, all participants develop in many ways and at many levels as a result of the sport experience, regardless of the specific manner in which the programme is administered. The importance of growth and development of individuals—physically, cognitively, psychologically, socially and spiritually—cannot be underestimated. Athletes learn about themselves, others and their world as a result of their involvement with sport. They learn verbally and non-verbally, and from hidden messages given in the sport context. Such growth and development accrue as a result of direct contact with people and encounters with various situations, regardless of exactly how the coach behaves or what the nature of the sport environment is. An athlete's interaction with any given environment always brings about change (i.e. learning). It is safe to state that an endeavour so meaningful and so profound to so many will lead to many important, albeit often personal discoveries.

It is not suggested, however, that all participants discover and/or learn the same things. The specific nature of the revelations and learnings will vary, paralleling the uniqueness of each participant and reflecting the individual's personal encounter with sport.

The final characteristic of sport to which we would like to draw attention is that the sport experience has educational intent. Coaches help athletes to learn and perform better, yet to do so athletes must undergo a great deal of personal development and deepen their understanding of how people learn and develop. In many sport environments these educational purposes are put in formal frameworks and publicly displayed and promoted. These frameworks serve to guide the leaders within the sport environment. In other, less formal programmes, the belief in a wide-ranging educational purpose is assumed yet often is not put into practice. Increased motor proficiency, physical development, and strategic sport knowledge are areas that most programmes tend to explicitly focus on in their intention for growth and development, but these areas only contribute to sport development. If we want to develop people who are self-aware, the more idealistic sport environments might focus on and actively promote additional valuable outcomes such as social relationships, moral integrity, sportsmanship and respect for others. The trend in coach development now is to look at the athlete in a holistic manner and, in so doing, develop the 'sports coach as an educator' (Jones, 2006).

Indeed, if the sport experience has an educational intent, coaches are responsible for enabling athletes to learn, which makes coaching a dynamic and extremely complex process. Like other learners, athletes develop understanding and learn more effectively when they are involved in solving problems and have ownership and responsibility for their learning. Important tools in the learning process are to develop new ideas, knowledge and the ability to make decisions. If leaders merely present knowledge (sometimes quite forcefully) to those who are 'non-expert' and make decisions for them, the athletes become disempowered. In other words, if athletes' needs do not influence their learning experiences, learning is minimal. The knowledge, understanding, skill and decision-making ability that athletes learn and apply can make the difference between performance success and failure as well as developing a long-term or lifetime attachment to movement.

Developing athletes' abilities in knowledge, understanding, skill and decision-making makes up the four goals of the sport experience, each of which can be well supported humanistically using an athlete-centred approach. When coaches use a humanistic approach to coaching—or, to use the term preferred in this book, follow an athlete-centred approach—athletes gain and take ownership of knowledge, development and decision making that will help them to maximise their performance and their enjoyment. This athlete-centred approach provides athletes with a chance to be part of the decision-making process that is involved in the organisation and performance of sports teams. Indeed, it moves athletes closer to a 'central' position in this profound set of experiences.

As the approach to coaching we are advocating, then, *athlete-centred* or *humanistic coaching* has many meanings. For this chapter, after an outline of the current practice of coaches, athlete development is addressed and then an athlete-centred approach is defined and discussed in the sporting context. Also introduced are practices that coaches use as part of their athlete-centred approach, including three main practices that are highlighted in some form by all coaches and athletes in this book: Teaching Games for Understanding (see also Chapter Eight), questioning (see also Chapter Thirteen) and team culture (see also Chapter Six). Then key characteristics of an athlete with ownership and responsibility are identified before the final discussion on how to create an athlete-centred philosophy. In the ensuing chapters, coaches and athletes discuss and provide illustrations of ways in which an athlete-centred approach can be put into practice and the constraints that they have met in doing that.

Current Coaching Practices

There appears to be general support for the view that sport is an important institution of modern society that carries considerable weight. The institution of sport, reflecting as it does society's beliefs, values and norms, has the potential to significantly influence participants in all of these areas. It has been pertinent, then, to review the potential benefits that are often attributed to participation in sport, particularly those related to personal growth and development. The common view seems to be that these benefits are obvious and already have been established as a result of athletes' involvement in sport. Indeed it is the great potential that sport has to offer that really forms the basis to this book: that is, we are exploring effective ways in which coaches can enable athletes to develop and learn according to their needs and desires.

Unfortunately, in too many cases, little proof of the benefits of sport has emerged. In the current environment the actual behaviour of coaches in the field is all too often based on goals thought to be more closely related to winning and motor proficiency. When winning is the only focus, the development of the individuals involved tends to diminish. Winning is one of the major reasons we compete, but the opportunities for winning and especially learning are minimal when the process of development is not the focus.

To maximise athlete development and performance, coaches, like leaders of formal organisations, combine the power of their position with a particular leadership style. Although coaching today encompasses a wide variety of approaches, the traditional leadership style has given coaches a licence to 'exploit' their power by taking the choice and control away from the athlete, especially when winning is the only focus. When a coach takes total control and athletes have basically no say, the approach is *coach-centred*. This approach tends to be prescriptive. Sometimes it has been identified, mistakenly, as an important element in coaching success.

A coach-centred coach endeavours to control athlete behaviour not only throughout training and competition, but also beyond the sport setting. This kind of coach espouses all knowledge to athletes and actually disempowers the athlete by taking total ownership of the team. A coach-centred coach tends to coach athletes as if they are on a factory assembly line. Athletes of a coach-centred coach are often 'hooked' into a limited form of learning that emphasises memorising, mimicking or aping rather than understanding or solving problems. This limited approach encourages athletes to be robotic in their actions and thinking. They do not experience themselves as having an active role in contributing to or being a part of their learning.

In the professional arena, the performance objectives of many coaches depend on winning. The expectation is that coaches may be held accountable for many uncertainties beyond their control (e.g. injuries, exceptional play by the opposition, poor officiating, the weather). In reacting to this pressure on them, coaches can give athletes extraordinarily gruelling training sessions that demand more than the athletes can give; sometimes they use dehumanising practices to enforce their control (Pratt and Eitzen, 1989). Unfortunately the pressure in this professional 'must-win' environment becomes so great that coaches like these 'take over' in an attempt to ensure their athletes are winning. The directions become coach-centred, rather than mutually identified and recognised by both the athletes and the coach.

This disempowering form of coach control actually contradicts why many athletes participate in sport. A coach-centred approach can have detrimental effects on athletes who are controlled. The coach can also suffer when the athletes reject such control. In these controlling situations the benefits of winning can be limited. If a team is winning, the athletes smile, but if a team loses or tires of being bossed around, generally the team environment deteriorates. As the coaches in this book suggest, once the team environment deteriorates, it is difficult to win. Winning and success are difficult to achieve without quality team culture.

On the other hand, if athletes truly learn and take ownership of the direction of the team or competition, success is more likely. From the athletes' point of view, *success* is rarely defined solely as winning; it usually involves achieving their goals. A coach-centred coach often does not attempt to understand and makes mistaken assumptions about what athletes need (to win) and seldom determines why athletes participate in sport. Conversely, as part of an athlete-centred approach, one of the coach's first roles is to determine the reasons why each athlete is participating, and to establish a mutual vision and direction for the season that both the athletes and the coach own.

As the above discussion indicates, the opposite of athlete-centred is coach-centred, just as the opposite of empowerment is disempowerment. The traditional coach-centred approach disempowers athletes, yet it is still prevalent in many sport teams. Under this coaching style, reading the game is largely a prescription from the coach (like playing a chess game). Yet this kind of coach-centred coach often fails to realise that the competition itself can be a learning experience that encourages athletes to understand and choose options based on informed decisions. The need for an athlete-centred approach is obvious in many sports throughout the world—specifically, those sports that involve long periods when the coach is not directly involved in making decisions on the field and has limited opportunity to communicate with the athletes. More broadly, in every sport informed decisions by athletes are essential to performance success, as in every sport it is the athlete who competes, not the coach.

When coaching tactics and skills at training sessions, coach-centred coaches traditionally tend to give athletes specific directions on what to 'fix' or the exact moves to perform. In some cases, coaches believe that unless they are seen to be telling athletes what to do and how to do it, they are not doing their job properly. Coach-centred coaches believe that they are expected to win and that successful coaches are (and should be) hard-nosed and discipline-oriented. Others (athlete-centred coaches) view their role as promoting enjoyment and personal development, as being supportive and empowering.

Much of the research suggests that no matter what coaching style is used, athletes respond better to supportive coaches than to punitive coaches (Smoll and Smith, 1989). Ironically, coaches who follow the coach-centred approach often express concerns related to low athlete productivity, poor performance quality and lack of motivation and commitment by athletes (Usher, 1997). In contrast, athletes with supportive coaches show greater intrinsic motivation, enjoy participating and competing in sport, make informed decisions more rapidly in the ever-changing tactical manoeuvres and demonstrate that trust is mutual (player–player, player–coach, coach–player, coach–coach).

Although a coach-centred approach is necessary in some instances, traditional coaches can abuse their influence. Coaches hold the 'power' within a team and this status leads to an unquestioned acceptance of a coach's leadership style among athletes and significant others (parents, administrators, public). In this environment coaches do not and cannot listen to their athletes, as they believe that if they listen they will be perceived as losing their 'power'. Loss of face equals loss of power in many coaches' eyes. Such an environment ensures that coaches do what they want regardless of the personal and collective needs of the athletes. Coach-centred coaches make many assumptions about athletes. For example, they may assume that because athletes are participating, they want to be champions and they will pay the price required to achieve this end. Often teams with this style of coaching have short-term success at the beginning of the season, but start floundering later in the season as they continue to be unable to make decisions, especially as the competition heightens and the need for faster and more frequent decision making increases.

A very different pattern may be evident with teams coached using athlete-centred principles. Wayne Smith (International rugby coach) agrees that if teams can keep their cool, react to what they see, talk and guts it out and be relentless, they can get to the top every time. Wayne suggests that teams with an athlete-centred approach tend to be:

> ... middling to fair earlier, but as athletes are developing a team culture, developing a way of learning, they are actually going to be more knowledgeable and understand the game better as the season progresses.

In the changing world of sport, the coach-centred approach has been rightly challenged. This book argues that a coach-centred coaching approach takes success away from the athlete and emphasises the coach's total domination of his or her sporting teams (and/or individual athletes). The coach-centred approach also emphasises a very narrow definition of winning and success. The information here supports and encourages a humanistic, athlete-centred coaching approach. It is one of the most innovative and effective approaches to coaching, enabling athletes to succeed in and enjoy their sporting participation. Through it, athletes can create something significant and perhaps different from current practices within their sport. Athletes and teams can lead the way by using innovative ideas to make the game or competition more exciting. In the humanistic process coaches and athletes work for similar purposes within a motivating environment. An athlete-centred approach helps to motivate athletes and gives them a sense of satisfaction in being part of a common vision so the 'team' can grow in the same direction and individuals can grow and develop.

Humanism and Athlete Development

This section outlines how participation in sport is assumed to contribute to individual growth and development under five domains: physical, cognitive, psychological, social and spiritual. Against this background it is possible to identify the goals and potential contributions of humanistic, athlete-centred coaching, as proposed in this book. This information should facilitate the process of determining how and to what extent the humanisation of sport can contribute to the individual involved.

Physical Benefits

It is assumed that the physical capabilities of the athlete in any given sporting environment will be improved. Improved strength, muscular endurance, flexibility, cardiovascular efficiency and neuromuscular functioning are expected outcomes of regular participation in sport activities.

As a result of involvement in sport, it is anticipated that the individual's physiological status will be improved. Participation in sport can help to develop physical fitness. Sports participants may improve in one or more of the components of physical fitness as they strive to improve their performance in a particular sport. Physical fitness is often enhanced, at least temporarily (i.e. for the duration of the specific sport season and depending on the sport involved). Indeed, the goal of physical fitness may well be the most often-cited rationale for participating in sporting activities.

Participation in sport should serve as a vehicle by which athletes discover the boundaries of the physical capabilities of themselves and others. At the very least, even if physical development does not result, athletes should become more aware of their physical being, encountering their bodies in a number of ways not usually experienced in other daily pursuits. Sport, if coached well, provides opportunities to feel and observe the body working in stressful situations. In many ways such opportunities foster self-awareness and self-understanding.

Improved motor performance should be another outcome of participation in sport. In conjunction with, and building upon, the improved physiological status of the performer, the athlete's motor performance should become more efficient. Timing, power, agility, accuracy and other motor-related capabilities should all be enhanced, resulting in better performance. Kinaesthetic awareness should also be improved, leading to a gradual decrease in variability among performances. That is, the athlete should demonstrate a higher level of skill in the activities that are regularly practised. Motor behaviour and motor performance should, in general, be enhanced and the individual should become more proficient at the tasks practised.

An additional consequence of sports participation relates to future motor skill acquisition (see also Chapter Eight). The regular instruction, the multitude of practice sessions, corrective feedback about performance, conditioning programmes and other facets of coaching and training should facilitate the acquisition of motor skills and enhance the individual's future motor behaviour and performance. The sport experience, in effect, makes the individual more ready to learn, participate in and perform motor activities in the future.

Finally, involvement with sport is assumed to be linked with positive physical effects over the long term. In any educational experience—be it academic, sports-related or in another field—an intention behind learning is to maintain or improve the participant's interest in the subject at hand (Penney, 2006). The worst possible outcome of any learning experience would be for the participant's interest in the activity to decrease. The subjective experience of learning has been overlooked for some years but importantly the affective domain, which focuses on satisfying, enjoyable, valuable, interesting, challenging, delightful learning experiences, is coming to the fore. Relating this domain to sport specifically, essentially a fine sport experience, assuming it has enhanced athletes' interest in sport and the physical aspects of it, increases the chance that athletes, at a later date and hopefully throughout their lifetime, will repeat the activity or continue on with some form of movement experience.

An excellent sport experience can have this effect. It can make the sport encounter so enjoyable that athletes will come to value physical activity and incorporate it into their lives so that it contributes to their physical, emotional, cognitive and social vitality for many, many years.

Cognitive Benefits

Many elite coaches have suggested that the one ability they wish their athletes came to the sport with is the ability to make decisions. This ability lies in the cognitive domain of learning. In terms of individual growth and development in this domain, the least that athlete should learn is the rules, strategies, tactics and skills of the sport. The individual's understanding of the specific cognitive and mental aspects of the sport should be broadened through a quality sport experience.

The athlete should learn the 'how' and 'why' (i.e. rationale and reasons) underlying each phase of the sport. The depth of thinking required means that athletes should develop higher levels of cognitive functioning (i.e. evaluation, analysis, synthesis), rather than focusing on rote memorisation. In addition, meaningful decision-making opportunities, inherent in all sports, often require critical, creative and imaginative thinking abilities. Perceptive coaches fully understand that cognitive development and involvement occur constantly in sporting events; however, humanistic/athlete-centred coaches capitalise on the cognitive outputs from the athletes' encounters with sport. The true humanists, as Lombardo (2001, p. 35) observes, are those coaches 'who encourage, expect and demand original, independent, and creative thinking for their athletes'. It seems logical, then, to emphasise the processes involved in such high-level, conceptual work. Skills in problem solving and decision making are expected outcomes of the sport experience.

Another aspect of cognitive development that authorities in sport feel should be emphasised is that the experience of sport can encourage critical thinking (Coakley, 2009) and can serve as a 'change agent' or a vehicle for societal change and ethical decision making (Cassidy, Jones and Potrac, 2009). Because sport encourages participation and therefore interaction among all levels of society and all peoples, it can stimulate wide-ranging change. In the learning process, the learner is actively involved in constructing knowledge and meaning, and it is recognised that this learning occurs in and is influenced by social and cultural contexts (Howarth, 2005). When we also consider the present circumstances in which various media outlets are increasing the visibility of sport across many sectors of the population, the potential for influencing and initiating change in society through sport appears quite powerful.

Self-evaluation, introspection and self-analysis are other forms of intellectual activity that should be connected with sporting experiences (Whitmore, 2002). Athletes should be encouraged to think critically and creatively about their performance, and thereby foster the growth of their mental capacities. Opportunities for self-analysis and self-evaluation are pervasive within the athletic context. Indeed, such situations are a vital part of the sport experience, where athletic leadership could enhance the experience by focusing on it.

Psychological Benefits

The sport experience should also give rise to several important psychological outcomes. It is important for athletes to discover their capabilities, their limitations, their strengths and their weaknesses, as an awareness of these facets will lead to a better understanding of self. Numerous opportunities for self-discovery of this type exist in sport. Moreover, by providing experiences that foster self-discovery and understanding of self, as an athlete-centred approach encourages, the encounter with sport can assist in the process of self-acceptance.

A major assumption stated by proponents of sport at all levels is that sport builds character; that sport contributes to the development of positive character traits. Participants in sport have a multitude of opportunities to experience success and develop these traits. The phenomenon of a 'successful' (however that is defined) sports career is assumed to be translated and carried over into other aspects of daily living. The recognition, validation and confirmation of an individual's worthiness, which can accrue from ventures into sport, can become a continual source of satisfaction, pride and self-esteem.

Because participation in sport is often a source of self-esteem, it can contribute to the development of a strong, vital self-concept and thus greater self-confidence. If success in sport is defined as the completion of the tasks involved in participating in sport (e.g. preparation, training, planning, competing, self-evaluation) rather than using the more limited, albeit more popular definition of success as conquering the opposition, then success is well within the grasp of all competitors. The satisfaction derived from successfully harnessing the capabilities of the mind and body to achieve a level of motor proficiency, as well as the completion of a complex task, should result in social approval as well as reinforcing the individual's intrinsic motivation. This phenomenon should foster positive feelings about self and, thereby, an enhanced self-concept.

Well-designed sport environments structure the athletic experience in such a way as to maximise the individual's success. In other words, sport environments that contribute the most to their participants ensure that each athlete is validated, confirmed as a worthy person, and successful.

Experienced athletes are often assumed to have a high degree of mental toughness—if for no other reason than that the sport experience continually places them in pressurised, competitive situations. The athlete who remains in sport must become comfortable with competition and must develop mental toughness to survive the often tough, cruel arena that is sport. Social evaluation, continual comparisons with others, and repeated self- and team analyses require that the athlete develop not only a 'thick skin' but also the ability to deal regularly with the anxiety that such experiences engender. If an athlete cannot develop in these ways, he or she will usually drop out of the sport. It is for these reasons that many feel that the individual who has had extensive sport experience can deal with competitive situations and, they argue, bring such abilities, experiences and traits (i.e. competitiveness) to other aspects of daily living. Through problem solving and operating in authentic contexts, an individual can practise this expected mental toughness.

Self-discipline is often a direct result of participation in sport. The ability to take charge of one's life, to make decisions relevant to one's world, and then to carry out such decisions, leads to positive, psychological growth and enables independence. The commitment to sport, which often entails an explicit promise to attend all meetings, practices and games, places the burden of responsibility on the athlete. Often, quite a bit of personal, social and familial sacrifice is required. Adherence to training regimes often mandates self-denial on behalf of the participant. The experience of establishing a team goal and generating plans and activities designed to facilitate the attainment of this goal requires the athlete to employ time-management skills and long-range planning. In short, the sport experience often develops self-discipline, which in turn often leads to intrinsically motivated individuals, at least among those for whom sport remains attractive (i.e. those who do not drop out). Such individuals have learned how to manage and take control of their own lives and often are (or become) highly independent.

Sport can foster the development of self-direction and often enhanced levels of intrinsic motivation. Improvement in ability can then be attributed to the individual's efforts, rather than the result of efforts external to the athlete. In this case, the individual will take pride in his or her accomplishments. The feeling of being confident and competent will develop, possibly leading to a more self-efficacious individual. The motivation to achieve and to be competent quite possibly develops into a personal characteristic as a direct result of the sport experience.

It is expected that the athlete will be able to control his or her emotions better as a result of the sport experience. Encounters with rules, officials, opposing players, and fans (both supportive and non-supportive) require a measure of emotional strength and control. The experience of striving for limited rewards, working with a team against another group, within the context of rule-invoking referees and partial onlookers, and displaying abilities in public that may often elicit harsh, realistic, severe social evaluation demands a modicum of emotional stability and control. The performers, at some point, must develop the ability to manage their reactions to the arousal and resulting stress that is ever-present in sporting events.

Athletes must learn to modulate and adapt their emotions related to victory and defeat. More importantly, they must develop a level of emotional balance that enhances, rather than detracts from, motor performance. That is, athletes have to learn to control their arousal and anxiety levels in order to maximise their performance.

The experience of sport can also contribute to the emotional development of the athlete, if it is structured in such a way that the performer is permitted to express his or her enjoyment and excitement related to the sporting event. Encouragement of such emotional expressions or release will support athletes in their efforts to express and discover their inner being.

Sport furnishes the participants with unique opportunities for non-serious exploration with their universe. It makes sense therefore to emphasise its playful aspects so as to focus more attention on its non-serious nature and the unlimited potential for experimentation and exploration that it presents to the athlete. The outcomes of sport should result in a state of pleasure, satisfaction and enjoyment, bringing the performer a joy that is surpassed by few other activities.

Social Benefits

Sport is a very effective socialising agent for those who identify with and value it. The encounter with sport can socialise such predisposed individuals into the prevailing normative order and value patterns of the adult society that they are about to enter. In effect, as a reinforcer of culture, the experience of sport can contribute significantly to the process of enculturating or integrating the individual into society (Coakley, 2009).

Responsibility to others and commitment to group goals are experiences that individuals often confront directly for the first time in the sport situation. It is often during the competitive experience that individuals become aware of how their choices and performance affect others as well as of the need to focus clearly on both short-term and long-range objectives. Being a part of a team or group committed to sport means that an individual must fill specialised roles and follow through on many duties, both of which can nurture greater social awareness, sensitivity to others and responsiveness.

In an attempt to resist and combat the forces of homogenisation, impersonalisation and bureaucratisation in society, sport can and should provide opportunities for individuals to express themselves, to proclaim their uniqueness and subjectivity, and to provide evidence that individuals know themselves. Sport can be a vehicle that facilitates the development of several positive social variables, so important in our complex modern-day society where many people experience great difficulty establishing meaningful contact and maintaining ties with others. Participation in sport can be a major force in the development of such aspects as: (1) the ability to get along with others; (2) cooperation; (3) the ability to compete in a socially approved manner; (4) comradeship; (5) social and communication skills; (6) personal responsibility for one's role in society; and (7) satisfaction of socialising needs.

Affective and Spiritual Benefits

Kretchmar (2005) suggests that there is an element of delight that athletes should strive for when competing in sport. Indeed an encounter with sport should increase the individual's desire to participate in the activity. This desire should continue for life, with benefits for the individual's health and wellness as discussed above. It is quite possible that simply having increased affection through participating in sport could lead a person to take up physical activity, which in turn will positively enhance the individual's physical being. The effects on the individual's lifestyle would certainly be beneficial.

The spiritual element of the thrill of movement needs to be considered as well. The spirituality of sport, the personal meaning, can help to shape our identity (Edwards, 2007). This personal meaning is crucial in helping athletes to believe in sport as a means of developing their spirituality. Phil Jackson (1995) in *Sacred Hoops* alludes to the spirituality of the sport experience: that the lessons learned in sport are of the heart and mind in preparation for battle. An attempt at honing in on that electrifying experience, one that exists within the heart and mind of each athlete, is one of the main reasons for competing. So focusing on the lessons to connect with life mysteries that Phil Jackson describes is a domain that needs further attention in sport. This spirituality is unique to each human. The aesthetic enjoyment experienced by each individual is sometimes insular, set apart from the everyday life meanings of the world.

With this insight into the holistic nature of each individual, it is easier to understand the rationale behind a humanistic approach that focuses on the person. It is timely, therefore, to turn the discussion to how coaches can enable the development of athletes as people.

Athlete-centred and Humanistic Coaching

At the outset, it is important to understand that the key to the athlete-centred approach is a leadership style that caters to athletes' needs and understandings where athletes are enabled to learn and have control of their participation in sport. Although both *humanistic* and *athlete-centred* may be interpreted in many ways, at a general level both terms describe a process by which people gain control over the decisions affecting their lives. When a coach considers the athletes first and thus gives them choice and control, the athletes take ownership of and personal responsibility for their decisions. In other words, through training, athletes and teams gain some choice in and control over what happens in their sporting life as well as in their general lifestyle.

Some of the main advantages of using an athlete-centred approach to coaching are that athletes are motivated to learn and they have a greater understanding and stronger retention of both tactics and skills (physical, cognitive, psychological, social and spiritual), which are so important to success in sport. A humanistic coach facilitates athletes' learning but does not control it. This approach is clearly beneficial given that athletes must be self-sufficient in their performance, decision making and option taking while participating in their respective sport. In particular, an athlete-centred approach encourages athletes to become self-aware and self-sufficient, allows them to make informed decisions and emphasises individual growth and change.

Many coaches, who use many different styles, highlight the importance of gaining trust and respect from their athletes to enhance performance (Potrac, 2004). In an athlete-centred approach to coaching this trust must be mutual, and establishing it is largely dependent upon the coach. Mutual trust and respect between coach and athlete do not mean sameness. Athletes must trust their coaches to make suggestions and decisions and to ensure athlete responsibility in the best interests of the team. Athletes trust coaches to be knowledgeable and prepared, and to provide a safe and supporting environment (Shogan, 1999). Through mutual trust, athletes take responsibility for the learning and performance of themselves and the team, thereby enhancing the team environment. In turn, coaches trust athletes to be serious about their performance goals and the goals of the team. Humanistic coaching (learning through enablement) promotes a shared, dynamic power relationship between athlete and coach. Using an athlete-centred approach is a pedagogical strategy that will assist the development of the trust and respect that so many coaches seek (Kidman and Davis, 2007).

An athlete-centred coach helps athletes learn and enables them to understand how to exceed their current limits. This kind of coach nurtures involvement and autonomy in the athletes' learning (Usher, 1997).

All of the coaches, authors and athletes featured in this book base their performance on an athlete-centred, humanistic approach that encourages self-awareness of their own skill execution and tactical play. Their approach is concerned with problem solving rather than prescription (Hadfield, 1994). When coaches set problems and encourage athletes to ask questions, they enable them to take ownership of their learning and athletic environment. The coach who uses an athlete-centred style divests himself or herself of power, however gradually, and gladly shares it with the athletes (Kidman, Hadfield and Chu, 2000).

With the athlete-centred approach it is not suggested that the coach should give full responsibility to athletes. Rather, coaches should exercise their leadership by guiding athletes towards decision making and enabling their own responsibility for sport participation. Clearly in some situations, with some athletes, coaches need to be more prescriptive, but the aim should always be to encourage self-reliance through decision making.

Many people practise coaching without really understanding its process. The coaching process is dependent on the complex dynamics between coaches and athletes, their individual attributes, their desires and ambitions, and the training and competition context. Athlete-centred, humanistic coaching considers all these complexities, but with an emphasis upon the development of the athlete, while always respecting the individual athlete's ability to think and actually solve problems.

Some Key Components of a Humanistic, Athlete-centred Approach

The case studies in this book highlight three major components of an athlete-centred approach that enhance decision making and help to form a quality team culture. These primary coaching practices are Teaching Games for Understanding (TGfU), questioning, and establishing a quality team culture—as discussed further below). In addition, the coaches have highlighted other aspects that they believe contribute significantly to athlete ownership and responsibility, such as the strategies of developing a team full of leaders and rotating athlete roles within the team.

Teaching Games for Understanding

Teaching Games for Understanding (TGfU) (see also Chapter Eight) is a games approach that has been adapted and modified in various contexts and under various names, including Play Practice and Game Sense. The common feature across these variations is that a purposeful game is used for athletes to learn the skill, technique and tactical understanding of the sport. The ability to use an understanding of the rules, of strategy, of tactics and, most importantly, of oneself to solve problems posed by the game or by one's opponents is the basis of TGfU (Launder, 2001). The TGfU model is understanding in action and providing opportunities to enhance athletes' ability to respond or make decisions, even when new situations are presented. TGfU is about applying game sense—'reading the game'.

With TGfU, athletes can learn about the game and practise skills and techniques within the context of a game rather than separate from it. Learning in context provides a sound understanding of the game and opportunities to apply skill and technique under pressure. When athletes are allowed to play or practise in a situation uncluttered by coaches telling them what to do and where to go, they are more productive in terms of learning in context, and become more motivated through challenges, social interactions and decision making (Kidman and Hanrahan, 2004).

TGfU is a physical application of game-like situations to help athletes in their decision making process. Games are used as the learning tool for many aspects of playing the sport. Play Practice (Launder, 2001) uses three rationales to support learning in action within a game context: Shaping Play (manipulating variables, continually changing, teaching through the game); Focusing Play (teaching in the game, pointing out similarities and differences between training games and real games, developing and refining skills); and Enhancing Play (improving performance through meaningful games).

Developing the game to meet learning outcomes is the key to planning and designing games. Some of the ideas around which games could be developed include: freeze replay, shaping applied to invasion games, attacker:defender ratio, altering the size and shape of playing area, nature of the goal, primary and secondary rules, conditions applied to the game, control and development of good players, differential scoring, playing time, tactical time-outs, and user-friendly balls and equipment. Tactical aspects include: deception, risk, shot selection and placement in relation to opponents, time, stage of game, space, decision making, field setting, defensive patterns, minimising angles of attack, attacking patterns, and keeping possession (Australian Sports Commission, 1997).

TGfU fits into a humanistic, athlete-centred philosophy because it enhances athletes' motivation and thus the intensity of their performance through their own problem solving. Athletes increase their effort because of the meaningful challenges offered. These challenges also create opportunities for athletes to respond to the pressure inherent in sport competitions. Achievement is also enhanced as TGfU enables athletes to do something well, to problem solve, and to take ownership of their own learning, and thereby provides many opportunities for coaches to listen to and respect athletes' thoughts. Of course, enjoyment is also enhanced because games are fun. Through games, athletes share success and failure; they learn how to trust each other and to know each other's ways of competing and making decisions, which enhances team culture. Chapter Eight by Ian Renshaw discusses TGfU, its conceptualisation and its relevance to current skill acquisition theory, namely the constraints-led approach.

Questioning

The technique of questioning (which is further explained and discussed in Chapter Thirteen) is one way of helping athletes learn to problem solve. It is not simply a matter of asking questions; effective coach questioning requires purposeful questions phrased in a way that encourages the athlete to respond. Stimulating questions are an extremely powerful means of inspiring athletes and enhancing intrinsic motivation (Butler, 1997). Questioning also engages athletes at a conscious level, enhancing their concentration and thus their intensity, which transfers well to competition itself where the pressure is great. Moreover, given that questioning athletes opens up an opportunity to listen to and respect their thinking, the technique contains the implicit message that athletes' thoughts are important.

For various reasons, there is a degree of resistance to the technique among some athletes and coach-centred coaches. Because coach questioning is less prevalent than direct coaching, in their early encounters with this technique athletes may be reluctant to respond to posed questions. To draw out the athletes, coaches need to work on building trust to demonstrate their respect for athletes' answers. In turn, the athletes need to recognise the coach's willingness to consider, listen and respond to the athletes' thoughts and answers. Then, once they become more accustomed to this practice and see that it gives them ownership of their learning, they will be more accepting of the questions and become more cognitively involved in the sport environment.

Among advocates of a prescriptive coaching approach, there is a perception that coaches who ask questions do not know the answers themselves. Asking questions is perceived by some to show a 'weakness' on behalf of the coach. Indeed, coaches may find it difficult, and at times daunting, to design questions that generate high-level thinking from the athletes. Yet to create situations where athletes learn best, coaches must listen to their athletes' responses, then redirect, prompt and probe for better or more detailed answers. Succeeding with such a technique demands an in-depth understanding of the game, the athlete, and the context in which a solution is applied.

Athletes will undertake problem solving with enjoyment and ever-increasing effort if given the opportunity. By generating their own solution, athletes gain more self-awareness; the subsequent enhancement of their performance is well documented (Cassidy et al., 2009). For example, athletes who take ownership of the content of their learning will remember, understand and apply it more effectively than those who are told what to do, when to do it and how to do it. When they solve problems through coach questioning, athletes discover, explore, create and generally experiment with a variety of movement forms, skills and tactics or strategies of a specific sport. The effect is to enhance their long-term learning (Thorpe, 1990). The process and outcomes of the technique are well suited to competitive sports which, by their very nature, are an endless series of problems to be confronted and solved via usually simultaneous thinking and motor activity.

Coaches should test their questioning strategy in each particular situation and adapt it to meet the purpose of the training session and athletes' needs and expectations. Sport and physical activity offer relevant contexts to involve athletes in high-level thinking. Coaches are often surprised and excited by how much athletes really do know, how easily they self-learn and how increased enthusiasm and enhanced self-esteem are additional spin-offs of this approach.

Team Culture

One key way to encourage self-reliance is to pursue a quality team culture in which athletes gain responsibility for establishing and maintaining a direction for the team (also see Chapter Six by Gareth Jones). According to Thompson (2003), 'team culture consists of values, (explicit and congruent), rituals, shared vocabularies, two-way communications, and a feeling of family' (p. 150). Team culture, a major philosophical underpinning in athlete-centred coaching, is defined as the ability to bring individuals together for the pursuit of a common goal (Yukelson, 1997). In this multi-faceted process, the team's pursuit of a mutual goal informs the quality of its functioning and success. Without quality team culture, success, learning and often winning are difficult. Thus a major challenge for coaches is to bring athletes together for learning and success.

Many athlete-centred coaches have multiple ways of developing the vision (the overriding direction) and the values (ways of acting or of ensuring that the vision is met) of the athletes on their team. Their mix of methods may also differ from those of others with a similar philosophy, as the range of descriptions from coaches in this book demonstrates. One belief that all these coaches share, however, is that either the vision must be mutually created or athletes must buy into an existing vision. In addition, values form the backbone of the team's actions; many coaches and athletes identify values such as commitment and communication. Expectations are often derived from these values. For example, if commitment is a value, then it is expected that athletes, coaches and managers will live by that value. An accompanying action might be to apply that commitment to punctuality or to the team members and coach. Whatever values are developed for each team, it is important that the team understands the actual meaning and intent of each value, and that they agree to or buy into that definition. If the athletes themselves develop the vision, values and expectations, they take ownership of them, live by them and take responsibility for monitoring each other.

The notion of team culture is also encompassed in an arguably important Maori word in the New Zealand Health and Physical Education curriculum document (NZHPE)— namely, *wairua*. According to NZHPE, wairua means spirit or the action of spirituality. In a team context, wairua is the spirit of the team, the notion of oneness that all athletes on the team have, a spirit that guides their actions. The team works together as one and develops a sense of spirituality that enhances each individual's well-being. Wairua encompasses all that is positive about team culture: that is, supportive values and attitudes, respect and trust, caring and concern for others. Without wairua, the quality of team culture is diminished and therefore the chance of success is limited.

All of the coaches cited in the chapters ahead identify quality team culture as the key to any team's success. Among the prerequisites for ensuring a quality team culture are constructing team standards and having spiritual appreciation. The existence of a quality team culture helps to meet the psychological and social needs of the athletes (Liu, 2001). Further than that, as Liu (2001) puts it, in a team culture all members voluntarily have a 'common faith, valuation view, morality, spirit pillar, ceremony, intelligence factor, and entertainment life' (p. 28). One important outcome is true cohesion, whose foundation, Jerry Lynch (2001) suggests, lies in 'selflessness, willingness to see that the team goal is greater than the goal of any one athlete' (p. 77). Thus the coach who allows for self-responsibility by enabling athletes to make decisions on team direction enhances selflessness, benefits the team vision, goals, values and strategies, and in so doing ensures a quality team culture (Kidman and Davis, 2007).

It is important to note that the chemistry of each team is unique. Its individual members have unique attributes as well as some commonality with other athletes. Teams also participate in an ever-changing context. The combination of these components means that a team may develop its own unique culture. As a consequence, what works for one team does not necessarily work for another team. An athlete-centred approach to coaching will take uniqueness into account by focusing on nurturing athletes and enhancing the positive aspects of each environment in which they participate.

It is clear that establishing a mutual direction and goals for a team enhances athlete and team performance (Carron and Dennis, 1998; Liu, 2001; Yukelson, 1997). The purpose of establishing a vision is to formulate season goals so that all athletes strive for the same purpose. In turn, values serve to establish 'rules' for the team and form the basis for setting up strategies to meet team goals. When establishing the vision, values and goals, it is important for the coach to include the athletes in decision making so that they take ownership of them and assume responsibility for monitoring them.

Other Coaching Practices in a Humanistic, Athlete-centred Approach

One of the most important reasons for using a humanistic, athlete-centred approach is to encourage athletes to take responsibility for and ownership of their actions and contributions to any team. By providing a humanistic-like atmosphere, using an athlete-centred approach, the coach encourages athletes' responsibilities not only in relation to problem solving but also in other areas that will aid the team. Thus some coaches create mini-groups, each of which has responsibility for something that benefits the team.

Using mini-groups in such ways promotes a sense of shared leadership—in other words, a team full of leaders. Many of the coaches featured in this book discuss the benefits of giving everyone on the team the experience of being a leader by giving each team member responsibility for an aspect of the team. By this means, everyone takes ownership of the team culture, and each athlete, coach and manager has certain responsibilities to monitor or lead. When training, each athlete should feel like they contribute to the play on and off the field or court. Hadfield (2002) proposes four reasons why teaching athletes to be leaders enhances the team environment. Specifically, shared leadership brings the benefits of: maintaining high standards and motivation; preparing a team that is mentally tough; gaining athlete input to maintain team chemistry; and adhering to team values and expectations.

The issue of captaincy often arises in sports teams. It highlights a difference of approach between those who advocate that a team has a captain as the one who has total leadership responsibility for it and those—such as several coaches in this book—who prefer a team to have a captain for media representation and name only. Significantly, a decision to single out the captain as the only leader often means that responsibility falls on the captain's shoulders and the ownership from the rest of the team for various aspects of the team environment declines. This lack of assumed responsibility by the majority of the team, where athletes divest their ownership and responsibility to the captain, can be detrimental to team unity. Most teams tend to have a captain because of tradition and because sport competitions require it, not because one is needed. Coaches must take into consideration the roles of a captain and assess what is best for their particular team.

Role Rotation

One of the key features of the process of developing decision makers is the use of role rotation. A major value involved in this practice is trust.

Two key ideas underpin role rotation. First, everyone on the team should be trusted enough to be able to play at any time during any competition. The athletes must believe that others have faith in them to do a given job when called upon to do it. Role rotation can therefore mean that within the team, all athletes play for an equal amount of time and contribute equally to all aspects of the team culture.

The second central aspect of role rotation is that athletes are allowed to play in a variety of positions to establish empathy, understanding, decision-making skills and tactical awareness of teammates. For example, in basketball a centre could play a guard role at training to try to understand the skills and tactics needed to play that position. A back in rugby might participate in a line-out to determine the roles of the forward in that position. These role experiences increase cognitive development regarding others' roles. They give athletes a sense of empathy and knowledge about a particular position which enhances their technical and tactical understanding of the game. Inadvertently, as part of this experience, athletes also learn about coaching as they gain a broader understanding of the sport. It provides self-awareness and team awareness which aids in technical and tactical analysis.

Among juniors, who are still developing physically and cognitively, no athlete should be 'stuck' in any one position and should not specialise until puberty. Athletes change as they develop; a good centre in basketball today might be the best guard in basketball tomorrow.

Creating an Athlete-centred Philosophy

It is useful and important for all coaches to formulate a coaching philosophy or personal statement about the values and beliefs significant to their understanding of sport and life. This philosophy provides the foundation that directs the way they coach (Kidman and Hanrahan, 2004). After thinking about why they are coaching, coaches should write it down and analyse it. Although it can feel quite threatening to put their own philosophy down on paper, the process of thinking through their philosophy is enlightening.

As coaches learn, they tend to change their attitudes and values in accordance with athletes' needs. Because these changes will affect a coaching philosophy, reviewing the philosophy regularly and altering it to fit with each coach's experience are important features of the process of developing a philosophy.

The value systems that underpin a coach's approach are crucial in determining the needs of both coaches and athletes. As the basis of the coach's knowledge, these values will be important to guide any of the coach's actions. In addition, it is the coach's responsibility to communicate this philosophy to athletes so that they are encouraged to achieve their goals. Every sport setting needs a philosophical base so that the team or individual can develop and learn according to a consistent, coherent way of thinking.

Under an athlete-centred philosophy, part of a coach's facilitation role is to define the nature of these guidelines and to follow the athlete-centred philosophy in his or her approach to coaching. As mentioned above, one goal of an athlete-centred approach is to establish mutual visions whereby the coach facilitates the process of setting priorities for the good of the team and/or athletes. By developing an athlete-centred philosophy in which athletes are encouraged to become self-aware and self-reliant in decision making, the coach provides a foundation that contributes to the holistic development of individual athletes. The whole season should be built on the belief system that athletes and coaches have created mutually.

The holistic development of the athlete is central to the success of an athlete-centred coaching approach. The athletes are the main focus of any team and determine the success or failure of the season. The quality of the athletes' experience of a season will depend on the value systems, principles and beliefs of both themselves and the coach. Successful coach Wayne Smith describes the holistic, athlete-centred approach he incorporates in his sound empowering philosophy, in which his role is:

> … to create an environment so that the players feel comfortable in making decisions. In this way, they can cope with responsibilities and they can take ownership of their learning. Players should own the team culture. They should set their own expectations, establish the team protocols, … create the vision and the values. We [as coaches] guide them and facilitate them, but it is their total 'buy in' [collectively] that we are after. It's their programme, their campaign. So my philosophy is to create empowered players and to have … a holistic type approach so that the players are not just sport jocks, not just training for rugby, but have outside interests. I believe coaching is all about trying to develop better people, not just better players and it's important to enjoy the whole experience.

Worcester Warriors rugby coach Mike Ruddock's philosophy, as summed up in his onion analogy, is very similar:

> I like to promote a team that is a thinking team. It's a positive team, that understands the game, that gets involved in key decisions, either through formal or informal communication with the coach and coaching staff, then they know what they are doing. I haven't been overly prescriptive in making us do this in this part of the field and in that part of the field, but I feel I always try to let the players make decisions based on safe or different options we have and giving the boys a bit of rope so they can make their own decisions. This process can be a longer way to do things at times, because you tend to lose a few games and make the mistakes before you come out on the other side with a bigger and better bowl of knowledge about what works for you. Like an onion, there are so many layers.

A philosophy is based on ideas formed from experiences. These experiences stem from influential teachers, coaches or mentors who have had a positive or negative effect on aspects of your life.

Specific steps to follow in developing your own personal coaching philosophy are to:

- ask why a particular teacher/coach had such a meaningful impact on you and what happened;
- determine how or whether those experiences may direct personal coaching actions;
- develop opinion(s) based on the knowledge that you have gathered over the years; and
- identify your hopes for the future.

> I like thinking of possibilities. At any time, an entirely new possibility is liable to come along and spin you off in an entirely new direction. The trick, I've learned, is to be awake to the moment. – Doug Hall

References

Australian Sports Commission. (1997). *Games Sense: Developing thinking players: A presenter's guide and workbook.* Canberra: Australian Sports Commission.

Butler, J. (1997). How would Socrates teach games?: A constructivist approach. *Journal of Physical Education, 68*(8), 42–47.

Carron, A.V., & Dennis, P.W. (1998). The sport team as an effective group. In J.M. Williams (Ed.), *Applied sport psychology: Personal growth to peak performance.* Mountain View, CA: Mayfield.

Cassidy, T., Jones, R., & Potrac, P. (2009). *Understanding Sports Coaching: The social, cultural and pedagogical foundations of coaching practice* (2nd ed.). London: Routledge.

Coakley, J. (2009). *Sport in Society: Issues and controversies* (10th ed.). London: Sage.

Edwards, M. (2007). Sport and identity in Aotearoa/New Zealand. In C. Collins & S. Jackson (Eds) *Sport in Aotearoa/New Zealand society*. Auckland: Thomson.

Hadfield, D.C. (1994). The query theory: a sports coaching model for the 90's. *The New Zealand Coach, 3*(4), 16–20.

Hadfield, D.C. (2002). Developing team leaders in rugby. *Rugby Football Union Technical Journal.* Retrieved 7 October 2002 from www.rfu.com/pdfs/technical-journal/Developing_leaders_captains.pdf

Howarth, K. (2005). Introducing teaching games for understanding model in teacher education programmes. In L.L. Griffin & J.I. Butler (Eds) *Teaching Games for Understanding: Theory, research, and practice*, Champaign, IL: Human Kinetics.

Jackson, P., & Delehanty, H. (1995). *Sacred Hoops: Spiritual lessons of a hardwood warrior*. USA: Jackson.

Jones, R. (Ed) (2006). *The Sports Coach as an Educator: Re-conceptualising sports coaching*. London: Routledge.

Jones, R. (2001). Applying empowerment in coaching: Some considerations. In L. Kidman, *Developing decision makers: An empowerment approach to coaching*. Christchurch: Innovative Print Communications.

Kidman, L., & Davis, W. (2007). Empowerment in coaching. In W.E. Davis & G.D. Broadhead (Eds), *Ecological task analysis and movement: Understanding movement in context*. Champaign, IL: Human Kinetics.

Kidman, L., Hadfield, D., & Chu, M. (2000). The coach and the sporting experience. In C. Collins (Ed.), *Sport in New Zealand society* (pp. 273–286). Palmerston North: Dunmore.

Kidman, L., & Hanrahan, S.J. (2004). *The coaching process: A practical guide to improving your effectiveness* (2nd ed.). Palmerston North: Dunmore.

Kretchmar, R.S. (2005). Teaching games for understanding and the delights of human activity. In L.L. Griffin & J.I. Butler (Eds) *Teaching Games for Understanding: Theory, research, and practice*. Champaign, IL: Human Kinetics.

Launder, A.G. (2001). *Play Practice: The games approach to teaching and coaching sports*. Champaign, IL: Human Kinetics.

Liu, Y.M. (2001). Discussion on team culture. *Journal of Capital College of Physical Education*, 13(1), 28–33, 60.

Lombardo, B.J. (2001). Humanistic coaching: A model for the new century. In B.J. Lombardo, T.J. Caravella-Nadeau, K.S. Castagono, & V.H. Mancini, *Sport in the twenty-first century: Alternatives for the new millennium*. Boston, MA: Pearson.

Lynch, J. (2001). *Creative Coaching: New ways to maximize athlete and team potential in all sports*. Champaign, IL: Human Kinetics.

Penney, D. (2006). Coaching as teaching: New acknowledgements in practice. In R. Jones (Ed.) *Sports coach as an educator: Re-conceptualising sports coaching*. London: Routledge.

Potrac, P. (2004). Coaches' power. In R. Jones, K. Armour, & P. Potrac, *Sports coaching cultures: From practice to theory*. London: Routledge.

Pratt, S.R., & Eitzen, D.S. (1989). Contrasting leadership styles and organisational effectiveness: the case of athletic teams. *Social Science Quarterly*, 70(2), 311–322.

Roberts, G.C., & Treasure, D.C. (1995). Children in sport. *Sport Science Review, 1*(2), 46–64.

Shogan, D. (1999). *The Making of High-Performance Athletes: Discipline, diversity and ethics.* Toronto: University of Toronto Press.

Smoll, F.L., & Smith, R.E. (1989). Leadership behaviors in sport: a theoretical model and research paradigm. *Journal of Applied Social Psychology, 19*(18), 1522–1551.

Thompson, J. (2003). *Double-goal Coach: Positive coaching tools for honouring the game and developing winners in sports and life*, New York, NY: Harper Collins.

Thorpe, R.D. (1990). New directions in games teaching. In N. Armstrong (Ed.), *New directions in physical education* (pp. 79–100). Champaign, IL: Human Kinetics.

Usher, P. (1997). Empowerment as a powerful coaching tool. *Coaches' Report, 4*(2), 10–11.

Weinberg, R.S., & Gould, D. (2007). *Foundations of Sport and Exercise Psychology* (4th ed.). Champaign, IL: Human Kinetics.

Whitmore, J. (2002). *Coaching for Performance: Growing people, performance and purpose* (3rd ed.). London: Nicolas Brealey.

Yukelson, D. (1997). Principles of effective team building. *Journal of Applied Sport Psychology, 9*(1), 73–96.

You cannot teach a man anything, you can
only help him to find it within himself - Galileo

Coaches have to watch for what they
don't want to see and listen to what
they don't want to hear. -John Madden.

Chapter Two

A Critical Analysis of an Athlete-centred Approach

The purpose of this chapter is to examine, in an objective fashion, the advantages and the disadvantages, the pros and the cons, the pluses and the minuses of an athlete-centred approach to coaching that has been proposed in this book. It is our intention to present a balanced analysis of this approach, in the belief that it will convince the reader of the viability of this approach to sport leadership.

Before launching on this analysis, however, it makes sense to examine some of the underlying reasons why we support such an approach. First, in the current milieu of sport, we are concerned about the way that coaching leadership is being manifested at all levels of participation. In particular, in many instances the health of the athlete is being overlooked, ignored or, at the very least, subordinated to a level somewhat below the coach's needs (e.g. the need to win). As a result we have youngsters being surgically repaired in their teen years (e. g. elbow reconfiguration surgery), American football players suffering from serious head injuries and concussions and being encouraged to put on extra pounds, the use of performance-enhancing drugs, the too-numerous cases of eating disorders, the worn-out shoulders of young swimmers, and the many tears to the anterior cruciate ligament (ACL) that young female soccer players are experiencing (Hyman, 2009). In general, many injuries are directly caused by 'overuse'—that is, by athletes, young and old, being enticed into competing in their sport all year long, despite the need for variety, rest, and time for their bodies to recover and repair from the stresses of continuous, high-level competition. Often well-intentioned but seriously uninformed coaches are encouraging specialisation, resulting in 12-month practice and training regimes, despite the voluminous growth and development research that supports the need for athletes to recover, rest, and not overwork the joints of the body. In many cases, these youngsters are not responding solely to their own interests, desires and needs, but rather are fulfilling the needs of the adult leader, the coach, the team, parents, or other significant 'non-players' in the experience (i.e. feeling the pressure from coaches, adults, peers to go all out to win). In essence, the underlying philosophical stance we present here is that decision-making capability should be returned to the performer. In recent years society has supported a major shift to fully empowering the coach, most often with the consent and encouragement of the parents. Too often it appears that this 'shift' has been detrimental to the health of the athlete.

Another major concern that has motivated our endeavour in suggesting an alternative to the current 'traditional' scheme of coaching leadership (i.e. the coach-centred approach) is the educational outcomes of the sport experience. With the exception of the highest levels of sport (e.g. professional sport, big time university sports, big time club sports), none of which profess to 'educate' their athletes nor to enhance the character of the participants, sport in general is claimed to provide specific educational experiences that enhance the learning of the athletes in all the domains of learning (i.e. physical, cognitive, psychological and social). In short, participation in sport is said to support the development of positive character traits. All these glowing, positive outcomes are claimed for the participants in the sport venture. In most cases, organisations have committed to such desirable goals in documents circulated and available to the public in support of their programme's educational intent. However, when one closely examines the outcomes of sport, the specific behaviours of coaches, the actions of those non-players who strongly influence the sport experience, one is hard-pressed to uncover supporting evidence for the often grandiose claims of programmes and/or individuals. In our experience, it is left to unsubstantiated claims, anecdotal data, and solicited testimonials from former players—rather than solid evidence—to support such important claims (Coakley, 2009; Fullinwider, 2006).

Traditionally sport has been considered a means by which children can learn values and discipline, as well as develop morally and socially (e.g. by learning skills in teamwork and cooperation). However, there is a dearth of research to show conclusively that participation in organised sport programmes leads to the development of appropriate values and attitudes, morals or other characteristics traditionally associated with sport involvement (Coakley, 2009). Indeed, contrary to these readily accepted and conventional assumptions, significant sources indicate that sport has been shown to teach inappropriate values and attitudes (Fullinwider, 2006; Shields and Bredemeier, 2001; Stoll and Beller, 2000).

Thus sport involvement does not necessarily lead to positive socialisation. Rather, significant others, including coaches and other adults, can contribute in both positive and negative ways to the building of character and moral development. As well as influencing whether children participate in sport at all, adults have an enormous impact on the types of sports in which they become involved, and whether that sport experience is positive or negative. In children's sport, it appears that a number of social influences often produce a clash of values between adult expectations of success and children's expectations of fun (Roberts, Treasure and Hall, 1994). Consequently parental value systems can actually limit children's ability to perform at their own level and for fun. Therefore adults have a responsibility to consider which expectations are their own and which belong to their children. This is a difficult task because it requires some degree of objectivity.

Again, the decision-making power—the same power that enhances the learning and full educational development of the athlete—has rather been maximised for the adult in control of the games of children and sport performers. If sport is to truly maximise its educational potential, athletes must be part of the decision-making, the thinking that goes into solving the problems that emerge endlessly, continuously and joyfully in all the situations of sport. We say joyfully, for it is the successful response to these minute to minute, continuous 'problems' that arise during a competitive sporting event that attract us to 'play' our games (see Chapter Seven). When adults limit, restrict or eliminate the athlete's participation in these decisions, in these thought-provoking interactions, then the athlete's enjoyment is reduced.

In short, there is little evidence that coaches intentionally address these claims of holistic development of the athlete. It is more likely that these outcomes in each of the individual's developmental dimensions (e.g. physical, cognitive, psychological, social) are expected to accrue simply by the athlete's interactions with such experiences—that is, the leader considers these outcomes incidental, does not address them directly, and does not focus on them in any meaningful way. Coach development programme materials and required educational opportunities typically overlook or downplay such goals, and instead focus on the technical aspects of the sport. Too often on those occasions when the coach could possibly address such important learning outcomes, the coach-centred coach ignores the opportunity presented and/or does not provide athletes with a chance to analyse, think through the situation, or practise other related skills.

In reality, many of these worthy objectives/outcomes do indeed occur, but not as a direct result of the coach's efforts, behaviour or leadership. We contend that an athlete-centred model of coaching leadership would take advantage of such coachable moments (if not organise the experience to maximise the occurrence of such events), and capitalise on the situations as they arise within the sporting endeavour. These coachable moments would be central, not peripheral to the sport experience. As such these 'moments' would ensure that learning occurs in all four dimensions (affective, cognitive, physical and social), not only in the physical aspect.

The increasing overspecialisation in sport is another reason to decry current coaching behaviour. Athletes are often expected to play and/or practise one sport all year long—increasing the risk of an overuse injury (as outlined above), often minimising or reducing the intrinsic outcomes of playing (joy, thrill), as well as reducing options for trying alternatives such as other movement vehicles or sports. Jay Coakley (2009), a pre-eminent sport sociologist, recently suggested that this intense, year-round specialisation has emerged in large part to support the various commercial ventures of the owners/managers of sport facilities (e.g. hockey rinks, indoor baseball facilities, sport training centres). In essence, Coakley suggests that the over-specialisation movement has been supported and encouraged by individuals who need to make money, keep their facilities open all year, and keep their trainers/coaches occupied, and whose position gains additional backing from the often false hopes of parents who want to believe that their child will be the next superstar.

Having established the basic rationale for our support for an athlete-centred approach, we now turn to examine those factors that can either support or negate efforts to implement such an approach to coaching leadership. What follows represents some of the major concerns of those who have attempted to lead athletes in athlete-centred programmes, along with critical comments from the critics/antagonists of an athlete-centred approach to coaching behaviour.

The Ego of the Coach

Although many current and former coaches claim that to lead others one must have a well-developed, if not strong ego (belief in self; centred self-confidence; strong belief in one's abilities), an athlete-centred approach requires that the coach's ego not be *the* major factor in the sport experience. Rather, the coach's ego must be numbered as one among many other egos: the experience and ego of the participants must be placed at least on a par with that of the coach.

Once a coach permits his or her ego to 'lead' the way, all sorts of negative, dangerous and inappropriate coaching is likely to emerge. For example, the coach's need to be a winner, in order to satisfy his or her status and feed his or her ego, often leads to coaching described as belligerent, loud and obnoxious; a kind of coaching that tears down athletes and makes them feel terrible because they have failed to perform to a level that informs the world that the coach is a great one! This kind of outcome often arises when the athletes have less of a need (less of need to feed their ego) to win in order to feel good about themselves. Too often, coaches often want to win more than their athletes (especially inexperienced, younger athletes, who may desire only to play, to have fun, and to be with their friends). As a result of such a conflict of goals and desires, the athlete may drop out of the sport, never to return.

Closely related to the 'ego issue' described above is the pressing need for and/or focus on short-term outcomes (i.e. winning), which may operate at the expense of long-term player development (e.g. full understanding of the game, motor proficiency, future development not only as a player/performer but also as a lifelong, physically active person/adult).

To many people, success is measured by how many games or competitions are won or lost. It is a criterion on which the jobs of many coaches depend. Success, however, is not just about winning. More important to the concept of success is *striving* to win. Mark Norton (Chapter Ten) emphasises that the high school boys he coaches and the nature of their experience are his focus and conveys a broader, more holistic definition of success:

I want to create a positive, enjoyable, and meaningful experience for the kids. I want the team and the team mission to become a focus in the boys' lives. I also want to create good volleyball players and a team that plays quality volleyball. I like to use volleyball and physical activity as a vehicle to teach the kids about themselves, other people and how to effectively interact and function with others. That's how I treat my teaching of physical education also. Volleyball, a game hugely reliant on teamwork and one's teammates, lends itself to do this superbly. At the end of the day, if the kids have developed as better people, I've been successful.

Certainly winning is a major factor in sport but success, as defined above, is more important. An athlete can win without performing well or can lose even though the performance has been outstanding. It is a major responsibility of coaches to emphasise this latter notion, reinforce it regularly, and model such a belief.

In any competition, it is difficult to win if athletes do not experience success, a quality team culture and an athlete-centred environment or balance in their lives. The idea of success as athlete learning, enjoyment, performance or growth is often overridden by a 'winning at all costs' attitude (often regularly manifested, vocalised, and modelled by the coach to such an extent that the athletes fully understand what is highly prized by the coach) which ignores athletes' needs and sabotages the pursuit of excellence with the result that sport participation degenerates into a means to an end (Boxill, 2003).

The Expectations of Society and/or the Media

Society, via the media, focuses on winners. Society expects everyone to compete. Society does not celebrate those who simply play for fun and enjoyment, or those who enjoy sport even if they do not win. Many might argue that society, especially North American society, has forgotten the true meaning of 'playing' or 'playing for fun.' (Specifically, we contend, when one truly 'plays', only the players make decisions. Non-players have no influence on those playing, etc.)

One only has to attempt to find stories about 'losers' of competitive events. There is no public/societal memory there. Losers are quickly forgotten, and are rarely celebrated. Indeed, even winners are seldom remembered for very long! It is unusual to hear news about a successful coach who provided a great training environment and encouraged athletes to do their best. The media rarely portray a successful coach as an educator. Nevertheless, one of the most important jobs in coaching is to educate athletes, preparing them physically, psychologically, cognitively and socially. Knowing how the athletes tick and drawing out their athletic capabilities are measures of success. Because coaching is a people-oriented profession, well-skilled coaches know how to facilitate the environment to bring out the best in their athletes and they need to be committed to the individuals with whom they are working. In addition, given that sport is only one part of an athlete's life, another measure of success may be whether each athlete continues to participate in sport (either with the same coach or another one), or at the very least remains a physically active individual.

Another issue to be discussed here is society's stereotypical image of the athletic coach. The coach as a 'field-marshal', 'commander in chief', 'general of the troops' is not one to be questioned. His or her knowledge is typically judged to be supreme and final. For such a 'general' to ask his or her charges questions would be to 'lose face' and show a sign of weakness. Society, expressed or manifested in the actions of unknowing, uncaring, uninformed parents, also has a hand in the current coaching scene. Parents, unwittingly, are often carried away with the wave of adoration and fame that their children accrue. In effect, many parents are living vicariously through and at the expense of their children. Parents, especially those without an extensive sports-related background (although many guilty parents are individuals with the exactly opposite experience—that is they are experienced, skilled, accomplished former athletes, who believe what is good for the goose is good for the gander) typically 'bask in the reflected glory' that their children garner. These parents often contribute (knowingly or not) to the too commonly observed abuses resulting in the sport endeavour today.

Unrealistic ambitions of parents add fuel to the issue. Rather than be happy that their children are participating in a meaningful and enjoyable pastime, parents too early and too often focus on what the experience will get for them and their children beyond mere enjoyment—university funding, scholarship monies, a professional career. The odds of youngsters ultimately achieving either a university scholarship or a professional sport career are very small: Hyman (2009) cites figures that suggest approximately 7% of athletes will receive scholarship money, and such money often falls short of a 'full-ride' (i.e. a full sport scholarship) as coaches attempt to spread the money across as many athletes as possible. Moreover, as Hyman (2009) suggests, it is likely that an academically strong student would receive a much larger financial scholarship than most athletes.

Society also expects coaches to be knowledgeable, to make decisions, to be leaders and to be active. Society does not expect coaches to ask questions, pose situations or encourage athletes to be critical thinkers. Society does not expect coaches to be facilitators; the stereotypical coach is loud and commanding, has an obvious presence, knows everything or at least acts that way and knows how to make decisions, is organised and has a 'take-charge' personality. Coaches who are quiet, are indirect in their leadership, ask questions, do not have a 'presence', appear to be unsure, or are not assertive often are demeaned and challenged by players, fans, spectators and programme organisers.

In conflict with such widespread responses are revelations by Goleman (1995) that better leaders are often those who do not have knowledge as they have to rely on their charges and as a result the group learns together. They may, in effect, 'lose face' but often gain the respect of the group. The lack or limited availability of coaching development programmes, and/or the often minimal requirements therein of coaching development programmes, has exacerbated this point. Coaches, who are often former athletes themselves and are working from a background of limited study of the growth and development of their athletes, simply coach the way that they were coached, thereby perpetuating the traditional coach-centred model of coaching leadership. These individuals have never experienced, studied or been exposed to an athlete-centred, humanistic model of coaching—in essence, through no fault of their own, they do not know of any other way to lead athletes. However, increasing the coach's awareness of alternatives may assist them to change and realise a better performance from the athletes who are able to take ownership of their learning.

Athletes

Athletes have different ideas about their participation in sport, including different reasons for participating, desires, interests, involvement and commitments. Sport offers a setting where athletes can gain a sense of competence, achievement and recognition. An effective coach is one who introduces individuals to sport and provides them with confidence, success and recognition so that the athletes want to continue in sport and with physical activity. A coach can make the athletic experience positive or negative. Our athletes deserve good coaches dedicated to their betterment and to the development of confident, motivated, successful and happy people. This dedication is embedded in the values and principles inherent of an empowering philosophy (i.e. an athlete-centred, humanistic approach).

Athletes themselves are often the most vocal critics of athlete-centred coaches, presenting a major obstacle to the implementation of such a model of coaching leadership. Never having experienced coaches who have used anything other than a predominantly coach-centred model of sport leadership (i.e. the coach as 'commanding general' of the troops), they may resist any other type of leadership and may be put off by coaches who appear not to be sure or confident of the tasks involved in sport. Athletes with such attitudes tend to criticise athlete-centred coaches and have less respect for a coach who fills the 'coach as facilitator' role than for the coach working in the model of the all-powerful, all-knowing general on the field. Further, many athletes find it difficult and/or uncomfortable to have to think when asked questions, as they have to work in such situations and take responsibility for their learning.

When first asked to respond to questions, or to resolve theoretically, or intellectually relate to the sport experience, athletes new to such an approach may be baffled, or disappointed, or rebellious. Coaches need to be aware of athletes' general lack of exposure to such an experience and consequently must implement such a programme, gradually. In effect, coaches need to educate athletes how to respond to an athlete-centred system, given that it will often be a new experience for most athletes.

Time Constraints

Coaches typically have limited time with a small number of athletes. Excellent coaches plan their time with athletes in specific detail. Although time is a major constraint, it becomes more powerful with the dominance of the coach's needs or ego involvement or both. If a coach is feeling pressured to win and believes (rightly or wrongly) that the number of wins influences the way he or she is evaluated, then techniques such as asking questions and having athletes analyse situations could represent a challenge to time management. In these circumstances, the coach will focus on telling, informing, lecturing, etc. and will simply dismiss an athlete-centred approach as too time consuming.

However, we again refer back to one of our basic concepts. If sport is truly educational, then coaches need to lead in a manner that enhances the athletes' motor performance and their understanding of all aspects of the sport experience. Time spent in having athletes think must be viewed as productive. Again, the time constraints become pressing only if the coach is focused primarily on short-term outcomes (e.g. winning) rather than the long-term, future development of the athlete as outlined above.

The 'Professional' Model of Sport

The professional or adult model of sport was briefly explained in Chapter One. This philosophy has become so engrained within the sport hierarchy that to question it is close to blasphemy. In the professional model, strictly defined, winning is all important, the coach's needs are all important, win at all costs predominates, survival of the fittest and the best rules is the philosophy, and all other factors related to sport, including its educational intentions, are less important. At the professional level of competition there is no pretence of sport making the participant a better person, or 'building positive character traits' via the sport experience. Winning is all that matters. Participants are expected to be 'gamers'—that is, they should be ready to do whatever it takes to win, be it legal or illegal, or virtuous or otherwise. Nothing should interfere with the pursuit of victory—no individual, not the opponents, and certainly not the rules, stated or implied.

We would somewhat agree that at the truly professional level of sport this outlook makes more sense (although the structure of professional level of sport needs further critique than what we have offered here) than it does at those performance/competitive levels that justify their existence by trotting out documents stating their many educational goals. At the professional level of sport, the holistic development of the athlete is not necessarily the primary concern of coaches and administrators. Professional sport is primarily devoted to winning, making money, being champions and all that that comes with these outcomes. The individual development of the professional athlete would be considered a distant second to the above-listed goals, and would not be the prime concern of the coach. In addition, the financial and employment security of several individuals, including the coach, are dependent on athletes performing well and winning championships. In these circumstances the personal, cognitive/psychological and social development of the athlete is of lower priority than the more tangible performance goals.

However, when the professional model intrudes on the sport experience at levels in which sport is justified because of its many educational outcomes, its character-building capabilities, and its impact on the personality of participants, then we would suggest that an athlete-centred approach is more appropriate.

One of the major issues in sport today is the 'creeping professionalisation' that has occurred, and continues to occur, in all levels of sport, even at the earliest ages of all activities (e.g. football for three- to four-year-olds, tee-ball leagues, biddy basketball). Professionalised sport places the coach-centred model at the centre of the sport experience. The needs and interests of the adult leader/coach take precedence over the needs, interests and/or abilities of the performers.

The Coach's Lack of Exposure to Alternative Models

Coaches typically coach in the manner that they were coached when (and if!) they were athletes. In many situations, unless they have undertaken study and professional development, the only models that they have been exposed to are those of their former coaches. How can we expect a traditional coach-centred leader to implement an athlete-centred approach if he or she has never been exposed to it—never observed it in action nor had the opportunity to study it? Indeed, if coaches have completed a coach development programme, did it include discussion of an athlete-centred approach? Currently coach development programmes are more likely to be delivered via the traditional lecture format, with little practical or hands-on activity, and minimal feedback, and it is certainly rare for them to focus on an athlete-centred approach.

In the past a segment of the coaches involved in sport were prepared to be physical education teachers. As such, it could be assumed that these physical educators/coaches had been exposed to a spectrum of leadership styles. Currently there are quality issues with coaching development programmes. With the influx of 'walk-on' coaches, the explosion of youth league programmes, year-round sport programmes (e.g. football for summer, autumn, winter and spring), and the resistance of some physical educators to coaching assignments for a variety of reasons (e.g. a combination of low pay, parental interference, and ambitious expectations of the community and/or society), the quality of the coaching leadership can be issue. As a result, ever-increasing numbers of unprepared coaches (e.g. volunteers; sport specialists versus school teachers) are leading athletes into action. These circumstances provide additional support for putting in place at the very least basic coaching development programmes and making them readily available to potential coaches.

Talent Development

An issue strongly related to moving sport coaching to a more educational, humanistic and/or athlete-centred approach is the need for coaches who fully understand the struggles that some athletes experience. Often the coach has had a very positive athletic/sport experience as a gifted, talented individual who struggled less to become highly skilled than many of the athletes who he or she is now coaching. It is easy to see how such a coach would not understand (empathise with) athletes who do not quickly and easily 'get it': given that the coach learned this skill or technique so quickly, why can't these athletes? In contrast, the average player who becomes a coach understands the intermediate steps, the hours of practice, the number of repetitions, etc. that it sometimes takes for a less gifted athlete to accomplish the same skill as the more gifted athlete.

This very real issue often causes conflict within teams. The demands of a coach who does not understand the variability of the motor learning process and the individual with average skills who must work twice as hard as others to keep up can result in, at the very least, communication issues, if not problems that could disrupt the team culture.

Recommendations

Many highly competitive adults tend to 'exploit' sport participants based on their own needs and values. It is not a question of blame: most adults are trying to do what is best for the participants, but sometimes they get it wrong. The solution is to give priority to the development needs of the athletes ahead of adult needs. Teachers, coaches and parents have such a major impact on the quality of participants' sporting experiences that we need to reflect on the opportunities we can provide for them. Our influence can help ensure a positive experience and a sound level of development. If participants are happy and successful, under little or no pressure to win, they enjoy their experience in sport.

Some recommendations based on the issues raised in this chapter are included here:

1. Reduce the adult influences on sport. Can we really prepare athletes to coach themselves? Can we at least invite them into the conversation?

2. Recruit leaders who have undergone appropriate coaching development. Coach development programmes can address many of the concerns related to how sport is managed today. It is important to require completion of meaningful coaching development experiences as a prerequisite for such leadership positions. The profession also needs to monitor such programmes so that they are valid and, current, and include a major section on the growth and development needs of athletes of all ages. The health-related growth and development issues must be studied in depth and coaches must demonstrate a clear understanding of the needs of athletes at all levels in order to obtain licensing.

3. Provide coaching development opportunities in ways that increase access, visibility, etc. (year-round offerings; many locations; inexpensive; keep local). Quality coaching education programmes must become a prerequisite to taking control of a sports team. Coaches also must be encouraged to value continued professional development (CPD), so as to ascertain whether they have maintained/sustained their knowledge of their sport and more importantly knowledge of their athletes.

4. Select highly skilled and empathic individuals as coaches (how to screen for empathy will take some thought-provoking consideration). The profession of coaching needs to develop policies and procedures to ensure that capable individuals are selected to lead our youngsters in sport. Unfortunately (or is it fortunately?), given the needs of the many school-based and/or recreation-based sport programmes in the world, the current demand for coaches clearly outstrips the supply. Certainly we do not endorse the cancellation of sport programmes because qualified coaches are unavailable. The shortage presents a serious concern for educators and coaches alike: how do we select and prepare a sufficient number of coaches to satisfy the need, while providing appropriate leadership?

5. Reduce the practice of 'over specialisation' and year-round programmes. Dr Lyle Micheli, a world-renowned paediatric sports medicine physician, suggests that the waves of new volunteer coaches have to be continually alerted to the fact that more training for children/athletes does not always equate to improved performance (McMahon, 2007). How can we encourage athletes to participate in a variety of sports and thereby reduce the stress on the body that participating in that activity all year, year after year, will cause?

6. Introduce emotional intelligence (EQ) to address the 'ego' issues related to coaching leadership.

7. Educate parents and society about coaching as an educational endeavour. Can we require completion of 'parental development' courses as related to sport participation for their children? Such courses have been organised in several parts of the world (e.g. National Alliance for Youth Sports, USA), where parents must attend one or more sessions in order for their youngsters to enrol and participate in sport programmes.

8. Begin to role model an athlete-centred approach so it becomes the norm with athletes, parents and onlookers. Leaders in coach development courses, expert coaches, and coaches working in educational institutions should be required to model an athlete-centred approach. Administrators supervising such sport programmes could be required to encourage their coaches to employ an athlete-centred approach as an employment requirement.

9. Emphasise that the development of athletes is a long-term (rather than short-term) process. All those involved with sport, at all levels, would need to support this goal. With this common emphasis, everyone involved at all levels of sport would be professing the many benefits of sport participation beyond winning and physical and motor development. A holistic set of expectations of the sport experience held by performers, parents, administrators and coaches would enable and encourage coaches to behave in a manner that would support an athlete-centred, humanistic approach.

> Those who know do not speak Those
>
> that speak do not know. - Lao-Tzu Tao Te Ching

References

Boxill, J. (2003). Introduction: The moral significance of sport. In J. Boxill (Ed.) *Sport Ethics: An anthology*. Malden, MA: Blackwell.

Coakley, J. (2009). *Sports in Society: Issues and controversies* (10th ed.). New York, NY: McGraw-Hill Higher Education.

Goleman, D. (1995). *Emotional Intelligence: Why it can matter more than IQ*. New York, NY: Bantam.

Fullinwider, R.K. (2006). *Sports, Youth and Character: A critical survey*. Retrieved on 30 December 2009 from www.civicyouth.org, Circle Working Paper 44: Center for Information & Research on Civic Learning & Engagement.

Hyman, M. (2009). *Until It Hurts: America's obsession with youth sports and how it harms our kids.* Boston, MA: Beacon.

McMahon, R. (2007). *Revolution in the Bleachers: How parents can take back family life in a world gone crazy over youth sports.* New York, NY: Gotham.

Roberts, G.C., Treasure, D.C., & Hall, H.K. (1994). Parental goal orientations and beliefs about the competitive-sport experience of their child. *Journal of Applied Social Psychology, 24,* 631–645.

Shields, D.L. & Bredemeier, B.L. (2001). Moral development and behavior in sport. In R.N. Singer et al. (Eds.) *Handbook of Sports Psychology* (2nd ed.). New York, NY: John Wiley & Sons.

Stoll, S.K., & Beller, J.M. (2000). Do sports build character? In J.R. Gerdy (Ed.) *Sports in School: The future of an institution.* New York: Teachers College.

People will rise to a challenge if it is their challenge. —Wayne Smith

If you want to build a ship, don't herd people together to collect wood and don't assign them tasks and work, but rather teach them to long for the endless immensity of the sea. -Antoine de Saint-Exupery

Leaders understand the power of choice -Anonymous

Chapter Three

Mike Ruddock

Worcester Warriors Rugby Coach

Background

Mike Ruddock is currently the Director of Rugby for the Worcester Warriors, a Premier rugby team in the English Rugby Union. At the time of interview, Mike was beginning his third season as coach of the Warriors. Previously as coach of the Welsh rugby team he saw his team achieve in 2005, for the first time in 27 years, the Six Nations Grand Slam (a major tournament in which Wales beat all five other competing nations).

Before taking up coaching, Mike played rugby for 14 years, starting in Blaina in Gwent, Wales. Mike's playing years took him from the Blaina team to the national Welsh squad. At the age of 26, a work injury saw him rehabilitating at a local rugby club, where he decided to help out. This marked the beginning of his coaching career.

The lure of coaching motivated Mike to do a formal coaching course to assist his new interest. He completed a series of courses, including the Welsh Rugby Union courses at Levels 2 and 3 and an Irish Rugby Union Level 2 course. Although he also decided began to study for the Level 4 in rugby coaching, the overemphasis on theory and the lack of actual coaching frustrated him. As a full-time, paid coach, the time required for writing not only took him away from the coaching he loved but also reduced the time available to research the future opposition through game analysis.

In his coaching role, Mike was a product of both amateur and professional eras. After coaching local teams Blaina, Cross Keys and a Second Division team Bective Rangers in Ireland, he was lured back by Swansea to coach his former playing club. He coached this amateur team from 1991 to 1995 as the coaching director. In 1995, when rugby became a professional sport, Mike was lucky enough to work for a club who could pay for him to coach. However, finding the funds for support coaches was more difficult so Mike essentially coached by himself for a number of his first experiences as a professional coach.

Mike's period with the Swansea Club proved to be very successful: the team won the Welsh League Championships in 1992 and 1994 as well as the Welsh Rugby Union Cup in 1995. Swansea also defeated world champions Australia in 1994. Mike was subsequently asked to be an assistant coach of the Welsh team for the 1995 Rugby World Cup in South Africa.

In 1997 Mike went to Leinster in Ireland where he was the first professional coach in the province. In 2000 he went back to Wales and coached Ebbw Vale for three years before moving on to the Newport Gwent Dragons in 2003. The team beat a number of highly rated teams, which influenced the Welsh Rugby Union to ask Mike to coach the national team, a role he then took on between 2004 and 2006.

The ever-changing professional era of rugby meant that Mike had a new role in the Welsh team: he became Director of Rugby. In that capacity, though he coached, he was also responsible for player recruitment (including player contracts and budgets) and for recruiting and managing a number of other coaches and support team members. In a little over 10 years, therefore, Mike went from essentially coaching by himself in 1991 to having to manage a team of assistant coaches, fitness and strength and conditioning coaches, physiotherapists, video analysts, a medical department and equipment personnel, to name a few.

After Mike left the position of Wales rugby coach in 2006, he spent what he calls a fantastic year with a Mumbles (in Wales) junior squad in an amateur coaching role. After experiencing the pressure (and politics) involved in coaching a national team, he enjoyed Mumbles so much he felt re-energised and realised that he missed professional coaching. Thus he accepted a position of Director of Rugby with the Worcester Warriors in 2007. As he reflects:

> I think I was ready to go back; I had a bit of a breather. I enjoyed actually working during the day and not worrying about all the ups and downs of rugby, but at the end of the year, I had enjoyed the [Mumbles] team so much, things were going well and it sparked my interest in getting back into full-time professional rugby.

During the year that he has away from professional coaching, he worked for a recruitment agency and was responsible for team building and culture development for interested Welsh companies. His approach to establishing a team culture is discussed in more detail later in this chapter and in Chapter Six.

When asked to identify his favourite coaching stint prior to the Warriors, Mike said:

> I have had a couple of really good ones that I thoroughly enjoyed ... For example at Leinster I enjoyed a good rapport with the players and we beat some really good teams ... It is really rewarding to the see the likes of Brian O'Driscoll, Shane Horgan, and Gordan D'Arcy for example, players that I offered their first ever professional contracts go on to become top players over the years ... With Worcester, I hope to enjoy the job, the role, again work with the people and be determined that the team go forward.

Mike's approach to coaching is athlete-centred in that many decisions and coaching ways he uses depend on the needs of the athletes. His responses to many of my questions demonstrate his passion for helping players to be the best they can be. As well as using the interview process to develop an understanding of his coaching, I had the pleasure of observing the Warriors coaches and players during the end of the season in 2009 and the beginning of the season in 2009–2010.

Mike's Philosophy of Coaching

Mike suggested that his coaching philosophy has changed over the years but it is evident that his basic beliefs have not. He has tried new things and focused on the current trends, but an athlete-centred philosophy has pervaded his coaching. He feels that his coaching is constantly evolving and discusses rugby philosophies as well as coaching ones. His initial reaction to the question about his philosophy was:

> That is interesting, because you examine coaching philosophy on a number of coaching courses and you write things down and you become a little bit one-dimensional … it changes, it continues to change as you grow and develop and mature and learn from past mistakes and strengths … You change things in your mind and how you adapt a philosophy based on those experiences. Also the game is changing, the laws are changing. It becomes pretty muddy in the end and is multi-dimensional. I guess the old saying is it is like an onion really: there are so many layers to it.

Mike acknowledges that the key to his 'onion' philosophy is enabling players to enjoy their experience and develop as rugby players:

> I like to promote a team that is a thinking team, a positive team, that understands the game, that gets involved in key decisions, either through formal or informal communication with the coach and coaching staff. They know what they are doing. I haven't been overly prescriptive in making us do this in this part of the field and in that part of the field, but I feel I always try to let the players make decisions based on safe or different options we have and giving the boys a bit of rope so they can make their own decisions. This process can be a longer way to do things at times, because you tend to lose a few games and make the mistakes before you come out on the other side with a bigger and better bowl of knowledge about what works for you.

In encouraging this thinking, Mike suggests that a major part of his coaching repertoire is to provide problem-solving activities for players. Here his coaching staff either pose a question or use a scenario where the players need to come up with a solution to a relevant problem.

To reiterate how his philosophy has changed over the years, Mike compares his first one-dimensional understanding of a coaching philosophy, often prescribed through coaching courses, with his realisation that the task of coaching players is complex and the environment and tasks at hand are always changing:

> … it is how you treat players, it's how you treat staff. In the old days, when I first started, it was so one-dimensional. You approached things in how you wanted the players to approach it. Now, there are all sorts of processes involved, that I feel you need to do with the players and coaches, i.e. decision making with input from the group, getting an understanding of what they think about the input, what is right, what is not right for this particular group and there's the questioning approach about boundaries that need to be implemented. Some players and groups find it confusing and others relish the fact that there are little or no rigid boundaries and that they are free to have or make decisions or set their own standards. Every group is slightly different and I think what I'd like to do is try to adapt a little to the changing times and changing groups, as well as [develop] key principles of how I want my teams to play.

This complexity of the sport environment and the way players perform and train is reinforced when there are multiple cultures, multiple personalities, a range of expectations and so many other unpredictable, dynamic factors. Mike's major premise is that it depends on the situation, the athlete and the context. He advocates for his players to be decision makers but acknowledges:

> In an ideal world you want all players to make decisions, but in practical terms, because you would have all 15 players deciding what to do next, [it] wouldn't work for a good decision-making process … The reality is certain players are going to do that [make decisions] better than others and you want to recruit, train, develop and nurture players who will be capable of those key decisions that run the team, to make those key decisions in the right positions for the team and have the latitude or formalised authority to make those key decisions at that time, with full support from the rest of the team.

Mike's experience with both amateur and professional rugby teams has allowed him to think broadly about the differences in decision making among players:

> … the game is the same at all levels, the biggest difference is the emotional and psychological elements. It is about obtaining a professional players' environment for everyone to be comfortable and challenged and confident in what they are doing … the amateur player doesn't have time to think about rugby everyday. He's got work and a family so basically

his thoughts about rugby would be only when he is going to training and only then does he start wondering about what the team will be doing tonight—'this is how we want to approach the game on Saturday, if I am on the team'—[or] wonder what his game time will be. He doesn't have much time to sit down with the team as a group and get into too much discussion about it. [With an amateur team] you have to pick out some key individuals who you know you can work with, like the captain, who you know you will see on a more regular basis, to bounce around some ideas on the tactical approach of the team … it is more one-dimensional… Whereas a professional rugby player can execute all the mental skills, fitness principles, and the same sorts of game plans, and practices, on a more regular basis … The full-time player, particularly the most successful, has an intellect and emotion, and the ability to think more clearly and deeply about the game because that's what he does every day.

Mike advocates a philosophy of 'discipline' in which the boundaries for the players in training and games are dependent on the level of the team, their expectations and reasons for competing in rugby:

Ideally you want some sort of discipline and parameters for people, but I don't want it to be the 'be all and end all'. I don't want discipline or rules to gobble up my team; I want collective sorts of actions; I want a happy environment and enjoyment to dominate if possible. I want a happy camp with people who have smiles on their faces and they enjoy the team, they enjoy working hard, they enjoy the challenges and they play good rugby. If the coach is walking around sitting on top of them all the time, they would be afraid to make a decision in case it was the wrong one and they would be afraid to give a 20-metre pass or offload in the tackle (for example) in case there is a mistake … I don't want people who have fear. It's coming up with a balance of having sufficient rules and regulations whilst having an environment that creates a sense of purpose and a sense of togetherness … Some groups are comfortable with getting more out of it for themselves and some groups want more rules, discipline and boundaries. It's about reading your group and going through that process. It does take longer to build a successful culture through player input and shared boundaries; however it is more sustainable over the long term because the players are driving the culture rather than being forced down a certain path that might not fit that particular group.

Mike's Development as a Coach

Mike has had 24 years to develop his coaching, and admits he has learned much in that time. Most of his learning about coaching stems from his experience in winning, losing, making brilliant decisions, making mistakes, knowing the players, and drawing on his own and others' technical expertise. These experiences include the complexities of coaching people to get the best out of them. The essence of his approach to coaching is a focus on the people involved—reading them and understanding them.

When Mike and I discussed why he coaches, he said with great conviction:

> ... you feel so passionate about it that it makes you want to go through the bad times as well as the good times. [Through the difficult times] I ask myself that question, if I really want to do it, for the game, through ups and downs, do I want to get myself in a position going from zero again? ... Yeah I want to do it, it's something that I enjoy doing; I enjoy the interaction with the players in particular.

In considering how he evolved his approach, Mike recognises that, although it has been a long process and he still hasn't learned everything, his approach depends on the particular team or group of players, the staff and the situation. Because the approach is so complex, it is difficult to put into words:

> You can't get into the process to the nth degree ... because there are situational differences and individual differences and in each different club there is a club chairman who acts in a certain way and has particular expectations and so ultimately the pressure is on. I am starting to feel for the first time in 24 years that I actually know what those processes are really about, that I actually know where we are going for the long term as a group in terms of a sustainable culture. Even though we have had some tough times I don't need to panic and be reactive about it, whereas in the past I might have, particularly if results were not great. If we stick to what we are doing and continue to put those processes in place now, we will actually reach the Promised Land. We will make mistakes and we will mess things up a little bit, but we will have successes along the way and most of all we will have a positive environment that has player and coach input driving it and therefore a culture that has a genuine sense of ownership about it.

One of Mike's most valuable experiences as a coach and developing this athlete-centred approach was with Swansea. He gives an example of player input:

> ... with Swansea in '91–'92, the majority of my coaching involved a lot of good communication with key players and tactical chats with the captain

in particular. The first session I ran with Swansea, I actually sent two boys away from the training session for being late. However, there was a prelude [to that action] in that I met with the squad some weeks earlier and gave them all a questionnaire, and asked them to identify what was needed to go forward for the club. I also asked them to put down what they felt would be an appropriate time to train; to allow people who were going to be further away to come to training on time, so we'd all start together and we would all finish together. At the first training, these two boys suddenly had an excuse, 'Well actually I finished work at half past five and the training is at six, and I have to travel 45 minutes and I am going to be late' … At the earlier meeting the players had all given a commitment and I had two boys turn up late, so I felt justified in sending them away as they had broken the agreed protocol—I hadn't just forced a time upon them. They had committed to that time! I look at setting the tone, people keeping to time and keeping to their contracts that we all agreed. I hadn't forced that rule on them; it is something that they had promoted at the team meeting as the perfect training time. After that incident, it all settled down. People got into the right habits and I involved the players a lot in decision making.

Throughout his coaching, Mike promoted the need to include players in making key decisions about the mutual direction of the team, by questioning, through problem solving about what the team wants their reputation to be. He believed that if the players contribute, then they *own* the decisions made and take responsibility for those decisions. Mike gave an example of one of his successes achieved through player input:

I remember we played Neath in the Welsh Cup … local rivals who were doing particularly well at that time. We had had a bit of a bad run prior to that game after three really successful seasons. We had been champions the previous year, but we'd lost a couple of players and we suddenly needed rebuilding … People were writing us off going to Neath in the Cup, which was in six weeks' time. We sat down [together] and agreed a policy with the boys … [The policy stated] that we would match [Neath] in terms of fitness and aggression as they were one of the fittest teams, if not the fittest in Welsh rugby at the time; however we believed we had the skill and the ability to play and beat them … We set out a plan to work really hard on fitness and contact skills … to go to Neath and win the physical battle and finish the game strong because we were in good condition … The week before the game, I said to the players, 'Well, we are on track physically, technically and tactically, but I don't know what will help our mental approach, but I am looking for a 1% or something that will make the difference in terms of our mental approach.' [When presenting this problem] I figured it might be a goal-setting exercise or an evaluation of anything we could do mentally to give us an edge. One of the players put up his hand and said, 'Well, we play in white and they play in black. It's just like a cowboy film, a guy with a white hat on rides into town, opens the bar saloon and there are all the bad guys in the background and it's a negative place to go. So if we could change that, we wouldn't feel as intimidated.' … We brainstormed that we had our away navy blue rugby jerseys which we hardly ever wore. We decided to wear those because it would clash with [Neath's] black jersey. We anticipated that the referee would make them change their jerseys as the home team. Their second kit was turquoise. We thought that Neath wearing turquoise jerseys wouldn't be so intimidating, so basically the players came up with that plan, whereby our Navy jerseys were locked up safely in the changing room until the last minute. We warmed up in our t-shirts and tracksuit tops. They didn't suspect that we'd change our kit till the last minute. We went back in and we put our navy blue jerseys on, the referee came in before the kick-off and said, 'This is a colour clash, I'll have to go tell the other team to change their jerseys.' There was mayhem, we could hear them shouting in the changing rooms, and they came out and called me everything under the sun. We went out in our navy blue jerseys, they walked out in their turquoise, much to the surprise of their home fans who wanted to see the big, bad guys in black, and we turned around and beat them in the cup. The headlines the next day and the stories in the newspapers were not about the game as much as the psychological aspects where they changed jerseys at the last minute, putting them off their game plan.

Due to his nature, Mike does not agree with the 'bullying' tactics that some coaches use and they are not part of his current approach. As a player, though, he respected all of the coaches, with their different approaches. He recognised the authoritarian approach had some advantages yet he also perceived its limitations:

… the thing that impressed me [was that the kind of coach] that had a lot of success was the more athlete-centred coach … [however] we had a fantastic [playing season]—my first season—under a bully coach. We won the Welsh and the Anglo Welsh championships, which is the unofficial table where all the Welsh and English teams play off against each other. We won that by a country mile. However we lost in the Welsh Cup final at the end of a long hard season. [The authoritarian approach] certainly made a difference to that team for one year. But in the following year, unrest started to settle in; people got disenchanted with this approach and in the end the club let him go ... I'd seen at first hand the pros and cons of the bullying approach. It can have an impact in the early stages and can create a reaction to that, but that reaction can be very much short-lived; that's my experience when I tried that approach as well.

Based on those experiences, Mike continued to be an athlete-centred coach. However, it is interesting that after this success in developing players and winning major competitions, in his last year with Swansea the team produced fewer wins than in previous years:

I think I always had strong years in Swansea where we won most things and had a great, successful record. Towards the end of my tenure, we sort of dropped away and we had been beaten by a side who was coached by a guy who I knew had an authoritarian style, a 'My way or the highway' style.

As his team was firmly beaten by a side who had a 'bully' coach, Mike embarked on a mission to coach as an authoritarian. Ultimately, though, he came to realise this approach not only did not help the players (despite the team winning a tournament in the first year), it also went against his nature:

I think I am always against bullying people, but I did go through a phase in '97,'98 at Leinster where I did try 'It's my way or the highway'. I thought I needed a change of style ... I thought that might have been one of the reasons why we hadn't done so well [in the previous season at Swansea] ... Perhaps I had been a bit soft on the guys in Swansea toward the end of my tenure. [The authoritarian style] did work the first year [at Leinster], but I found that after a while, it lost its impact ... Fundamentally I realised that to improve individually and collectively, players needed solutions not emotion. I also believe that the best solutions were the ones that included players' involvement. That involvement would allow them the opportunity to get a greater understanding of the problem that needed to be fixed and an understanding of a collective approach that would ensure a unified commitment to finding a solution. It was a good exercise in the sense that it convinced me to work with the athletes/players and not use the big stick.

Mike admits that some players need to be told and motivated externally occasionally. He gives a situational example:

... probably the first year, I bullied those guys a bit ... We didn't have a lot of support structures in place and video analysis structures, and we couldn't review what we were doing that often. I was on my own, so I couldn't delegate to coaches or pick up on their ideas. there was no way of changing things a lot with the likes of larger groups—e.g. 30 or 40 people, the squad—as I couldn't break them down into smaller groups or smaller activities. I tended to work on bigger activities and a drive to coaching around expectations of getting a commitment, an action on fitness and all those sorts of things.

Mike is a self-reflective person. In a generally informal approach, he questions himself to determine if there is a way to do things better. Interestingly, Mike suggests that there is so much in coaching with its multi-dimensional nature, he often encounters unexpected situations. To deal with these, he draws on his past experiences and reflects on the best way forward:

I would say that personal reflection on what I am doing is good and bad, but we have started doing some work at [Worcester], where we give feedback to each other as a group and try to work with a buddy on that, although I [personally] haven't been that successful with that. The timing is a problem, it is the kind of thing that I should be putting in my diary and saying, 'Well, come and tell me about how you perceive my coaching and I will tell you how I perceive a job that you are doing.'

Under the buddy system that Mike mentions, staff give feedback to each other about their coaching, or whatever role they are undertaking. Acting as a type of mentor to each other, they seek and provide feedback about their successes and difficulties related to their role. So, as part of Mike's current role as Director of Coaching, he reflects on this buddy system which leads him to suggest that, though the process sounds good in theory, it doesn't work particularly well for him at the moment. At this point in his coaching career, he is responsible in a more managerial capacity, such as dealing with players' and coaches' contracts, ensuring media are happy, dealing with budgets and answering to the club's major business associates. In examining the uncomfortable fit of the buddy system with this role, he says:

… reflective practice and being prepared to receive constructive feedback from subordinates is a battle as the Director of Rugby, perhaps it is sometimes just a feeling that by doing so you have some sort of insecurity by needing to get your coaching style checked out with other people … I suppose it's linked to the media and all the outside perception that the coach should be a strong guy, with an unfailing will of steel and never has any self-doubt and is always going to know what to do at the right time.

However, Mike sees value in holding group feedback sessions about various roles in the club. He feels that the pressure that others feel, given they are essentially his employees, is less when they can remain anonymous when providing feedback:

> I am quite enjoying the group sessions where people are giving feedback as a group. I think it is less threatening than at an individual level, because the individual can be part of a group of three or four who might deliver some fairly negative feedback without fear of retribution, whereas on an individual basis it would be difficult for someone who I employ to tell you how crap you are at certain things for fear of losing their job. Ultimately this process informs you of your strengths and weaknesses as perceived by those you work with. You don't have to do anything with or about the feedback; however the smart coach will probably want to work on a few areas to become a more effective coach.

As noted above, when Mike started coaching, he took many coaching courses to help him develop his skills in this area. He found these very useful as a way of getting him started:

> I hadn't done any teacher training, so how to organise sessions and split groups up and communicate to those people and to get the confidence to stand up and do that, was valuable in any approach you take when you are first starting off.

However, in contributing to his continued coaching development, the courses were less useful. Mike still found the knowledge useful, but what he really needed at this stage was to practise coaching:

> … one of the reasons I didn't go on to the Masters courses, was the game changes all the time. Whilst the theory of coaching is well documented to a point, the danger with immersing yourself fully with the theory modules is [that your main concern is] to get the written word right. I felt at times I was losing track of the practical side of coaching. While I was at the computer doing my module work, I wasn't looking through recent tapes of training or playing … I think sometimes the danger is that [although it] is great to know or have the knowledge, modules on fitness, modules on psychology, modules on the coaching process (which I think is really, really important) and all the other areas that go into building a degree in coaching, it's [a problem] finding the time [so] that you don't overcommit to one area on the academic side and lose track of the practical side. How you come up with that balance is a tricky one for anyone … I learned a lot on the coaching courses, but what they can't show you is how to get it right and win every game.

Mike decided not to continue formal coaching courses. Nonetheless he continues to seek opportunities for learning, as he indicates:

> I try to fill the gaps in my knowledge or performance by speaking to people who have special skills or knowledge in certain areas that can help me deliver exactly what I want. I don't have all the ideas or answers ... I have to utilise the services of other coaches who have expertise and skills in other areas.

The Process of Establishing a Quality Team Culture

Mike values team culture as a way to give players a focus or direction in their rugby as well as to help shape team goals. Through his years of coaching amateur rugby, he often informally attended to and monitored a team culture, but during his professional rugby career, he has implemented more formal team cultures and strategies, particularly during his time at Worcester. The team culture process is very important to Mike: he believes that solid teams can't win without it. At the same time, he has attended to the team cultures in many different ways, including inviting an external person to help. Ultimately, he says it depends on the particular team:

> It's trying to come up with an environment with give and take, there's a feeling that we belong together, that is what I enjoy ... where people are deadly serious about achievement; however they have got a smile on their face, are courteous, are friendly to each other, are focused and yet honest at the same time.

It is important to develop and encourage an environment where people respect each other and depend on each other to get the job done.

As the team members change quite often every year, he first gets to know the staff and players to develop rapport, trust and respect and he values what individuals bring to the team. He analyses them through informal chats and lots of observation:

> I want to get to know people and see how they are going, and let them know I value and support them 100% ... I want to find out what they are about rather than bring in people you know just because you know them ...

Mike believes that all members of a team should be involved in the formation of team culture, but sometimes because of the needs and past experiences of the particular players involved, he and his staff need to set up the initial structure and directions.

In attending to his team culture, Mike is keen to develop an open environment where all the players, coaches and support staff can learn from each other. He encourages all his staff and players to have an openness to learning, be able to think and be prepared to have a go. He believes this open environment allows players to make mistakes, as only 'doers' make them. The environment is such that players are not reprimanded for their mistakes, but encouraged to find solutions to mistakes that have been made. All these elements in his philosophy are reflected in his description of himself as a coach:

> ... we create an environment where I am prepared to accept criticism from my peers as well as [where] they are prepared to accept criticism from me and from my players ... You feel there is a sense of trust.

The team culture is developed around the players' needs and expectations. For certain teams, Mike realises that there needs to be a balance, whereby the athletes have ownership for the culture, but sometimes the expectations from he and his coaching staff have to be made clear, e.g. boundaries:

> [For the Worcester Warriors,] there is a template for our coaching responsibilities and trademarks that is documented and rugby-specific. All of our coaches have agreed on these key performance strategies and will incorporate those within coaching sessions ... We kept the ones established from last year (clinical, knowledgeable, united, expansive, ruthless) ... the players were quite happy to keep those. But in a workshop, I asked them to look into more rugby-specific trademarks ... what our brand is going to be on the field, what other teams' perceptions [of us] should be ... The players came up with specific trademarks that represented us. These were recorded and placed on view in our changing rooms as a reminder of 'what we should be about'.

The formal trademarks that the team has agreed to are monitored and facilitated by the coaching and support staff, but Mike is aware that he has the final say and the key decisions ultimately have to come from him. He believes strongly that honesty is one of the biggest values in practising his coaching and being part of the team culture:

> ... be honest about your thoughts and selection. When you want to really make a point even if some of the players don't agree with it, if they see that you are honest, I think they will go with you. And being able to say, 'I honestly don't know the answer', then I think they respect that. So honesty is important. If you've got that then you expect the players to have honesty on the pitch about their performance as well.

Mike also believes strongly in the social binding of the players to focus on the united value that the team culture portrays. The team is often together for social sessions because Mike believes that this socialising helps to bind the players:

One of our trademarks is to be united; however we have to work at staying united—it doesn't just happen on its own accord. I think people in rugby make assumptions that teams automatically have good spirit. When the opportunity presents itself we might go [and have a] few beers after the game and have a sing song as a team. Over the years it has become more difficult to do things like that because the perception is that professional players don't do that sort of thing. They might lose a bit of fitness for example, to go and have a few beers but we gain in the longer run in our team spirit, the sense of togetherness. When we win we win together, and when we lose we lose together. We come out on the other side stronger; we become more knowledgeable because we sit and talk about it after the games and become closer.

He also values the informal way that certain trademarks can be attained, again help the players to bind as part of a great team culture:

Last year, we had a bit of a song after we didn't perform well, [which we sang] after a game in the changing rooms, in the second half of the season. We looked to a team song which we sing together, representing the symbol of our tightness. Don't get me wrong, I might have given the team a rollicking at the end of the game; however we then made sure we took it on the chin and stuck together, with a team song being a tangible demonstration of our commitment to each other to put things right.

Ultimately Mike believes in displaying and monitoring these trademarks to bind the team together through the long season. Given the length of the season and the amount of change it can entail, he believes that it helps to keep the team culture fresh by revisiting the trademarks and ensuring the players review them.

Mike's Use of Questioning

Mike is an advocate of using questioning to develop knowledge and problem-solving skills. Through my observation of him coaching and dealing with players and staff on many occasions, it is clear he is a practitioner of this technique as well. The use of questioning as a coaching tool (see Chapter Thirteeen) is demonstrated in various aspects of his coaching, including in his focus on establishing team culture. Through his verbal questions and physical questions to prompt problem solving, players consider possibilities, rationalise them and come up with the best solution—and thus become better decision makers. Mike provides an example of his problem-solving approach with reference to a video analysis of a British Lions game:

I did a review the other day when the Lions played South Africa and I showed the clips where someone had been given a yellow card. I didn't show the example until after I'd asked a few questions of players. For example, 'How important is discipline for the modern rugby player?' I then explored why with the players. The answer came back that 'If you get carded you'd be letting your teammates down.' I said, 'Explain exactly how it would let your teammates down.' We went through that whole process. I then asked, 'When a team is down to 14 men, do you believe it would be more likely that the other team would score against them?' I asked the same player to give me the answer again, and he said, 'Yes, a team of 15 players have an advantage over 14 and during that period could score a try.' So, rather than just showing the video and then saying, 'You can't do this, or you won't be on my team', I asked a series of questions even though it takes longer … However I believe the players develop a greater understanding and a willingness to find solutions that fit them over the longer term.

Another outcome of having an environment that emphasises problem solving is that players also feel comfortable about asking coaches questions back. When observing the Warriors, I saw numerous examples of players asking coaches to clarify or challenging them on the tactics and principles and generally participating in the process of designing team plays. Players who act in this way are interested, motivated and involved in the team.

Mike suggests that on the rugby pitch, questioning the whole group can be time-consuming and, where it is continually used, it can affect the intensity of the session and can mean that some players are standing around while others are answering questions. However, what I noted in my observations of the Warriors' training sessions was that all coaches tended to use activities that were problem solving in their nature. Consequently the verbal questions were not excessive, yet the essence of an approach concerned with solving problems and enhancing decision making was evident. Verbal questions also have a place, in Mike's view, but it is more likely to be off the field:

I probably do more questioning in the classroom than I do on the field … I use it a lot in video analysis. Rather than point out a mistake that has been made, or a good play or the use of a certain tactic and deliver that from my perspective, I might ask a player to tell me what he sees and the strengths and weaknesses of the actions. I feel that the videos are a good way to actually check the players' knowledge and understanding, whether they see a particular movement. So, it is good for me, and it is good for the player.

The key to questioning effectively is to be able to read and understand your athletes and know when to ask the question, to whom and in what situation. Mike's philosophy of understanding individuals was evident in his method of questioning. Mike sees his use of questioning as arising partly because he felt he did not have all the answers:

> I think actually instead of trying to be the font of all knowledge at every session, and know every player's role inside out, I like to put the players under pressure to articulate their own particular role when challenged to do so. It is difficult to memorise, particularly on a team pattern, where every player should go at any one time. So rather than leaving myself open to saying the wrong thing to the player, it probably started off as a bit of a checklist for me, saying, 'Well where do you go? What is your role?' And then I could cross-reference that in my booklet if I needed to. Despite stumbling across this approach, ultimately I think it is just a better way of checking the players' knowledge base. I am still learning about that side if I am honest, even though I use it very often.

Although questioning can be very time-consuming, research on learning attests that using this approach raises awareness and compels thought and attention based on coaches' observation. Sometimes the time questioning requires, however, is time that teams don't have. Acknowledging this dilemma, Mike suggests that it is important to understand the situation and players' needs, which will sometimes lead to the decision to revert to telling:

> It depends on the level of development of the group. For example, I would use a questioning approach in a stable group where roles and responsibilities have been established. If that is not the case and the emphasis is on bringing a team together for a competition very quickly then I would probably spend less time on questioning and more on making sure that they are organised to a certain level in a short space of time. Questioning will take you longer, but I believe it is [a] stronger team for the whole experience if you give them time to be able to do it.

When the coach asks questions, athletes must find an answer, which in turn increases their awareness, knowledge and understanding of the purpose of particular skill performances or tactics in the context of competition. Questioning creates independent athletes by providing them with a chance to take responsibility for their own interpretations and understandings and make decisions. Questioning creates athlete curiosity as long as the coach is non-judgemental. It is also an extremely powerful means to inspire in athletes an intrinsic motivation to learn.

Mike and Teaching Games for Understanding

The tool of Teaching Games for Understanding (TGfU) (see also Chapter Eight) has been shown to enable athletes to become self-aware and solve problems, which in turn develops their ability to make decisions. Instead of using the traditional practice drills, which have no real relevance to the actual game (although Mike admits that some players occasionally need them too), Mike and his coaching staff use many games to meet the purpose of a particular training situation. The games themselves enable players to make decisions and sometimes (only sometimes) coaches need to ask questions to enhance that decision making. In TGfU the questions should come from and be geared towards achieving an objective the coach and team have identified.

One of Mike's strongest beliefs is in the value of using games as decision-making tools:

> It's good to have little chunks of training, even 10 minutes here and there, where they can work against defenders. That's a constant theme; we always try to put segments in where they have to make decisions with a dynamic defence. We can change the defence, even with little touch rugby games: we could say we might be playing against a team who doesn't defend by pushing up and out, it defends by jamming in. So we can tell our defence to change its tactics so we can get used to running certain plays against them.

Mike highlights the importance of integrating games into training:

> … ultimately I think everything we do should be against a defence if we can. For example, we run unopposed patterns for them to get used to each other. The trouble with unopposed rugby is that you can never judge how far away the opposition are, and [players need] to judge where the spaces are and when to make the pass or not make the pass, or make decisions. So, once we have mastered a certain skill or mastered a certain pattern unopposed, obviously we want to test that as a realistic experience. Even with scrummaging or line-outs, you can practise against a machine unopposed, but ultimately you need to intensify that particular area with decision-making purposes and do some defence. For example in line-outs, you need to be able to scan the defending team's line-out defensive strategy before making a call which identifies where the ball should be thrown in the line-out. We need to try and create those scenarios in training by using defence all the time. That's why I like to see a small-sided game with attack versus defence or in the line-out practice or team practice you are ultimately trying to get everything against some sort of defence policy. It doesn't have to be full-on contact to achieve the goals you want, but obviously the more realistic and the more game-realistic you make it, the better.

Mike also uses games based on video analysis to highlight tactics that can be used:

> What I did on that was the day before I had shown some clips on the South Africa versus Lions game. In one clip a player had sensed that he wasn't held on the floor, got up and made extra yards, passed to someone and scored. He had been aware that he wasn't held in a tackle and I guess if he hadn't practised that at some stage, then he wouldn't have ever scored. We practised that scale within the context of a small-sided touch game rather than just a drill situation so that the player had to make a decision when to use it rather than it being an available option all the time.

In observing Warriors' training sessions, I noticed that many of the activities were grounded in games, from conditioning to creating plays. In most activities, there was an element of competition involved and the boys demonstrated their enjoyment of and intense involvement in these games. These situations set the team up well for competition as they contain elements of pressure, reality and game-like situations and fitness. Mike offers this example:

> … today [we played] a fairly loose game of touch, just working on some of the little idiosyncrasies or skills that we want to particularly pick out. For this game, we appointed a defence coach to stand just behind the defensive team; we also appointed an attack coach to stand behind the attack team. [The rule established] was that the attack team has the ball all the time for five minutes and they have to try to score as many tries as they can, or make as many line breaks as they can. The defence focused to stop them doing that. It becomes very dependent on situations. It also gives the defence coach five- or ten-minute blocks to really work on key principles. Obviously it can be broken down into micro activities and eventually build up to the full-team type defence in a full contact game … Basically the challenge is there from the attack team to break the defence down.

As it was apparent that Mike is an advocate of the games approach and encourages players to learn rugby through game situations, I asked him what percentage of his training sessions would be drill based and what percentage would be games based. He estimated:

> Probably 50% of activities we do unopposed or against a fairly limited defence. I'd have to say that because we break the skills and application down quite a bit, sort of three- or four-player type of activities, e.g. where you have to clear out in a ruck or it could be passing activities, it could be catching, it could be making a pass unopposed. So a lot of activities

we do without defence. However we try to get 50% where we always get some sort of opposition or defence in some sort of form involved in these practices.

I wondered where Mike learned about using games as when he did the majority of his coaching courses, the games approach was not 'in fashion'. As he recalls it:

I think it's something I learned when I was a player. Players actually enjoy games and the challenge of dealing with opposed or semi-opposed practice, to see if we could beat the team in one shape or form. It put more pressure on your skills ... I guess that it is perceived now to be very beneficial to developing a bit more activities and skills and decision making ... I've always, in my 24 years [of coaching], used game-specific and game situations ... I think there is too much emphasis on drills, breaking the skills down into micro element[s] without introducing the pressure of opposition.

A major dilemma that various rugby coaches mention is that using contact games during the season is quite risky. Due to fear of injury, coaches tend to avoid putting many contact-type games into place. Mike shares this concern:

We rarely fail to wear contact suits when defending as these suits protect you from bumps. In a week of a league game, we would give short spurts of contact whilst wearing these suits. Through our analysis department we also monitor how many physical contacts each player is exposed to in each league game. This allows us to identify players who are carrying [an] extra load into training and thereby make decisions on their level of involvement particularly if we do some contact work. In between tough league games we tend to avoid contact and use small-sided games or touch games instead. Rotating the whole squad means we can manipulate the defensive policy so we can attack and recycle the ball without loads of contact for the same people. Constant rule changes in a game assist the coach's ability to coach several different skills; like today we looked at where someone is touched but instead of going straight down and presenting the ball back, they stay on their feet for another second or two and spin/rotate and try to make another half a yard behind the defence before deciding to offload or not. We then looked at a rule change where after the player is tagged he drops to the floor and rotates through 360 degrees before placing the ball. We promote this skill because sometimes there is heat on the ball from a defender who tries to get his hands on the ball. By moving your body a little bit and moving out of his immediate range, the attacker avoids a turnover in possession.

Mike again suggests that video analysis is helpful in that, by using clips of games, he, the coaches and the players can observe where certain situations need to be developed. Often he, the coaches and he players (all working together) then design a game to work on that situation. He gives an example:

> [In a previous game] we might have conceded a try or we messed up a couple of chances to score, so we will design a game situation to further develop that practice. I might set up the exact situation and ask players to play from that situation, so we can learn from it and hopefully execute it better the next time. Or for example, on Saturday we didn't score because we weren't getting our support lines right. So we would try to set it up to show that support and how it could be improved.

The use of games for many different aspects of training—fitness, tactical, technical, psychological and cognitive—is strongly evident in the Warriors' training sessions. All of the Warriors' coaches, including the academy coaches, use games extensively. The players enjoy the games, and the game situations set up are purposeful, always leading to an element of the Warriors' game that needs to be developed.

Implementing an Athlete-centred Approach

Implementing an athlete-centred approach requires some degree of belief in the value of athlete-centred learning by focusing on a player's needs. As Chapter One notes, although both *humanistic* and *athlete-centred* may be interpreted in many ways, at a general level both terms describe a process by which people gain control over the decisions affecting their lives. When a coach considers the athletes first and thus gives them choice and control, the athletes take ownership of and personal responsibility for their decisions. In other words, through training, athletes and teams gain some choice in and control over what happens in their sporting life as well as in their general lifestyle. Mike highlights his understanding of athlete-centred coaching when he discusses the benefits of varying his coaching style:

> I am going to make certain variations in what I do depending on the situation and the people I am working with ... In tough situations a player might need more direction or look to the coach for advice and leadership in a different form. In other situations, players might enjoy the interaction and empowerment ... I think it is based on trust, cooperation and communication. The good coach should be able to move things from one end of the scale to the other: be a bit more autocratic in some instances or other times be more positive and intelligent ... On that basis this group wants certain accountabilities and certain boundaries. Having

said that, they don't want and I don't want negativity through the team, so it's coming up with that balance.

Athlete-centred coaching is not pure empowerment; rather, it is about attending and understanding the players' individual needs and working with them to enhance their performance. Mike's approach matches this athlete-centredness well, involving attention to players' different types of needs:

Certain players want instant solutions and specific feedback whilst others know the answers and just need to be asked a question to draw the solutions to the surface.

A number of decisions that have to be made whilst the game takes place are dependent on what is going on at that time, e.g. what is the weather like, what type of defence is the opposition defence using, what's the score, what is our past experience in making this play, what areas of the game are we successful in and what strategies have the most likely chance of success? These are the questions that the players need to answer in a split second under pressure and so the more experience they have of identifying solutions the greater their chance of success.

Mike suggests that having the right people around—people with intelligence and intrinsic motivation—helps promote decision making and players' 'buy-in':

I think recruitment adds value to your team. It's making sure always that the new recruits are the right fit. Successful recruitment helps create a positive environment, and [ensures] that people are confident because they can see that there is more depth to the environment with good coaching and player recruitment. They are all important things in building a team and a philosophy.

In the culture of rugby, Mike has had to deal with players who were developed at many different levels and in many different ways. However, he believes that telling people how to do things does not enable learning. He also believes that his personality is another part of the reason why he does not tell people what to do:

Over the years my approach has changed and I have mellowed. Because the players have been involved in helping construct our team patterns, there's a great understanding from them in terms of where they are, what they do, where they go and how to execute these plays because we discussed a lot of that in the classroom when we put it all together.

From a Director of Rugby's point of view, external expectations can make it difficult to implement the athlete-centred approach. Often people observing training sessions criticise a coach who is not overly verbose and yelling instructions. However, the very nature of being athlete-centred is to stand back when the situation calls for that and enable players to solve problems, come up with their own solutions and implement them. For some coaches, the process can be quite intimidating because of these external expectations, as Mike indicates:

> I suppose it all depends on how comfortable you are in the process; even if I went on the field and never said anything and didn't actually coach one day, I could handle that. I don't like to dominate them because we wouldn't experience the team environment that we've got. I am comfortable that the whole process has been instigated, shared and nurtured by me. As part of my coaching style I don't just use questions with players, I'll use questions with the coaches so that I can keep updating my knowledge of all the detail that is being coached in different areas but also to propose certain concepts and solutions to the players and coaches at the club. So, rather than just say to the guys, 'Actually I think that this is the pattern and we should run it', I might say to one of my coaches, 'Tell me about that pattern, why should we run that pattern? And what is the benefit of that? And what are the perceived outcomes of this pattern? And how would you expect us to manipulate the opposition defence using this defence?' I am asking who should go there and why. From that come some good debates and some great ideas. I am quite happy that part of my role is to stimulate and shape those debates.

The Process of Enabling Athletes

To enable players to learn, coaches in this book include them in making informed decisions in all aspects of the team environment. As Mike points out, a coach needs to trust in the ability of the athlete to make these decisions:

> That learning, [decision making] and players' intellectual property means that they have got a desire to move forward. The modern player has an intellect, has a view of what he feels is good training, bad training, good coaching, bad coaching, good game plan, bad game plan, good performance, bad performance … Because players have developed the need to be involved and challenged to improve, it creates a common mindset that demands a high level of coaching and coach interaction.

It is interesting that Mike sees a difference in players of today's game compared with earlier years, though the experience they receive and the learning that occurs in their coaching is still generally limited. He comments on his observation of the development of his two sons over the years in different teams:

Well I see what happened to my own sons really, in regards to certain tactics and certain elements of the game, but with most teams they have not really being involved in the compilation of these strategies in a game. They might be doing it, but they do not necessarily understand why they are doing it. So the communication aspect between the athletes and the coach can often be missing.

I asked Mike where he gets and maintains the confidence to use this type of coaching to enable the players to have ownership of their learning and performance. He relates how it fits in with the multiple roles of a coach:

Ultimately you are who you are … but you can take many different roles … as a coach sometimes you can don your different hats e.g. sometimes go authoritarian and sometimes go with a more relaxed approach and sometimes in the middle. Sometimes you might get into the players for poor performance, sometimes you have to pick players up. Sometimes you have got to hire people and sometimes you have to fire people. The guy you might have had a very good working relationship with, might have dropped his playing and he has come to the end of his career and you have to let him go. So you have many different guises in terms of the roles that you do and the job part of a coach … I don't know all the answers either. Also I believe that by using everyone's expertise and knowledge we can find those extra couple of answers that make a difference.

Given his understanding of enabling players to learn, it is clear that Mike must have had a good role model at some time during his life, someone who prompted him to believe that the players should be so involved in decision making and establishing team direction. Mike identifies that person:

I think my dad was a good role model actually. He was a bomb disposal guy in the RAF and then afterwards he became a station officer in the fire service. When I met his work colleagues from time to time, they would go out of their way to tell me what a good man he was. When he passed away his colleagues would mention things like, 'Your dad's a good guy; he always has time for people, he helps people, he works with people and at times when he has to make tough decisions, he does.' So that is the sort of feedback [that] would come back to me when I was 14 or 15 years of age, when I started to get to know the guys he worked with. Obviously seeing him at home, weighing up family difficulties or issues or things, he was always pretty good at sitting down and discussing things and trying to get you to understand things rather than just telling you. He would ask my opinion on things. He would never say, 'You can't go down to the local pub and have 10 pints of beer on a Saturday night.' He would ask you, 'Do you think this is the best preparation for your rugby?' and ask me questions about all sorts of things to make you consider things logically yourself and come up with the answer yourself. His style probably influenced me.

Some Challenges of an Athlete-centred Approach

As with any innovative method or way to do things, the athlete-centred approach contains pitfalls. At times athlete-centred coaches are frustrated when things aren't happening quickly, or there are worries when players don't understand the reason behind such an approach. In taking this approach, however, what is important is to understand that every player is different and you need to be flexible in your approach to address the needs of the players, rather than sticking with only one particular method. As Mike says, one of the major challenges is deciding when to step in and when to stand back.

As suggested above, a major challenge in undertaking this innovative approach is dealing with the perception of the media and other external sources that perpetuate the notion that if the coach is not telling or yelling at the players, he or she is not coaching. Mike reflects:

> You read press comments about different coaches and I think certain press would still promote a stereotypical sergeant major bully-type coaching style that focuses primarily on disciplinary problems and stuff like that. They and many supporters of team sports feel that this coaching style would be advantageous and it could be a perception that athlete-centred or working with athletes or players to find solutions to problems with a sense of involvement is a sign of weakness. So there is still a battle to be won.

A major pitfall in learning and being an athlete-centred coach is failing to understand the players' needs and being unable to attend to them. A coach with high emotional intelligence tends to be committed to people and their needs, take responsibility for their actions, have an ethical outlook and focus on interactions and relationships. Mike, who encompasses all of these elements, appreciates the need to focus on relationships as one of the main mechanisms to enhance performance and commitment. Reading people, or empathy, is essential in understanding and forming relationships, as Mike notes:

> Getting to know your players is crucial. Reading their mood and levels of confidence is paramount to being able to get the best out of your players.

When using an athlete-centred approach, with its requirements of gaining input from players and enabling learning, time is always a factor. Mike agrees:

> It is definitely a longer process involved in the questioning approach … Time could be a factor, the situation could be a factor, all those things will come into the mix as to whether or not the coach can get the best out of them, or make them feel happy and comfortable with their strategies.

Mike believes taking the time needed to implement an athlete-centred approach is actually better in the long run for performance:

> I think what it does over time is give the players knowledge more fully of all the different concepts of the game and why they are doing what they are doing, why they are expected to do certain things at certain times. Ideally they will grow and become even better.

Conclusion

After 24 years to date of a great coaching career, Mike still enjoys coaching. In taking up a different role as Director of Rugby, however, he has become more of a manager and less of a 'coach'. He plans to maintain and continue to use his successful people skills, as well as to learn more about the business side of his role. He values informal learning opportunities and will continue to find ways of discussing the various aspects of his role. When asked when he will retire, he says:

> I suppose the fear of coaching is when you get to 65 you've got to retire. Probably when you retire as a coach it is the day you have a complete understanding of every aspect of the game. Sir Bobby Robson [former England soccer manager] who recently passed away has inspired me by proving that you can still be an effective coach/manager well into your 70s and so there is hope for me yet!

As might be expected from a man who continues to seek out learning opportunities, Mike acknowledges that the learning never stops, that as the game changes the social culture changes and one must adapt to meet the needs of the situation. However, there are plenty of experts out there and plenty of people to learn from and Mike values that opportunity:

> I have a million things to learn about my coaching. It changes all the time and evolves and you grow and you change a little bit as you get older and more experienced. In some ways the older you get the better you should be.

It was indeed my pleasure to be able to observe the Worcester Warriors and their coaches. Mike, as the Director of Rugby, is known for his people skills, and his manner of coaching is well respected. When asked about a magic formula for coaching, he said that no one has such a formula:

> No one can predict that if you do this or that on fitness, psychological aspects, leadership development, game plan, technical strategies you'll win the World Cup and be champions … We are all searching for that magic formula. That is the beauty of the game, the challenge of the game and the ultimate goal is to win. All a coach can do is the best he can to promote the development of the team and its individuals because ultimately the game belongs to the players and it's their actions that will decide the outcome of the game.

Mike's coaching approach is about the players, catering to their cultures, understandings, skills and intelligences, and understanding the whole player (or the whole coach as well, in Mike's role as Director of Rugby) and working with their uniqueness.

Learning an athlete-centred approach is not an easy task, but the benefits to the team and individual athletes are immense. The learning process is easier when coaches begin by considering *how* such an approach might be suitable for them and remembering that the process of implementation requires time. Coaches will make progress by trying new ideas and continuing to self-reflect on how the approach is working within the team. There are also techniques, such as questioning and understanding TGfU, that need to be practised. The more coaches practise, the better they will be at giving athletes ownership of their learning and a direction to their sporting and life experiences.

It is amazing what can be accomplished when
nobody cares about who gets the credit. -Robert Yates

Teamwork divides the task and doubles the success. - Anonymous

The way a team plays as a whole determines its success. Y
ou may have the greatest bunch of individual stars in the world,
 but if they don't play together, the club won't be worth a dime. -Babe Ruth

Asking the right questions takes
as much skill as giving the right
answers. - Robert Half

Chapter Four

Lyn Gunson

International Netball Coach

Lyn Gunson's coaching experiences are many and varied. Lyn coached both New Zealand and England national netball teams. She has also been the Director of Coaching for the South and Southwest England Netball Performance Unit and now is the Director of Netball for Netball North Harbour in New Zealand. I was able to observe Lyn's training sessions while on a visit to England in 2002. Watching Lyn's teams train demonstrated to me her emphasis on athlete-centred coaching so, when she visited New Zealand in January 2005, I jumped at the opportunity to interview her to find out what being athlete-centred means to her.

Sport has always been a part of Lyn's life. She grew up in a rural community in Waikiekie in Northland where her parents introduced her to sport as a means of establishing social networks. Lyn suggests that the influence on her coaching philosophy came from her farm and country upbringing. Her experience of sport had similarities to being part of a community, in that team membership was stable for a long-term campaign and teamwork occurred in response to an external need and with an identified and defined purpose, thus creating a mutual direction. This focus enabled a committed effort when striving for a goal for a given period.

Professionally Lyn has a background in teaching. She undertook a Diploma in Physical Education at the University of Otago, while beginning to play netball in the national team. She also played provincially at various times for Otago, Auckland, Northland and Waikato. Upon completing her diploma, Lyn attended Auckland College of Education and became a physical education teacher, as well as holding a careers and counselling role, at Melville High School in Hamilton for 11 years. While teaching full time, she coached the New Zealand netball team from 1990 to 1993. During this coaching period, Lyn aided New Zealand's win at the World Games for non-Olympic sports. The team then lost the World Championships to Australia by one point and Lyn was not reappointed.

Ready for a change, Lyn moved on to work as a physical education adviser for a short time before accepting a position at the Waikato Institute of Sport where she helped her organisation introduce a leisure studies degree at the University of Waikato. She then lectured in the management stream within the leisure studies degree. At the same time she completed a Masters of Business Administration (MBA), which she highlights as an experience of wonderful learning through her interaction with people outside of the sporting industry. It provided some intriguing background information that enhanced her understanding about different trends and how others outside of sport view the world.

Lyn lived in England from 1999 to 2007. In the first instance she was there to work at the University of Bath in an attempt to do her doctorate but she became involved in setting up a project to develop elite players and coaches in netball. During her time there, too, fellow New Zealand netballer Waimarama Taumaunu (England Netball Performance Director) involved her in coaching the English netball team, starting six weeks before the 2002 Commonwealth Games. Thereafter Lyn coached the team through the 2003 World Championships in Jamaica, in which England came fourth.

Lyn started her coaching in high school where she helped out with junior teams. She also spent much of her playing life in roles that enhanced her coaching—as a player-coach and captain. Within both these roles, especially the difficult position of player-coach, Lyn could not be autocratic in the style she observed in her coaches. So she developed much of her athlete-centred philosophy in coaching from having to work with fellow players.

Lyn's Philosophy of Coaching

Lyn's coaching philosophy is athlete-centred in her belief that 'each individual needs to have their own space and be who they want to and can be'. She also believes that 'people who are truly elite, often get there themselves despite everything else around them. It is the others just underneath that need more construction. Coaches can often limit these athletes.' External influences from coaches and others are insignificant compared to an athlete's internal desire. The coach's role is to encourage this internal desire by providing the right environment for athletes to express themselves in a manner that leads them to reach their capacity. Coaches are nurturers of internally motivated athletes rather than builders of motivated athletes. On tapping into this motivation through an athlete-centred coaching approach, Lyn says:

> ... ask the athlete, 'Do you really want to do this or not? You decide.' If they really do decide then they will have the passion and desire; it has to come from inside them. It is not just about motivation, it's about whether they can see that they can ... One of the things I have asked the players is, 'What is your capacity?' If an athlete can get to the point where [he/she] knows what that might be and have belief in that, then go on to look for more, you begin to have an international athlete. They may never discover it if somebody else is always telling them what to do, think and believe.

Lyn believes that coaches can create the environment to support athlete learning and performing but their role is 'one step removed' in that, when the athlete is ready to move on, he or she 'will come in and you can tell from a particular comment that something is happening and you know straight away, [the athlete is] identifying [his/her] need'. Sometimes athletes gain an idea or suggestion from an external source, or a realisation from some experience, but as a coach, 'the influence you have is to point them in the direction where they will find what they need. That is athlete-centred'.

It is always tempting to identify the answer for athletes and deliver that solution from outside. In a coaching role, when the pressure is on for a short-term performance, there are times when it is simplest and easiest to simply tell the athletes what to do. Yet although imposing that external solution may suit the short-term situation, it is not the answer to long-term needs as the athletes do not own it.

By learning in, through and about sport, Lyn has become very good at analysing and contextualising it. As noted above, doing the MBA helped consolidate some of her ideas on how outside views and trends might affect sport: 'I did it so that I challenged myself to see another world view and so that I could think about sport and its context and the way in which it was going to be affected'. Sport has notoriously focused on the short term, giving priority to an immediate result. This short-term fixation perpetuates the practice of coach-centred coaching and thus of creating dependent athletes. However, working in opposition to this current construction of sport is that many sport situations require independent thinkers and decision makers. In this regard, Lyn's analytical thinking extends beyond coaching to evaluate sport as a socially constructed industry:

> Sport is quite an exclusive society and it takes little if any responsibility for [creating these dependent people], but if you can actually have the athlete willingly participate in [taking responsibility] and making genuine choices, then it's much better than if they fall off the treadmill at the other end. Of course the question arises, is sport responsible, and therefore are coaches [and others] responsible for the athlete's holistic growth as a person? I think that sport [constructs] children. We tell children what to wear, we tell them when to turn up, how to behave, who to be involved with. Fine, it teaches them some good things. But what is missing [within this] constructed environment? Many sportspeople do not recognise how constructed the sports environment is. They then demand thinking players … not easy from an [coach-centred] environment.

In addition to her education, two other major influences in her life have shaped Lyn's philosophy. Both have been mentioned already: first, the rural community in which she grew up and the sport experiences in her junior years; and, second, her extensive player-coach and captain experiences. Lyn's present focus on community stems from her experience of locals pitching in to help out when needed. She gives an example relating to her community analogy that demonstrates what this collective effort means:

> … where there is a good community, there are some underlying principles. One of them is that you help your neighbours … the village and wider district coexists quite happily until the school committee decides they need a fundraising exercise or there is a fire somewhere and someone's house is burning. All of a sudden, a group of people come together who have previously been co existing and because of other and past experiences they become a very tight team. They put the fire out, they organise themselves … leaders emerge and people fall into specialist roles according to their skills. Somebody leads [the task of] putting the fire out and somebody else takes up the role of coordinating the relief and aid effort, food and clothing and whatever else is needed. All of a sudden, you've got this team operating. When the main bulk of that effort is finished, it just slides back into coexisting again. Over long campaigns, teams operate more as communities; I think the best ones do. That allows the freedom for the way in which it can develop and grow. There are of course some important aspects that make this work, like a sense of value and cohesiveness and finally a common purpose that clearly identifies the direction and action.

The philosophical base established through Lyn's community involvement as a child also supports the notion of getting involved. Lyn played any sport she could because small schools needed athletes in a variety of sports in inter-school country tournaments. Lyn would play a hockey game, then run and play half a game of rugby, then soccer, then netball, plus help out with her other community teams, all in one day. She says about this experience, 'it was all about this participating in the way that you put your shoulder to the wheel, the collective wheel because the school needed you to do this, so that's what you did'. The collective school points system meant everyone contributed even if it was only a few points.

Lyn believes that the best coaches are those who 'read' people. She is unsure whether this skill is instinctive or if people gain it through experience. She believes her skill in imaging situations, replaying them in her head and knowing what somebody is going to do before they do it comes from her farming background:

> … I have often been asked about how I instinctively know if someone is going to do something. Now, where does that come from? … Certainly what helped me develop it is part of the farm situation. I remember having

these experiences with animals. If a dog was going to bite you or a bull charge you, you had to know about it. They weren't going to tell you, it wasn't a person you were dealing with, so there were lots of other signals that you started picking up on, including the electrical energy and atmospheric situation around the animals you were dealing with. I started to really read the signs, and if I hadn't I would be dead now.

This need to read athletes is mentioned in different ways as part of their philosophy by coaches throughout this book. 'Reading people' seems to be an essential skill to coaching. Coaches need to understand athletes and their behaviours, as well as to have empathy for their individual situations and needs. As Lyn says:

Anticipating situations is huge in coaching and it's how you get the information so that you do start to anticipate things … I think that it is quite strongly in you and that you either develop what is there or it just stays dormant … I think part of it is that there is the physically obvious, which is often to do with biomechanics and seeing through the external body extremity. Then there is a whole lot of other material around the energy and the non-observable. Some people seem to almost be able to see them. Others just feel them and others are just completely not aware that they exist … some image by seeing pictures, but I feel energy and myself doing the activity as well … this is a completely different level of imaging. It's much more complicated, but people can use all their senses quite instinctively depending on all manner of experiences. Coaching a variety of cultures has taught me a great deal about the differences in how people view the world. The English [netball] team has been interesting from this aspect. Many live in large cities and their view of the world is quite different depending on which part of the country, which culture they are from and how they have grown with their environment.

The instinct or art of reading people and situations is just the beginning. Once you have anticipated the situation, the next important step in successful coaching is timing. As Lyn explains it, the coach must be able to make the challenging judgement of what to offer the athletes and when they are ready for learning:

It is such an intertwining of observing what's happening, looking at the contextual relationships and then deciding is this the time and is this the way forward? Does this intervention need this type of information, process, experience, support … not just what to do but when to do it. That timing is incredibly difficult to teach. I experienced this when lecturing teachers in training. I have seen people [who'll] react to [a situation] or they'll get a piece of information and they'll react to it. Two days before or two days later they might react completely different to the same piece of information or activity, so it's matching up when that person is ready to take on that experience or information; in other words, are they ready to learn?

Reading people and empathy are dominant characteristics of Lyn's coaching. She describes how she uses them with Bath athletes and coaches:

What we have done at Bath is try to make it completely athlete-centred and we are trying to read all the time …when different things are needed and when those players are ready. What I find is that if [I] can match up [their readiness], the learning is extremely fast… [the learning] entrenches itself very quickly and they work with it straight away. They use the feeling, emotion, information or behaviour and start to work off of it themselves … They lock in one piece of something and take off with it in an integrated form … the ripple and domino effects cascade to many other actions. To find that timing means you've got to listen to them a lot and hear what is happening behind the words and actions, see their reactions and see what's going on … all of a sudden when you do this, that information that they might be receiving back and analysis makes them able to go away and apply much more themselves. There are some good international tennis players at present who can do this.

Lyn also believes that the capacity to analyse situations and then 'translate them into something practical' is a key to athlete learning. She uses analogies in her coaching to convey particular points to her players. The analogies are real situations or experiences, sometimes unrelated to the sport, that athletes can relate to in their own lives so that the information is translated into their own cognitive understanding. The athletes remember the ideas better through hearing them as stories or analogies, as Lyn suggests:

You are not telling them what to do, but you are drawing or focusing their attention on something that they are already doing and engage in themselves and then, all of a sudden, they make a connection because their awareness has been raised.

Lyn follows these coaching beliefs in developing and teaching athletes. However, for national teams, coaching by this method becomes more complex as coaches do not have the athletes all the time and the general demand is for instant results. To deal with these problems, coaches tend to revert to a coach-centred style. Lyn observes:

Often when people take a national team … it feels easier and quicker to take on a directive approach as it suits the 'measurement by winning' required by public and administrators. Athletes are often controlled both on and off the court … The athletes are almost emotionally blackmailed as coaches want to know every little piece about them so that they can be manipulated. While it is helpful to know some of what happens, players need their own space as well or they are limited by their coach and do not grow as much as they can.

Against the general trend, Lyn practises her philosophy of athlete-centred coaching even for national teams. She finds that people's perception of her coaching is problematic because they have different expectations often brought about by their previous experiences of coach-centred coaches. Nevertheless she adheres to her beliefs:

> … people want instant results next week for a one-off test series regardless of its place in a long-term plan. The modern-day event series in netball does not allow for the lead-up games where less experienced players are able to be conditioned. Consequently some teams are developmental at the national level in stages of a four-year cycle depending on the prior experiences of the athletes. If the context domestically is highly competitive, the prior conditioning into this level makes it easier to step straight into the national arena. So, to [be athlete-centred] is extremely difficult as it seems slower. It can be seen as more analytical depending on how it is achieved. But I have always tried to do it because I believe it is the most permanent way to get change of behaviour and produce long-term success.

Long-term goals can leave a coach and team open to criticism when competing in the international arena. Because of public and societal expectations that have been constructed in the past, sport tends to focus on creating robots rather than human beings. As Lyn sees it:

> Good international performance should also push the boundaries of performance. In the national, high-pressure situation, most sports now have events that they want to sell as commodities in the commercial arena and each year there is a big event. [In netball] it might be the World Youth Champs followed by Commonwealth Games followed by the World Champs … Each year there is a big event and so if [we] want thinking players who own their performance and own their own development and are supported by the coaching staff, that's completely different. It's much easier and much faster to be autocratic. Or so it seems. That's the problem. It depends on your philosophy, which one you are going to activate or which combination of effects you want at any given time. It can be fast if you are skilled enough once you have got past the barriers. Many players like autocratic as they then have someone to blame when things

do not go right. The athlete-centred way demands they take responsibility for their performance and learning.

Though athlete-centred coaching is more difficult, its advantages of developing better performers and thinking athletes represent a key to long-term success.

Lyn's Development as a Coach

Lyn's coaching development began in high school when, in her rural community, she was needed to coach the younger ones. There were many participants and not enough adult coaches, so everyone just pitched in. Lyn also recognises the huge influence of her parents on her coaching. As a youngster she used to tag along to all her mother's netball coaching sessions, learning so much about people and coaching from watching and being there. Being involved in many different sports also assisted by widening her range of experiences.

Although she believes her physical education lecturers gave her some ideas, Lyn feels most of her coaching evolved through time and personal experiences. Another major influence on her coaching was her teaching experience at Melville High School. Again, the philosophy of a collective community was pervasive in that school, where the rate of sports participation was high. As Lyn says, it was not 'winning' that made this school excel:

It wasn't known as a sports school but, when I became Head of Department there later, I did an analysis of it ... We had over two-thirds of the school participating in sport, but not one of the teams were the top teams in the area. You wouldn't say that that was the best school for sport because we weren't winning a lot of competitions, but the students were actually involved and many as individuals were achieving national honours both in sport and academic studies, which did not make sense. It was a good school because it had a huge heart ... it had a lot of different divisions in the school and the staff there were fantastic. I felt quite privileged teaching there because the people had that collective focus. People pitched in and really helped each other. It is such a precious thing and it allowed the flexibility to let the students feel as though they could achieve whatever they really wanted to. The school often turned around difficult children because of the approach of the staff and I began to realise the way in which excellence and excelling was really being achieved. We often had students achieve well outside their recognised capabilities and I felt [the collective focus] was the cause. I began to evaluate properly how narrow sport coaching was.

Lyn's player-coach experiences in netball ranged from actually being a player-coach for several teams to taking on the role of coaching the team as part of her role as captain, which was her position on several teams. The first of these experiences was in Otago, where players, especially Lyn, were required to help out. She gained quite strong coaching experiences through these roles. Taking on the role as leader within each of her netball teams was a necessity. Lyn says she:

> ... coached using examples or just sharing ideas. It was more of a leadership role because I was playing as well ... you certainly can't be an autocratic coach when you are a player ... If you try and [be coach-centred], it simply does not work, it is more a collective effort, but it was extremely difficult not to [coach autocratically] because of the nature of what was happening [within the team]. I suppose in lots of ways, I always tried to help other people to believe in their own ability and act as an agent for that. [I guess] you call that coaching ...

Lyn notes that it was difficult for a captain to take on a player-coach role as well. All the same, the experience obviously developed her as a coach. She recalls:

> There are a lot of things which have shown me what *not* to do, not *what* to do ... I spent a lot of my time hatching up ideas that I thought were missing. In actual fact, it made it extremely difficult to be the captain because I was doing more than I should've been doing as the captain. It was a completely different way of captaining when you are responding to your environment ... One year we had been away and won a tournament and I didn't play, but I coached ... I just felt that at that particular year, they needed all my energy off the court, as opposed to on it.

Lyn's player-coach and captaincy roles gave her some real insight into coaching based on situations and needs, which contributed to her development:

> I think any captain that is any good is going to respond to their environment. If they were 10 years later and they were in a different environment, there would probably be a different captain. Responsiveness is a basic leadership skill; it depends is how you lead in that particular time.

Most coaching Lyn experienced as a player was autocratic. Again, it was her wider life experiences that had the greater influence on her coaching development. She reflects:

> The main bulk from me, came from a wide variety of experiences I had, not only in netball, but in other life experiences, but I think that a lot of things for me came from my rural community upbringing and the fact that you lived so far away from others, you had to do it yourself anyway.

The Process of Establishing a Quality Team Culture

Lyn's emphasis on community pervades her thinking about how to form a quality team culture. Like other coaches in this book, Lyn believes that team culture is the glue that holds a group together and that, without it, athletes aim in different directions. Lyn believes that teams should have a direction that is purposeful to the team. She also believes that to bring a group together, a coach must enable them to accommodate all the different cultures in the team. Lyn explicitly works on developing this community by instilling meaningful principles.

On any team, there is a variety of athletes, and therefore the team comprises a community. Lyn describes how it operates:

> Of all the teams I have taken, there are sometimes five different cultures in the team. Netball seems to be a game where there are socioeconomic differences, intellect differences, age differences and life experience differences. I actually believe more in the concept of community. You've got a community of people on your hands for a period of time … depending on how long you've got these people. It may be that you are part of a four-year cycle programme and that you have to think about how you want to be at the end of that. When are the big events? When do we have to put the best performance out that this team is capable of producing? Also you need to leave a door open … for competitive pressure outside [and] for those people who will grow and develop within the group … who come from other aspects, like another country. It would be highly unlikely that you could pick a team at the beginning of a four-year cycle and have the best group and it remain the same for all that time. The culture rises out of the group you've got. However, I strongly do believe in having some basic principles which establish a connecting forum from which to go [forward] and pulls them together.

To pull this community together, coaches need to think about how to start with a new group. Initially, Lyn believes that a coach needs to analyse, reflect and observe the cultural elements of the new team and where each member has come from:

> For each team I have taken, the first thing I have done is look at the team and say, 'What have I got in here? Have I got older players, younger players, less mature players? Have I got people who are used to being in charge? Have I got people who need information?' and have a complete assessment [of] who this team is in its current form. I don't ask them, I just see them operating …

> If we would have new knowledge, we must
> get a whole world of new questions.   -Susanne K. Langer

The culture of the New Zealand national netball team was of interest. When Lyn started coaching the team, the senior players had just been part of winning the World Championships. Lyn explains how she began looking at that team culture:

> Many members of the World Championship team were about to or had retired. The team had [been together] for a long time … many wanted to finish at the World Champs, which was understandable because they had been to a couple of World Champs anyway. Some of them had hung on, partly because I think someone talked them into it, it wasn't me, but this produced its own challenges for me. The first thing I did was actually recognise that the coach is often the new person in a functioning group and there is plenty of residual culture left over from prior experience. I needed to pay attention to the obvious subgroups within the team. I called a meeting of the senior players to discuss their contribution in support of the captaincy. We discussed their roles and the expectation that they could lead by action in a variety of ways and in support.

Lyn's major theme in creating a quality team culture is to instil and practise life principles. Her four major principles with the English team were having direct communication, taking responsibility for your own and the group's performance, being honest and celebrating difference. She elaborates:

> Those basic principles that I think are important in any group of people operating anywhere, are, [first,] direct communication—[for example,] there is no point in me discussing [something] with you if the person it affects is sitting on the other side of the fence. My view of that is that women's groups gossip a lot and they get a lot of negativity into a group by not really getting directly to the issue and sorting it out and it continues to develop and fester rather than killing it and moving on. My view with players is that if they don't want to sort that out, then they shouldn't be talking about it because that's how we undermine group behaviour.

> The second one is take responsibility for your own performance but also for the group performance. The third is [honesty, which] we can operate on [through direct communication]. I discussed with the players, 'This is how I think we should approach this, from these principles. If we can manage these … then we are going to do okay as a group …' and the most important for me is to celebrate difference … When you have got people of the variety that you have in some of these groups, trying to make them be the same is not only impossible but also undesirable. It is much better to approach it in the community sense and get them at least adhering to similar principles that can then make their differences co exist rather than saying, 'You have to like each other'.

Lyn discusses activities that she has used to instil the principle of celebrating difference:

> I think there are important exercises you can undertake. One is to change the discourse of the group to reflect the principles. Enlist the senior players to take leadership actions. There are functional ways to achieve [a celebration of difference] as well—e.g. group meetings, individual interviews, use of outside activities in order to create situations where people understand how each other perform and think … I try to create situations where people can either get to know one another … and understand how each other think about something, or can demonstrate the behaviours they might display in situations of stress. Therefore, if you can get them accepting the difference and then working with that, that's much better than getting into conflict …

The importance of establishing principles and values is recognised by all the coaches in this book. However, one key concept in developing principles is that the athletes should have a say in developing them so they can own them and thus take responsibility for living them. To create these principles with the English team, Lyn says:

> Normally … I would try and draw those out of a group [my]self … it depends on what the situation is; you would want all of the group to come to the same types of principles that they had all bought into. That is the classic team setting, the environment. In the case of the English team, we didn't have a lot of time, six weeks before the Commonwealth Games. What we did was more directed to begin with; we said, 'Here are some things that might help this group right now' … I put them up and asked for additions and deletions. It was quite fascinating to watch that process because they virtually just took them on … I am quite a strong believer in discourse as a way of changing social behaviour. So we gradually start to eliminate some of the words and phrases that people were using, by introducing new phrases and words and ideas that would get them to start to understand what was around them differently. The players needed knowledge and to be involved mentally in what they were doing. They then had a chance of taking ownership. However, one of the real issues is whether the support staff also behave in this way.

With the English team, due to a lack of time, Lyn had to be proactive in promoting her own principles:

> I did some other things like establish some continuums of behaviour where they physically stood where they thought they were on these continuums. It was a public acknowledgement to their group of their own thoughts

about their contribution. It was trying to get an openness and honesty that wasn't there before. One of the things that we talked about was that if you are not honest about what you are doing, the opposition are going to be more than honest about what you are doing and [their words] are not going to be very nice … We gave them some examples of what some other team might say about their team … What I was trying to do for that particular situation was say, 'Here's how you have been operating and you can all see that is not successful'.

After considering the context of a given team on its own merits, Lyn decides how to establish the team principles for that particular team:

In other situations, I'll get [the athletes] to formulate the principles. I often want to see what the natural behaviour is first because the natural behaviour will develop according to who is in the group … You only have to take one person out of a group and put one person in and it can change a lot. So, each time, it is better to just let them go for a while, see what's going on and gradually just draw an activity together. It might be really important with that group to have [the principles] written down.

How does Lyn gain athlete ownership? She says:

Mostly by asking questions, to focus and refocus players by highlighting various instances or behaviours—sometimes in a general way; other times very much one-on-one, and at other times casual.

The key to these principles in the end is to practise them and try to live them. Lyn suggests that, in many cases where you are bringing together a group of very different backgrounds and cultures, the group would normally not mix well. It may go all right for a while, but with one glitch the whole community can be broken apart. So Lyn uses these principles to pull them together. Each situation that arises, there is a lesson to be learned, so to revisit the principles and ask the athletes if they are adhering to the set team principles is an ongoing process of learning, as Lyn explains:

In netball, it's timing and it's a very quick game which requires a lot of trust and a lot of cohesiveness in a very short space of time. These people are going to have to try to share … In some games, you can go and score, but in netball, one half of the court can't do that. So it's equal ball, and very much a team game. You can't get mad at the other person for not doing their job because you can't go and do it for them. You've got to actually somehow contribute even more with what you can control … People get really angry if they are contributing a lot and they can see another person not contributing as much. So that's why teams need some form of common ground … I have seen teams scrapping inside themselves within their team, but they bind like concrete when they have an external threat … where a group is not cohesively going very well, we've said, 'Let's stop focusing internally and let's focus on something external … establishing the purpose. The real threat is what that opposition is going to do to you. Let's focus on that and stop the internal focus' … we have magnified issues that are external to the group to make them bind as a group.

The external influence is one factor that can bind a team to a common goal. Lyn makes this point with reference to a wonderful example of a tour that she was on:

> David and I saw [the team bond] on a bus trip once. For three weeks no one had a cross word to say and didn't get on anybody's nerves at all. There were 58 people. The reason was that they all hated the tour director. That was the external source. They respected his knowledge, but they didn't like him as a person. So the entire group coexisted quite happily because of the focus on this external influence.

Lyn has never been a proponent of team-building activities that centre on external motivation:

> The [English] team did a lot of external team building and, while it gave the administration of the team an idea of what was happening, the transferability of the activities was quite limited.

By contrast, the types of team-building activities that enhance the team environment have a mutual meaning to the team, enabling them to go in the same direction. Lyn relays an example relating to the English team:

> Team culture to me is best established when there is common purpose and that common purpose is meaningful to the group and highly transferable. There is quite a bit of research about team building in external situations that shows low transferability. Some of the team-building activities that I have seen that work best [have] been when it is related to what you are trying to do … For example, we found there were some financial constraints going into the English development campaign. So we got the players in and said, 'We've got some issues here about how the finances are and what the priorities need to be. What do you guys think you can do to help this problem?' They were fantastic. They got together as a group, one or two of them took the lead automatically. They started doing things differently and they produced a significant cut in their spending behaviour. That was a project that had meaning for them. So if I was to engage in a

team-building type of activity, it's more about what has meaning for the group.

When another opportunity arose for Lyn to put a problem to the athletes and thereby enhance the team culture, she grabbed it. This is the sort of purposeful team-building activity that Lyn uses:

> … the English group was … taking two-and-a-half to three hours to get taped before games because the one physio was doing it all … That is not a good amount of time to have the tape on. I asked for the group to do as much of their taping as possible in a half-hour period. There were moans and groans about that at first but, because we identified why and that it was a constraint, they could see what the purpose was. The interesting thing in observing that was that after a while, it became a team-building activity: players coexisted doing something that had meaning and it gave some a sense of control over themselves [which] they needed before playing. The time was cut to 27 mins. Obviously, people [who] were injured were taped by the physio, but there were others who were preventive taping and quite capable of taping themselves. I favour those types of team activities which have meaning for the whole group and in effect build team. In our efforts to support international players, we sometimes take away their sense of responsibility and ownership.

So this example again demonstrates the practical application of Lyn's philosophy of community and athlete responsibility, which perpetuates her belief in creating a quality team culture. She also favours establishing principles for the team, preferably with the athletes. Of interest is her view that it is valuable to find an external threat to bind the team. Lyn also advocates that team-building activities are only useful when they serve a team purpose and are meaningful and transferable to that situation, at that particular time, with that particular team.

Lyn's Use of Questioning

Coach educators are highlighting the need for athletes to become more skilled in decision making along with increasing their awareness and knowledge of the sport. Lyn believes that questioning is an important method of enhancing the learning of a particular experience, which is achieved not just through applying the correct technical process of asking the question, but also through the art of timing the question, formulating it and choosing it appropriately. In England, she says, coach educators:

> … have been encouraging the coaches to start questioning. What I find interesting is that they are taking the pieces of activity in isolation without

that integrated approach. It doesn't work. People are saying they want more athlete decision making and taking responsibility, [therefore] we have to use more questioning. I have been asked to take sessions about this a lot. Some of the coaches have really attempted this approach and I have seen them struggling with it.

Lyn relates how her experiences in her careers and counselling role at high school focused her attention on questioning as a technique:

What I noticed in guidance groupings, was that although people said things about what to do and what you should do with interviewing people, the one thing that they didn't talk about very much was how did you genuinely feel? Many went into a mode of behaviour that was quite false, I felt. This goes back to what I feel about understanding how the emotions and the energy fields are because if you translate that, even though you are saying the right thing, if [the person's] feelings are different or you think a particular way, you will actually communicate it … So, if you genuinely can't like the people who you are trying to help, then it makes no difference how trained you are. I saw it time and time again where people tried to help other people, but they didn't genuinely like doing it so it didn't work or it had very short-term effects.

Lyn has been asking questions for years because athletes need to learn to be better players of the game and to make better decisions. She can ask one good open-ended question, which appropriate to that person in that situation at that time, and get the athlete to think in depth. Lyn believes in asking the question relative to the need, personality and desire of the player involved. To ask a good question, coaches must consider 'the timing and the mood' and the question must be 'totally open-ended and leave ownership with the athlete'.

In saying this, being time efficient has a great effect on the ability to think in depth. Any training session involves a variety of experiences, creating a context that coaches must be able to analyse so that they can coach according to the atmosphere at the time. Lyn suggests that the major consideration in formulating the question is what outcome is required:

What is the question that is going to open up the outcome possibilities? It's being conscious of the situations all the time. We constrain [players] by our inability [to ask questions] and focus their attention … How do you know that person you are dealing with doesn't have the next revolutionary idea about sport? [For example,] who started two-handed backhands? Who starts wearing their cap on back-to-front and sets the trend? Where is the one who has the confidence to do that? So are you going to be a follower or somebody who keeps ahead of the game? Coaches have to allow [innovation] to happen, otherwise the game doesn't develop and champions do not emerge.

As Lyn implies, using well-formulated questions is a key strategy for an athlete-centred approach. She understands why coaches take the coach-centred approach: it is certainly easier. A truly athlete-centred coach faces the challenge of catering to the learning of the athlete and his or her individual needs. Any coach who pursues 'athlete thinking' must be:

> ... very brave in this current world of sport. For me, I don't have any question as to what I am going to do, but I can understand the constraints of a lot of coaches who aren't given the time by administrators to actually get to that point where [developing thinking athletes] is having an effect because it may appear to take longer and look softer ... People who have come through sport might have come through another method, so they are looking at this [athlete-centred] person thinking, 'What is this? This isn't coaching.' They are already judging [the athlete-centred approach] because of their own experience. My experience is, it is more demanding on the athlete.

Lyn advocates the use of questioning because she is committed to enabling athletes to learn and develop. The athlete-centred approach is different to the dominant public perception of coaching. To take this approach, coaches must strongly believe that the athletes' needs are most important, despite the pressure from outside groups. Even though it is difficult to shake of the influence of our predecessors and the media, coaches must ask themselves, 'Who am I really here for?'

Lyn and Teaching Games for Understanding

In observing Lyn's coaching, it was evident that she uses Teaching Games for Understanding (TGfU or Game Sense) to teach athletes about the game. To develop international players, Lyn believes that teaching the athletes game sense is crucial. Many players she coaches come from other clubs or associations who have not taken the time to get athletes to think about the game. 'Many of their backgrounds and experiences are limited', says Lyn. She believes in 'getting athletes to experience those feelings about spatial concepts'.

Lyn began using TGfU in New Zealand, making up different situations and games to satisfy a need for athletes to become game aware. By focusing on game understanding, Lyn stresses her belief in developing international sportspeople, rather than just athletes who play for their country:

I think they are two different things because quite often the player who plays for his/her country is aiming to do things just well enough to get on the national team … so if they are just going for the national team, it is all right if it is the top individual side in the world, but then everyone is chasing you so you have to be better than that … there is a difference in actually understanding what the context internationally is and what you have to do for it. It is important to continually get better and make sure that you can answer whatever anybody else will put to you. If you can't do that, then you are not an international sportsperson. You are only a national player. To be an international sportsperson, there is decision making, there is a whole contextual difference, there is a difference in the variety of physical skills and the way in which you use them and in what you have to understand socially. All the social implications [some external] of being in international sport can crush the person who may be physically talented before they even get off the ground.

These international players are developed according to how they are oriented. As Lyn says, 'If they are only oriented in the motivational sense, in being excited by the challenge of getting better, then that is how they will approach the international scene'. What she is aiming for with her athletes is for them to be able to sit on the sideline or go to a training session and be able to analyse the opposition in a totally unemotional and rational way. Once players get this international feel, their training goes up another notch. Lyn explains:

It's whether you want to be the best as measured by somebody else, or whether you want to be the best your capacity can manage. If you take the second attitude that most people use, then in the first one you are just edging out the opposition all the time. You see it quite often in athletics, where somebody has a world record and they run against the clock really well, but when they get into an actual event it all changes for them. Some people will win to beat other people, but they won't crack a world record. Other people will crack a world record, but never win a race … In team games, it expresses itself by teams that get ahead and they can't pull away, they are just winning all the time. The New Zealand team is like this.

To develop players' ability to analyse and strive for that extra notch, and in this way to nurture an international sense, Lyn's training sessions are full of problem-solving situations to enhance their game sense:

The best example is that we have a bunch of players who came into the team who did not have good spatial awareness and game sense awareness, just in a general sense. So we said, 'How can we combine training, make it fun and do some other things as well?' We started making up these games in the morning and they would have whatever the fitness element was (speed, endurance) then we created invasion games that had spatial concepts which were teaching them about some of the spatial context that they need in netball and some of the game sense that they were missing. We added other elements that tested their attitudes to rules and other team players by changing rules and making up red herrings. We simply pressured them mentally. What we were doing was just constantly trying to create a game environment situation. I don't go and find the games, I just make them up from the elements that they need and that they need to learn.

Lyn suggests that when the players begin training with her, they often have great knowledge and ability to train and play in discrete units but do not understand how to integrate these units into a full game context. Lyn has really noted a difference in the English team using TGfU, she can see a big change in her players' application and understanding for the game of netball.

To enhance the international game of netball, Lyn uses TGfU to teach for pressure situations that may arise on the court:

We use [games] all the time to make decisions and add pressure, like risk taking, pressures. We want people to take risks ... There is a time to skill and drill, hone something up technique-wise, but the rest of the time, once they have got that technique right, they need to apply it. They can have the best techniques in the world, but if they can't apply them, then it is a waste of time. We quickly get to the application which has risk taking, decision making and pressure ... The other thing is recognising that they are in a ball game and they should be using the ball as much as they possibly can.

Through TGfU, Lyn creates a learning environment that enhances the desire for athletes to get competitive. What kind of environment that should be depends on the national culture in which you are coaching. She says that coaches need to be aware that:

There is a real art in a strongly competitive nation where there are a huge number of people participating; you can have a harshly competitive environment. But if you've got a quasi amateur situation with a small population, then you have to handle that differently.

When I ask Lyn if she learned the TGfU approach through any particular training, she responds:

I probably picked up on it from teaching, actually ... When I first started teaching, I was teaching a lot of home room and disadvantaged groups ... they taught me a lot about human behaviours. They didn't do what you expected, they never did. They never responded to language as you expected either. So it taught me a lot about what I was effectively doing and how people will respond to different pressures. These groups were bluntly honest about everything.

Lyn has been using TGfU throughout her coaching life without putting a label on it. Her intentions in training have always been to create situations in which athletes develop an informed understanding of the game or situation in a holistic sense and with integrated training. She has also seen it as essential to develop this understanding by creating pressure situations through using games to train the players.

Implementing an Athlete-centred Approach

One of the major challenges Lyn has faced in her athlete-centred coaching is that many athletes have experienced only coach-centred approaches before starting with her. She says it is important to help the athletes through this process of change:

... the players, when they first experience how you are doing this, they think you are soft and confusing. It is a whole change of behaviour for them. At times, they don't cope with that very well. Sometimes you have to be autocratic, e.g. 'Stop doing that and do this', and then they feel comfortable. If you are really, genuinely trying to help them get into this whole scene, you do have to assist them through that process of change.

The challenge continues for her athletes as, when they go back to coach-centred coaches, they must adjust again. However, Lyn feels that these athletes, having been enabled to think and learn about the game, have an advantage as they begin to use their knowledge and experience to enhance their performance under each different leadership style. Going back to a coach-centred coach, these athletes may also begin to challenge the coach's ideas, which many coach-centred coaches cannot cope with. In Lyn's view, it is important to give athletes some guidance about how to return to such a situation:

It is interesting watching [the high performance players] who've come out of a highly autocratic system and into this completely different way of doing things and there isn't one of them that does not now like it. They are having great difficulty at the moment going back to ... very autocratic coaching and teaching situations. Of course what you've got are athletes who challenge, who ask questions, people who think about things and say, 'Excuse me but you are not making sense to me'. So it is a much more challenging to the coaches who are autocratic now and we've had to counsel the players who have gone from that programme back into autocratic coaching, to teach them how to cope with that. It is quite specifically different. What is interesting for me about that is when I first went there, I didn't realise I was that different [in my coaching approach]. I have now realised that it is extremely different.

Players who will be the best international athletes will have a special passion. That passion exudes through training if you can offer them an opportunity to enjoy what they are doing and know why they need to understand certain situations. Using an athlete-centred approach, a coach can enable athletes to gain that passion. Lyn relates two other analogies to illustrate what can be achieved with passion:

It happened in [one of the last] World Championships when Temepara [Clark] came back on the court in the final of the World Championships. Australia would have won that game, but Temepara came back on that court and got two interceptions. She was sent off but when she came back it was with a controlled and very passionate drive. This player had the complete drive at that moment in time and she was going to get out there and do this well. In fact, it was the last thing she did ... That does not happen by drilling. Another example is 100-metre sprinters who often run faster in a relay than they would ever run in just a flat race. That shows that element of people's desire and passion within them that will drive an exceptional performance at a particular time.

Lyn believes strongly that athletes have many learning experiences without coach interference. In many situations that Lyn sets up (e.g. a game or practice), the athletes set off to do things in their own way. She often waits on the sideline until she can determine that the athletes are stuck or an athlete asks for clarification. Their learning is enhanced because they are discovering and taking ownership of their understanding of the situation(s). Often when implementing activities or games, coaches tend to interfere, to jump in and tell the athletes how to solve the problem. In effect, athletes are giving the responsibility of understanding back to the coach and the coach is taking it away from the players. However, the coach's role should be to try to set conditions that will enhance the learning and accelerate it.

Freedom is the opportunity to make decisions. . . - Kenneth Hildebrand

My grandfather once told me that there were two kinds of people: those who do the work and those who take the credit. He told me to try to be in the firstgroup. There is much less competition. - Indira Gandhi

Conclusion

Lyn says that she continues to learn about her coaching and from the athletes:

> I think you learn all the time in different environments but you have to pay attention. I'd rather something emerges than is specifically created because people buy into it as something they own. I think the discourse crucial. If I expect people to be courteous to one another and share and perform to win, then how I spoke about that was really important. It wasn't the words, but the ideas behind the words. So by changing those you can set an environment that will indicate change in a lot of people's behaviour and expectation. I can remember teaching a seventh form [class] at school and they were talking to one another in very negative terms, as young people did at that time. We talked about it and suggested an experiment: to play a game of softball in the class and see whether they could actually not say anything negative. We agreed on a penalty if they did. They all bought into this and off they went. At the end of the session, they debriefed. They realised they couldn't get through the game. People would start to say something and then they'd stop midway and realise what they were about to say. They were all great about it, but what I was trying to do is just show them where they were at and what they were doing unconsciously. I didn't have anybody tell me to do that or teach me how or when to attempt it.

Lyn is an astute, insightful coach. Her ability to read people impressed me in watching her coach and interviewing her. She has a highly analytical mind, with a key ability to focus on the big picture.

Lyn also believes strongly in focusing on a quality team culture through the notion of community. This community is a group who come together to strive for a mutual direction, often an external goal. Through a coach's efforts to ensure this community works well together, it is possible to create a quality sport environment in which values and principles are adhered to and practised as individuals work together for a common purpose. To develop and maintain such a community, Lyn advocates the four principles of having direct communication, taking responsibility for your own and the group's performance, being honest and celebrating difference.

Lyn's use of athlete-centred coaching has been an asset to those athletes she has influenced. Her curiosity has inspired them to develop the same quest for knowledge. Through her, athletes have also been exposed to many valuable experiences that have enhanced both their performance and their holistic development.

Schooling, instead of encouraging the asking of questions, too often discourages it. - Madeleine L'Engle, US civil rights leader, clergyman

If you don't have time to do it right,
when will you have time to do it over?
- John Wooden

Chapter Five

Matt Powell

Rugby Player, Turned Coach

Athlete learning is the essence to athlete-centred coaching. In the UK, the Football Association (FA) is making some attempt to encourage people to use an athlete-centred coaching approach.

Recently one of the coaches of football (soccer) skills held a workshop for the specific purpose of enabling coaches to understand the purpose and idea of athlete-centred coaching and Teaching Games for Understanding (TGfU). After the programme, one of the participants went back to his classes and implemented a session to have a go at enabling the athletes (students) to take ownership of and responsibility for their experiences. After the session, the participant (teacher) asked both athletes and other teachers who were involved to share their experiences. He subsequently emailed the FA skills coach with a report on the insightful and positive responses that were forthcoming from this discussion. The teacher reported on a football training session involving a mixed ability class of 10-year-olds that 'gave me one of the most rewarding feelings since the programme started if not since I have been a coach'.

As this participant relates it, the session involved the medium-term objective of developing attacking skills using travelling and sending skills in random, variable practices and small-sided games. Based on the athlete-centred coaching approach, four to five students were to plan the warm up for the final session, which was to involve fundamental movements with and without the ball and some dynamic stretches. The class as a whole asked to play some skill-based games as part of the warm-up related to movements with a ball.

The response, as the participant reports, was 'fantastic':

> The day of the session I was greeted with four of the biggest smiles possible and the children [in charge of planning the warm-up] had a session plan on a cork board and A3 [butcher's] paper and quoted 'this is our visual aid like your whiteboard.' My only contribution was 'Good afternoon and welcome coaches'.

Evidence of broader student empowerment soon emerged when, while the original workshop participant was talking through the programme with the class teacher during the warm-up, a student:

… stopped the class and said 'who can tell me how we can improve using our success words from previous weeks'. SPACE was the answer and she followed up with 'what parts of space?' 'Looking for it', 'Making it', 'Going into it' and 'Keeping it' were the responses and the children went off and space was majorly improved. I was totally amazed the information the children were asking and coming up with.

Following on from the fundamental movements the children had all the class with a ball except four children who were taggers who scored points from touching a ball that was not under control. They were also told that no TACKLING should take place for safety reasons. After playing for a few minutes the four leaders asked the class how can we challenge ourselves? [Responses were]: 'More defenders', 'Using different parts of feet', 'Smaller area', 'More skills'. They then played again and this time were asked to put thumbs up if they needed more challenge or thumbs down if it was already challenging enough.

The icing on the cake for me was when I said to one of the coaches for the day 'one minute left'. [The leaders] called all the children in and asked the class the effects on the body the activity had. (I felt like I was taking the session myself!)

The difference in the approach was clearly apparent to the head teacher who, on observing part of the session, asked whether the children were teaching today and, following a discussion with the workshop participant, commented, 'It's amazing what they can do when you show them respect and give them some ownership'. Further reward came from the feedback from those directly involved in the session. As the workshop participant reports it, teacher feedback included:

Very impressed by the Coach; Lessons were extremely well planned and structured; Delivery of the lessons was totally appropriate for this year; Group, tone, discipline, class management and organisation were all excellent; Lessons were stimulating, challenging and differentiated where necessary to ensure all children were fully involved at all times; Superb subject knowledge and skill levels made this an exciting opportunity for myself and my class; We all learnt lots.

Some of the comments from the students involved were:

Taking the warm-up ROCKS; I wish we could plan all our lessons!; I was unsure whether I'd like football but I did!; I really liked how we had to decide personal challenges; The pace suited everyone; They were excellent as we had lots of key words to focus on and I liked the way we could lead the final session; Everybody could do it even the ones who had played before because you made it harder.

The above example demonstrates the motivation and importance of enabling athlete ownership of and responsibility for their performances.

The purpose of this chapter is to highlight the insights and experiences of one specific athlete who recently became a coach for the Worcester Warriors rugby club, Matt Powell. It focuses in particular on Matt's perspective of various coaches he has had in his 20 years of experience as both a child and a professional player.

An athlete who played many sports, as encouraged by his family, Matt began playing rugby in Brecon, South Wales at the age of about eight years. Perhaps not surprisingly, given that his dad played rugby and he was growing up in a rugby-mad country, Matt began to take rugby quite seriously when he went to a private school at the age of 11. He thrived in the environment and particularly enjoyed all team sports. Reflecting on this schooling experience, he acknowledges the changes in sporting fortune that can occur due to individual growth and development:

> I was quite well regarded around 11, 12, 13, but then others started growing when I was 15 or 16, and I didn't, so I went off the radar a bit during that time. However, in my sixth form, I played for the First XV for two years and I started [to] play well and gain more confidence and began to gain recognition nationally.

His experience at the private school included a geography teacher who took an interest in his rugby to the extent of writing to Saracens (a UK rugby club) about him. The letter sparked Saracens' interest in Matt and subsequently they offered him a university scholarship and a contract to play for the club. Between school and this great opportunity at Saracens, Matt decided to take a year out (gap year) in Christchurch, New Zealand to help a school and further his rugby-playing experience with a local rugby club.

New Zealand was a good experience; he enjoyed coaching the children at Medbury and developed his rugby-playing experience at the same time. Upon his return to Saracens, he played rugby and started a sports science degree at Brunel University. He then played with Harlequins for three years, during which time he completed his degree. For most of his first year with Harlequins he was a starter at the number 9 (Scrum Half) position but then, after the coaches changed, he became a second-string player.

After the conclusion of his contract with Harlequins, Matt considered his next move:

> I was getting a bit stale really, I wasn't playing a huge amount and I kind of wanted to go somewhere and do something different. Even in those

days I was thinking that I might stop playing rugby and start thinking about doing something else. Then the opportunity to play in the premiership [highest-level rugby competition in the UK] came about [with Worcester Warriors], even after I looked at France and Japan.

Coming to Worcester was the next step for Matt and he was ready for a challenge:

I think I was just drifting through. If I had a bad game or a good game, I didn't have much pride in my performance. I was stale at Harlequins, so in coming here with someone who was expecting me to always perform at a high standard it was really good for me.

Matt was one of a number of scrum halves (rugby position number 9) with the Worcester Warriors where he played for six years. During his stint with the team, he dealt with eight different coaches. Also during the process (for many reasons), he lost the drive and motivation to keep playing. When I asked him why he stopped playing, he responded:

It wasn't anything really, I was just ready to do something else and I really wasn't getting [as] excited as I should be about playing as I [had] 12 years ago. I think I have probably been through four or five relegation battles [a positional situation whereby the team is lowest on the league table and must not come in last place or they will be 'relegated' to the next competition level] and that's a tough season for every one of those [battles] and also particularly at [Worcester], I didn't think I was the answer to what we needed … and I wouldn't want to be on the bench, I want to carry and do battle and be part of the team so, I didn't think I could really … But I think mentally I was ready to do something else.

This decision left Matt with a few options about what he would do next, but then Mike Ruddock asked him to join the coaching staff at the Worcester Warriors. After much consideration, Matt decided to take up this new opportunity, as he enjoyed Worcester and Mike's coaching and saw it as a major challenge. Matt is unsure as to whether he will pursue coaching, but this first season will probably give him some great experience.

Throughout his playing years, Matt has had many coaches and has experienced a variety of coaching methods, actions and politics. The next section discusses some of those experiences.

Coaches

Matt's favourite coaches along the way seem to be those who gave him the most respect and those who were honest and sincere about his performance and his contributions.

When coaches didn't demonstrate these characteristics, his experiences were quite negative. As a player he maintained a high level of motivation, even in despite of his experience of some coaches and the way they coached:

> I was really self motivated … I enjoyed working with Mark Evans, he coached my first year I was with Saracens, before taking on a senior management role. Things were going so badly, he thought he would come and coach … he rubbed some people up the wrong way, but I respected his knowledge and management of myself. But I knew he believed in me. I knew he liked the way I played; he trusted me with the game plan; he was very complimentary towards me. So that gave me quite a lot of confidence and I enjoyed that … I think if I knew [that] someone liked the way I played, then that got more out of me. I knew I was never going to be, I was never the type of player who was going to be multi-phase rugby and [to do that] you have to have highly skilled passing line and that wasn't me.

Matt also had a great respect for coaches who were intelligent and knew the game of rugby. As he explains it, his learning was enhanced when coaches who knew rugby challenged him to think about the game:

> Keast was a very intelligent guy, very organised. I enjoyed the tactics and the way to play the game … Andy Keast was tactically and technically one of the best coaches. He knew a lot about the game and I learned a lot from him, but his man management [ability to deal with players] was diabolical. But I probably played my best rugby under him. I almost played in spite [of him] really, but I improved my performance with him. He made me analyse my performance, he really made me look hard at my own game.

When challenged with analysing his playing performance using video footage from games and training sessions, Matt's rugby playing seemed to thrive:

> [One coach] kind of encouraged me to and – he told me really that I had to [watch videos]. We used to do loads and loads of video sessions … We did video sessions [video analysis] with just me and him sitting there for hours and hours and I learned quite a lot about myself, my game. He would try and break certain players in the squad and build them up in his own weird way.

The coach's ability to manage people ('man management') appears to be important to Matt as, when the coaches respect the players, the players work harder for the team. As a result of some of his experiences, Matt believes that a coach could expect too much player input to the point where he felt that he and the players were doing the coach's roles:

> … last year, it was very much player-centred and [the players] made all the decisions and there was a tactical group, a leadership group. Now I think it has come back a bit, to take a bit of pressure off players, because there was far too much [player input] last year. We are really player-centred here I think. [Now] players are never afraid to stand up and say, 'We should be doing this' or 'Let's try this'.

When I asked him what he thought 'player centred' was, he responded:

> I think it means players having ownership and having a say in the way they play and the environment they play and train in. So, I've been in teams [that] have been dictated to, like … for example, you were told this is how you are playing and there is no discussion.

Unlike some players, Matt really needed a challenge and to have ownership, but he suggests that his self-motivation was what enabled him to perform well. Relying on the coach to understand him as a person was also important to his performance and development:

> Phil Larder was an interesting person, he acknowledged the current system and he was … so complimentary: 'Matt when you are playing everything ticks. You are an organiser and you play well and you are there'. I thought that was very kind. He might be going around saying that to everyone, I don't know. But I believed him and I really enjoyed playing in that style. I have a lot of respect for him … We were 16 points adrift, we were in danger of getting relegated (moved down to the next league) at Christmas time, and he came in and took over on January 1st and just sorted our defence out. You would walk on the pitch and he managed to get everyone's attention and everyone just sparked straight away. Again, he put structures in place and I reacted to that, but he really believed in me and he was very kind of complimentary towards me … just talking [things] through with this guy. One of the things that he said was, 'I think you could have been a much, much better player, but I don't think you have ever been managed by a coach, to get your understanding'. I can kind of see his point really … if [Phil Larder] was still here and I was working with him for three or four or five years I think I would be a far, far better player. I worked my brain more when he coached.

During our interviews, there was much reflection and Matt demonstrated his player self-awareness:

... I felt that I could never get to perform, when I played a few games and I get dropped and have only played a few games. The only times I play well is when I have six or seven games and I feel like I am on automatic number one, then I play well. It is very difficult to get [to that point] as [the role] is very complicated when just given a few games. In some ways, I like[d] Mike as a coach when I was playing under him, but I knew he really didn't want to pick me. I knew I was never going to be that kind of player.

I asked Matt how he learned to play the way he did: did coaches have anything to do with his need for structure? He reflected:

I think it could've been the coaches as well. Then again, I don't have raw pace, I am not going to make 10 breaks a game, whereas Justin Marshall will cuz he's quick, he's physical. Danny Care from Harlequins will make 10 breaks a game and do that. [A player] could be [making those breaks] because he is physically capable of doing that, but he doesn't think about it, and doesn't know where the others are. Whereas Justin Marshall is physical, he is quick and he knows where others are ... Yes, I don't think any coach made that difference really.

Matt appreciated coaches who took the reins when things were not going well. He gave examples of how his team lacked direction when they had a coach whose training regime consisted of playing games only. After this games-only coach was sacked, for reasons unknown, and a different coach came in, Matt was more comfortable:

... I remember we were playing Leicester on the Saturday and he [the new coach] came in on Monday morning and said, 'Right, the following weekend's game, [the games-only coach] won't be with us and I am taking over until further notice' ... he said, 'We play Leicester on Saturday and this is how we are going to beat Leicester' and he had flip chart, and he said, 'Right we are going to keep to this guide and we are going to kick it, we are going to play in this half and we are going to kick it here and then we are going target this player and this is how we are going to do it and that's it. That's how we are going to win on Saturday.' And we trained for that and we beat Leicester. I liked that approach.

The basic premise to being athlete-centred is to identify and cater to athletes' needs. The approach used by the new coach in the above anecdote was athlete-centred because in that particular situation at that particular time, the coach perceived that the players were in need of specific direction because they were floundering and, for at that time and situation, it was important to give direction to get the team back on track. However, if he continued to be directive, then it is likely that the learning would have stopped and his approach would no longer have been athlete-centred. Matt acknowledges an appreciation for a more athlete-centred approach when he speaks about Mike Ruddock:

> The thing about Mike, I really like his style of rugby, it's the best style of rugby I have come across. His man management is brilliant. He is great with the boys. He has a vision of how he wants to play the game and I agree with that … The way he brings the youngsters through … he realises that actually if he doesn't understand the defensive system, [he is] going to get a defensive coach in … to do that … all those systems … or like line-out, he'll get [a coach] to do that. I actually respect that more than not doing a great job at it … Initially when I started coaching, Mike took a lot more interest in what I doing with the patterns. Initially, he wants to know who, why is that, what does that look like …

Additionally Matt observes that over the few years he has had Mike as a coach, Mike has constantly reflected and changed according to the needs of the team:

> … last year, he wouldn't have even paid attention to it. I think he is changing as a coach … I really respect Mike as a coach, as a coaching Director of Rugby.

Matt feels that the knowledge of the coach is essential in gaining credibility with the players:

> Interestingly, what I found over the years is that we have all these patterns of play that most [of] the guys don't actually know because [the coach] didn't know them himself. So he didn't know where you were supposed to be. So if you went off the first phase, why didn't you go in that direction? He would say, 'Well you should know as it would be easier for you. You can't predict maybe three phases down, but the first two, you should know where you are going.' But one of the things I really want them to say is, 'These are our attacking systems and this is where we are going', so I know myself where every single player will be. I think the players should know that as well. When we go on the field, they could get wound up if someone hits the wrong ruck [a type of rugby play] or doesn't run the right line on the side plays …

Being Questioned

Athlete-centred coaches advocate the use of questioning as an important way to help athletes solve problems and make decisions. Robyn Jones (2001) suggests that one of the major challenges that athletes need to overcome is how to respond to questions when they are unaccustomed to being asked for their input. Matt says he does not like being questioned, especially in front of others. But from our discussion it emerges that it is the way the questions are posed that has a negative effect on his desire to be questioned:

> I haven't been too much of a questioning bloke. I kind of liked it when the coach said to me that you should be able to do this and be able to do that … I prefer not too many questions and pointless [questions]. Like [a coach] would pause [the video recording] and say, 'What are you thinking now?' And I would not know. Then he would say, 'Wouldn't you agree that it was better to pass the ball?' And of course I would say, 'Well, yes'. Then he would say, 'Well, why didn't you then?' and 'Was that good execution?' – 'Well, no that wasn't good execution' …

Clearly Matt's frustration here is with the way some of the coaches question and the apparent pointlessness of questions themselves. He was also unfamiliar with this approach during his rugby-playing life such that, when he first came to the Worcester Warriors, he found it difficult to answer questions.

As David Hadfield (2005) observes, implementing an empowerment approach and using questioning may be uncommon and, to some, may feel unnatural. Athletes may initially be surprised that they can have input to solving problems and thus their immediate response may not be favourable. However, if questioning becomes part of a coach's repertoire and the coach focuses on questioning well, then athletes will enjoy solving problems and will experience success, especially where the coach clearly respects athletes' responses.

In some cases, as Matt discusses, some players didn't really like to analyse their performance too much, but he admired them for the skill they showed:

> You kind of want a combination of an intelligent 9 [scrum half], like [a named player]: he is skilful, he has [a] really good pass and he is in really good condition and he doesn't think about the game much. He won't think that this is where the space is going to be, he just goes out and plays and doesn't think about things.

TGfU

Through his years of playing rugby, though Matt didn't understand what TGfU was, he subsequently acknowledges that the more realistic the situation, the better equipped the players are to apply their learning from training sessions to the games:

> Yes, I think there is a time and a place for your two on ones, your passing drills, but you have to replicate what you do out there on the field and

unfortunately the two on ones, that guy, isn't necessarily going to go; the defenders will do it for the sake of the drill and do what you want them to. But out there in a proper game, it is real competition, so I really enjoyed doing games at training … Since Mike arrived, we do a lot more of them.

However, Matt acknowledges that it seemed pointless to just play games without any apparent purpose:

… [One coach] was into that. I don't think he thought why we were doing it; it was just a bit of fun and he could join in too … I guess I am better with structures and [a coach] was like, 'Just play and enjoy it and see what happens', which was the way he played, but nobody else could really play like that unless you were highly skilled. No matter what, I wouldn't have classed myself as a player who was highly skilled, probably a lot better with a structure.

Matt believes that a challenge to using a games approach is that some players tend to social-loaf in the game:

I find it frustrating because there are a lot of people who can hide in these games. One of the things I started to do straight away was get cameras on individuals and just see what they are up to. I generally pick an individual who I know is … involved … Maybe that has helped, I don't know, maybe the culture of the boys has changed, but now everyone is contributing, everyone is working, everyone is looking for work, we are getting lot more out of the games at the moment I think.

With the Warriors, Matt has noticed quite a different approach and culture. The Warriors also use games but for the specific purpose of working on fitness and conditioning. Most of the players acknowledge that using games for fitness increases their intensity and enjoyment when doing fitness sessions. When I asked Matt if the games approach affected the positive environment, he answered:

I think the games have improved because of the team culture of the boys, and an enriched programme. The games are challenging, they are good fun, [the players] enjoy competition; they hate losing to other teams.

Matt also noted that tactics can be learned through performance analysis of videos of play. However, if players rely on the videos alone and gain the cognitive understanding without applying it on the field, it is difficult to transfer that understanding to matches:

[One coach] would expect you to do it all in your head rather than on the field. He didn't put you in the situations. He would rather you watch the video and expect you to remember once you are on the field … I had a good understanding of the game. But I think with a lot of the boys, they have to be in that situation 100 times.

Using video analysis to help players to improve is known as a useful tool in coaching. However, using the pressure involved in the games approach to apply that analysis can assist in transferring the knowledge to actual match play, as Matt observes:

I don't think you have to show them. You can still do video work afterwards and show [the players] you are going to get lots and lots of opportunities. That is a bit of a worry for me because [the players] let it go or are happy with it not working, and they think they will get it right next time. That creeps into our game. We have to take every single opportunity we get and that is how we finish off. If we do that, we'll be very successful. Like today, there was a bit of peer pressure from the boys, but there were lots of dropped balls. They need more pressure on them to execute moves a lot better.

Designing the games to meet a purpose is the key to using TGfU and enabling realistic situations under pressure in training is essential to understanding various match situations. Matt acknowledges:

Playing the game with a goal [or purpose] … the game can be played so they don't get another chance, like that conditioning game. It's the design of the game. Yes, but you want to get them to try to [do] new things, and sometimes they might think, it is easier if I don't make that long pass … You could get points for innovation and for whatever you were working on.

Many coaches suggest that if athletes work too much in games, there is no opportunity for them to learn skill. It is difficult to convince these coaches that skill learning is part of the process of becoming self-aware and a game-like experience provides the stimulus to learn the skill. Yet it is evident that Matt incorporates these principles successfully into his own coaching:

Even with skill drills, doing line passing, I would still try to make a game of it … this morning we were practising ruck lines, or running off groups of forwards or setting up random situations that may occur in the match. I was telling them, 'You have to try [to] manipulate what you want these guys to do. You are defending these guys and you have to make one of them look like a complete idiot, so it is a game between the two.' That's how I think they should look at it, even [then] they are practising their skills …

Interestingly Matt gained much of his skill work through watching others. This method of learning fits in with social learning theory, which Rod Thorpe (2005) highlights as an important component of TGfU in enabling players to get the most out of learning opportunities. However, as Matt acknowledges, if the person they are observing has a higher level of skill, it is problematic and demoralising to try to repeat that skill:

> There was a guy called Paul Turner actually – very, very skills-based coach at the Newport Dragons. He was an absolute wizard with the ball … He really pushed the skills; it was such a challenge doing training with him cuz he could do so much other stuff. In the end it became so demoralising because he was so good and he expected you to do all this stuff and you couldn't actually do it …

Social learning theory would suggest that the motivation of the player to copy or try to replicate someone else's skill is what encourages him or her to try harder to do that skill. Such modelling is about finding the right balance, as when observing someone with such advanced skill as in the quote above, some athletes might see it as easy for the expert, but too difficult for them. However, Matt believes that a player does need to be challenged above his or her level of playing:

> … any skill you are doing, should be [a] challenge, [have] some game involved in it, even it is a game with yourself … if you say, 'I have 100 passes and I have to get 97 out of 100', that's how I play my game. I did a lot of stuff on my own as we lived on a farm and I used to take a ball down to the yard and I used to pick something on the roof and do conversions onto the roof of the barn. And I used to think, if I make it, I am going to play for Wales and if I missed it I couldn't play for Wales. So, let's have one more go and see if I could do it this time.

Generally, in reflecting on TGfU, Matt suggests that:

> … most players love [purposeful games], they are all rugby players so they like competition.

Athlete Input

Matt suggests that athlete input is a key to ensuring players take ownership. An autocratic and directive coach might be able to compensate for the lack of input somewhat with strengths in organisational skills, which would give him or her the credibility needed for athletes to appreciate and go along with the coach. Matt tells of one such coach in this recollection:

... we had a good bunch of boys who got on well. No one expected us to do well, but we ended up winning quite a few games. But we were reasonably well organised. We didn't have a great side, but we were very well organised and that is what he was good at ... All of our patterns and our systems, they were pretty thorough. Yes I quite liked it: I am organised and I quite like structure. So I kind of did enjoy that. I probably ended up playing the best rugby of my life, which was weird.

Even if there was a lack of people management, therefore, good organisational skills would mean the team would play despite the atmosphere. However, Matt was disenchanted with the shenanigans of a coach who couldn't acknowledge the contributions he and his fellow players could make:

If I had a good game, he would say things like, '[I] don't think you've made it ... and you are not on par' ... He was like that with all the players really; he was just a difficult guy. In some ways ... we put it in almost in spite of him. But no one really enjoyed the atmosphere, [the players] all got along with each other, the players had a really good atmosphere, but he wasn't someone who you'd go out and want to play for ... the players kept the team together.

In cases where he had a coach-centred coach who didn't ask for athlete input, Matt felt that, as a player, he had no ownership of his playing or team direction:

Yes, I mean if you were to question him why he would do something, you probably wouldn't get selected.

Matt is keen for coaches to know their players and to try to work out what makes them tick. He values coaches who have the flexibility and/or adaptability to adjust their leader behaviour to satisfy the needs of the athletes, and who know their players well. Reflecting on his own experience of coaches, Matt considers that coaches who responded to his needs probably were not doing so as part of a deliberate strategy:

I don't think Phil Larder saw me and thought, 'Actually if I make out I really believe in Matt, I will get a lot more out of him'; I thought it was just his style. He probably went to everyone and said, 'We really need you in the system; without you playing, we are not going to do well.' From my perspective it is quite positive feedback, but it came across as very sincere. I don't know if he was that good a coach that with certain people out there, he had to give them a bit of confidence boosting. Like 'Matt, he is a guy that needs reassurance' ... People are different; looking back, I don't think I have had a coach who has been that sharp enough to know that 'This guy needs this' ... I may be being unfair, but like with Mark

Evans, even though we got on really well, he was really too busy being wrapped up in himself to think like that.

Matt discussed the current culture of the Warriors and the amount of player input Mike was giving to the players when he played. When asked for his view of the percentage of input that players within a team should have, Matt responded:

Player-centred wise we were probably 95% and at the moment we are about 65%. Last year we were about 90%. I think a good place to be is around 60% [athlete input].

An interesting interpretation of athlete input from Matt is that:

[Players] might like to input, but I don't think [Mike] would like to be in the situation last year where the [players] had pressure, like doing the coaches' work. [Coaches asked,] 'Will you analyse these videos?' Then, [we] said, 'Are you going to do it as well?' and the coach says, 'Nah'. [The players] were thinking that 'You should do it as well; you are the coach.'

Team Culture

In his reflections on team culture, Matt first explains his perspective of what it is:

It is the environment that you are working in … you got to get a group of people who want to work for each other … you have to break a few barriers to get people to work together and obviously the first day of the season [if you expect] to break a few barriers and get to know each other [instantly], that is not going to get you anywhere … different teams have different identities. At Worcester, we were a very, very physical side and no one wanted to come here and play, and we were just horrible people – you know, nice off the field, but on the field … then we started to lose that reputation really. Now we are trying to pull some of that back, a different sort of style, different trademarks.

Matt acknowledges that having a good team culture was crucial to success of the teams he has been with. He values the current team culture of the Worcester Warriors, which he sees as having developed significantly since he was a player with the team:

The culture is good … [The coaches] want thought from the backs, they want to be organised. I think it is a team culture, but that it is the culture that Mike introduced. [The team culture] is just getting stronger and stronger as we go on. At the end of last year, we didn't have that and I have never been in the situation before [with fellow team members] who would say, 'You played really well last week, but you have to do that again.' I have never seen conversations like that happen between players, so that was really good; you don't want to let that mate down and we have to make sure we carry on that form for next year.

In other teams, Matt never really experienced an explicit focus on working on team culture, except for the social aspect. His teams would put values together just to please the coach, but there was no obvious work to set up an environment where players develop self-awareness and examine their own personal impact on the team environment. However, the Worcester Warriors with Mike Ruddock as Director of Rugby have focused on achieving team cohesiveness through identifying and nurturing trademarks (values to live by) and constantly focusing on how they can work together. The culture now pervades the Warriors coaching team as Matt has observed since joining the staff this year:

> I think as a coaching team we are bit more cohesive now … Last year we worked separate and one guy would say, 'Well my line-outs are fine … or 'My scrums are fine', but now it is all about winning as a group. So the line-outs don't matter as long as there is a win.

In 2008 the Warriors hired a person from a company called Leading Teams who focused on designing an agreed, explicit team culture with the underpinning value of honesty. This honesty value was established through team meetings and feedback sessions with the players who used their honesty, through problem solving and self-reflective activities. Because of this experience, one of the overall Warriors trademarks is an expectation of honesty from both the coaches and the athletes which Matt believes is a key to establishing a good environment and team culture:

> We got to the stage last year where the boys were honest with each other and they were feeding back with each other. I probably haven't been in an environment like that where you could actually say to someone, 'You actually didn't get enough whatever on the weekend; we think you need to work on this a lot more.' I don't think many teams are able to get there like we did.

As Matt's latest coach, Mike Ruddock has explicitly tried to establish trademarks with the players. Matt thought this was positive as it was a focus for the players to work on:

> In some ways, we would put up on [a notice board in the players' common room] if they had attended to their trademarks or not and if they didn't hit their trademarks, then they would've got an X. [As a player,] you look at it and think, 'Well actually I didn't get my trademarks, so there is a good chance I won't play on the weekend.' Some of the players were saying [to

another player], 'You were really physical, you did this, you did that, you get a tick, you are so much better, but we didn't get the energy from you, so I am going to give you a X.' So, in some ways, that can be perceived to reflect in their playing, [e.g.] he played well and he didn't play well.

Interestingly, until his time with the Warriors, Matt's experience of team culture was largely based on social engagement, such as going out for a beer. Matt considers that none of his other teams explicitly worked on establishing a vision and values that the team could live by. In contrast, these 'trademarks' agreed to by both the players and the coaches of the Warriors were a consistent focus:

> I think it has been great, the [trademarks focus] … here. I haven't been in many teams who focus on it, until … Leading Teams started here. When Trent first came in, we evaluated and we started to open up to each other and we started to look at yourself and your performance. I haven't really seen any teams be honest with each other like that. I found that really, really good. Every team I have been involved with there has always been kind of a social culture and we'd go for a few beers now and again.

Matt notoriously was responsible for much of the social engagement when he was with teams who focused on that area:

> I guess cuz I was quite organised and apparently I am really good fun after a few beers, so probably for that. It was probably my downfall at Harlequins because in my last two years I was probably better known for organising 'piss-ups' [social gatherings with alcohol] than actually playing … The boys would ask, 'Matt, what are we doing this Saturday?' and I [was] kind of quite keen to get rid of that.

When I asked Matt how and why the primary focus on beer and social engagement affected certain teams, he answered:

> I don't know if it is mentally or whether we have to be month to month having beers together, I don't know. It probably does break [down] a few barriers. I am sure that many successful sides that haven't gone out and socialised together. So I am not sure if it – it might be a rugby culture thing.

A theme of 'team reputation' seems to underpin many of the rugby team cultures. Even at the Warriors, Mike Ruddock suggests that a team culture is based on what others perceive their team to look like. Matt acknowledges that with the Harlequins, reputation was a major emphasis:

> Within Harlequins, we were told what our trademarks are and helped them with the input by telling them what reputation we want. When I joined

Harlequins, they had a reputation of being fancy, [having a] Barbarians' [an all-star world rugby team] playing style, not a bunch of guys who were willing to put their bodies on the line and grind out a win. So, when we got there, the process was trying to change our reputation, so our team culture was based on that. In my time at Harlequins, that didn't happen. It wasn't until I left and Dean Richards took over and focused on changing the image and team environment that it changed.

In Matt's experience, many of the teams made trademarks but the trademarks themselves become only a bunch of words, with little follow-up to ensure players were actually practising them:

There are players ... who say the right things at meetings, but then on the field, even though they back it up, they say everything the coach wants to hear ... [When coaches ask what their thoughts are, the players say,] 'Well my thoughts are this, this and this and next weekend I think you should all keep up the good work.' They talk about what would happen if you get a yellow card ... Then the next weekend in the first minute of the game, he gets a yellow card and has to go off. 'Sorry guys, I let you all down, I let the team down, I let the coaches down' ... it is good to say things if you mean them. But actually, if they don't really buy into it ... It is all very well having these trademarks but I think it needs to have more of a challenge.

Matt feels that the trademarks have to be measurable, tangible or goal-oriented:

... if we [coaches] sat down and said, 'What are our trademarks for this season?', they [players] won't know it. So people say these words, like, 'Let's be clinical, aggressive physical' ... but they don't actually know what they mean. You can go play clinical, but you have to put something tangible to that, like, 'Let's get the best defensive record in the league'. So whatever we have to do to get that, we do it. [For example,] 'Let's score the most tries off the first phase in league.' So now we become a team focused on breaking down teams in attack. 'Let's have a low tackle focus' ... that is then what we are all about ...They are tangible things that I think where trademarks should be made ... we have had the same trademarks for the last three years – do they understand? I don't really know.

Another system is to reward players when they follow the trademarks:

Billy and I were talking about it, 'Let's look at defence, let's say to the boys, "everyone put 10 quid in and let's have a £500 bet that we are going to have a the top defensive record and the best first-phase try score record this year."' Then we would get, at the end of the year we would have five grand to go towards a tea social, then it is like a real challenge and all the boys would be thinking about this defensive thing. That's fun, if it is for money. I think that is better than the trademark, a defensive trademark.

Matt sees one of the first steps in initiating such an approach as setting up a team of people to help promote athlete-centred philosophy and practice. He sees the merit of finding the right people for the job who will thrive in an athlete-centred environment:

When we recruit guys now … I want the right people who can slot into this environment … mentally tough consistently every week, people who are motivated and carry similar value[s] to the club.

Matt also suggests that having a great bunch of people to learn from is a major part of his development as a player and coach. He describes some of his learning from Mike:

[He] makes a conscious effort to [focus on the people culture], by having the Leading Teams company, and having a leadership team, giving the players a bit more ownership, like the duty team, the club, the environment, that's all the culture of the team. That's all about developing team culture.

Conclusions

As Matt moves into coaching, he wants to learn more about the athlete-centred approach – not an easy task, but the benefits to the team and individual athletes are immense. The learning process is easier when coaches begin by considering *how* such an approach might be suitable for them and remembering that the process of implementation requires time. Coaches will make progress by trying new ideas and continuing to self-reflect on how the approach is working within the team. As Matt develops his approach, he can draw on his reflections on his playing days and what enabled him to play well. There are also techniques, such as questioning and TGfU that need to be practised. Matt didn't like to be questioned when he played, but acknowledges now that players will improve their understanding of the game through game problem solving and responding to questions. The more coaches practise questioning, using games to problem solve, the better equipped their athletes will be to take ownership of their learning and have a sense of direction in their sporting and life experiences.

Finally, I asked Matt based on his experiences, what kind of coach he hoped to be. His answer captures the evolution of his own self-reflection from his wide variety of his experiences:

I would probably have the personality of Mike, with the coaching knowledge of Andy Keast, and then that [coaching] person [has] got Phil Larder influence and a bit of Scott Johnson as well. Scott is out of the box and I like that, probably a bit more radical. Balance is the key …

References

Hadfield, D. (2005). The change challenge: Facilitating self-awareness and improvement in your athletes. In L. Kidman (Ed) *Athlete centred Coaching: Developing inspired and inspiring people.* Christchurch: Innovative Print Communications.

Jones, R. (2001). Applying empowerment in coaching: Some considerations. In L. Kidman (2001) *Developing Decision Makers: An empowerment approach to coaching.* Christchurch: Innovative Print Communications.

Thorpe, R. (2005). Teaching Games for Understanding. In L. Kidman (Ed) (2005) *Athlete-centred Coaching: Developing inspired and inspiring people.* Christchurch: Innovative Print Communications.

We do not believe in ourselves until someone
 reveals that deep inside us is valuable, worth
listening to, worthy of our trust, sacred to our touch.
Once we believe in ourselves we can risk curiosity, wonder,
spontaneous delight or any experience that reveals
the human spirit." - e.e. cummings

There is no point in coaching unless the teaching
you do helps the student to overtake you.
—Rene Deleplace, mentor of Pierre Villepreux

If you believe you can, you probably can.
If you believe you won't, you most assuredly won't.
Belief is the ignition switch that gets you
off the launching pad. - Denis Waitley

To give yourself the best possible chance of playing
to your potential, you must prepare for every
eventuality. That means practice. - Seve Ballesteros

Talent wins games, but teamwork
and intelligence win championships.
- Michael Jordan

Chapter Six

Team Culture

Guest Author: Gareth Jones

University of Worcester

What is Team Culture?

> Team culture is the way that things are done on a team—it is the social
> architecture that nurtures the team psyche. A healthy team culture creates
> a climate for success. (Martens, 2004, p. 40)

Team culture is transmitted through language, material objects, beliefs and rituals and
is the predominating attitudes and behaviours that characterise the functioning of a
team. It is concerned with both the formal organisational working systems and the
informal social interactions of the team. It is also the team spirit; without a cohesive
culture the team would not grow into an effective unit.

Attention to developing and growing a positive team culture plays a significant role
in athlete-centred coaching. As Lynn Kidman (2001) has suggested:

> One major way to encourage self reliance is the pursuit of quality team
> culture through which athletes gain responsibility for establishing and
> maintaining a direction of the team. Team culture is a multifaceted process
> in which mutual goal pursuit informs the team's functioning and operation.
> Without a quality team culture success, learning and often winning are
> difficult. Thus, a major challenge for coaches is to bring athletes together
> for learning and success.

It is important at this juncture to set out some basic assumptions of this chapter. First,
success is defined as not just winning but as endeavouring to win. Second, and related
to this definition, is that the process and subsequent performance are more significant
in athlete and team development than the actual result. A clear example comes from
Wayne Smith (now an international rugby coach) who has suggested that his most
successful season was in his first year of coaching the Canterbury Crusaders rugby
team:

> It was a brilliant year, the best year of rugby I'd ever had in my life, either
> playing or coaching. We didn't even make the semi-finals, but we built
> a lot of self esteem. We had players who, in interviews at the start of
> the season, said that they didn't feel they should be on the same field
> as Auckland. Just getting them to the point where they could hold their

heads high, where they knew they understood the game better than most players around the country was satisfying. We were starting to do something special and we knew it. It was a process of building self-confidence and belief. It was rewarding and enjoyable.

The development of a positive team culture is vital to success in modern day sport. Yukelson (1997) identifies the following core components as necessary to consider in building a successful team and developing a quality team culture: shared vision and unity of purpose; collaborative and synergistic teamwork; individual and mutual accountability; a cohesive group atmosphere; team identity; open and honest communication; and peer helping and social support.

The creation of an environment that clearly defines the purpose of the team establishes a framework that the athletes, coaches and management can subscribe to collectively. It is a means by which, in other words, everyone is singing from the same hymn sheet! The acronym TEAM 'Together Everyone Achieves More' and truism 'There is no I in TEAM' are clichés now yet they highlight the importance of the collective efforts of various sporting groups. By mobilising their efforts towards a common and mutual team goal, the individual team members together achieve success. The development of this team ethic frequently denotes acceptance of roles and responsibilities at the sacrifice of personal gain and ambition—for example, 'Take one for the team!'

The coach also needs to be aware of key elements in the successful cultivation of a positive team culture and the establishment of a clear direction for the group. In particular, the process has to be inclusive rather than wholly coach driven. Involvement of the athletes in deciding the team vision, goals and values is of paramount importance in the coaching process.

In recognition of the crucial role that team culture plays in the success of teams and coaching, this chapter outlines the development of a quality team culture with examples from sport. It also highlights the importance of cohesion and how it is critical for coaches to gain an understanding of group dynamics.

Groups and Teams

We all belong to various groups such as family, work and sporting teams. This sense of belonging has a substantial impact on our lives. This impact is reflected in a common definition of a group as when two or more people interact with each other in way that involves reciprocal influence.

The study of groups and group behaviour is of specific interest in sport and in particular coaching. An effective sports team is normally a very strong group, rather than just a collection of individuals. Woods (1998) outlines four key defining features of the sports team:

1. interaction between the members—communication is extremely important in sport on and off the field of play;
2. feelings of interpersonal attraction between members—players trust and rely on their teammates;
3. a distinctive collective identity—it is clear that players belong to the team by the uniform they wear and the behaviours they display both on and off the field of play; and
4. a sense of shared purpose or goal—it is the inclusive process by which a group of individuals come together to form a successful team.

At the same time, each individual within the team is important. It follows that coaches need to understand each individual and draw all the individuals in the team together to establish a quality team environment, as Don Tricker (see Chapter Eleven) highlights:

> ... the common denominator in sport is that it is played by individuals, each with different needs and expectations. Therefore, when building teams, it all comes down to ensuring that individual expectations are satisfied when developing the core components of the team culture. The components include ownership of a shared vision or common purpose, clearly defined values, standards and role definitions.

Carron, Hausenblas and Eys (2005, p. 13) define a sports team as:

> ... a collection of two or more individuals who possess a common identity, have common goals and objectives, share a common fate, exhibit structured patterns of interaction and modes of communication, hold common perceptions about group structure, are personally and instrumentally interdependent, reciprocate interpersonal attraction and consider themselves to be a group!

Sports teams are characterised by vivacity, growth and development—they are continually active. That dynamism is manifested in the developing nature of the structure of a sports team, its cohesiveness and its collective efficacy (simply the team's confidence in its abilities prior to an upcoming competition). This unity is also demonstrated in the interaction and communication among team members, group decision-making and team achievements. The structure of a group consists of roles, norms, positions and status. "When individuals begin to interact and communicate, status differences evolve, positions are assumed and role expectations and norms begin to form" (Carron, et al., 2005, p. 13). For example, in a rugby team, positions are established almost immediately. Status differences evolve because of differences in ability or knowledge and because roles (e.g. captain) and norms (e.g. physicality as a style of play) develop from individual interactions and communications.

Teamwork

Coming together is a beginning;
Keeping together is progress;
Working together is success.

Henry Ford

Don Tricker is a firm supporter of an athlete-centred philosophy. As he sees it, the athletes should take collective responsibility for the development of roles and responsibilities, as well as taking ownership of the team and its operation. He sees his coaching role as facilitating the whole process, as he demonstrates in this example:

> ... the athletes were the principal architects of our defensive patterns. The Black Sox culture encourages creativity; every idea was respected and cherished. As coaches we would facilitate discussion with players about how we really wanted to play. The coaches' roles were more about facilitation. It was clear we had a lot of input to provide, but we were leveraging off the knowledge and experience within the side. It wasn't about saying, 'One person has got all the knowledge here, so this is the way we'd better play it.' It was like, 'No let's respect each other; we have all got something to contribute here and we want to play out every scenario to ensure we have got it right and that we believe in it. Then we will practise it, then we will test it and if it's going to deliver what we are expecting, then we will implement it in a real competition.'

It is also important to understand how groups form and develop into effective teams. Tuckman (1965) identifies four distinct stages that a group goes through:

1. *Forming:* Team members begin to get to know each-other and decide what part they will play in the group.
2. *Storming:* Conflict can occur as team members seek to establish their roles and status in the group. The roles that athletes go on to assume with the team are shaped in particular by the degree to which they demonstrate three types of behaviours (Bales, 1966):
   - Activity behaviours involve contributing to the team's effort, such as by encouraging teammates (both on and off the field of play) and speaking up in team meetings, time-outs or at half time.
   - Task ability is the expertise of the athlete and his or her capability in contributing to achieving a team goal.
   - Likeability covers social behaviours such as performing a moderator role or indeed arranging team social activities such as a party.
3. *Norming:* Co-operation will start to replace conflict and group cohesion develops as team members start to work towards collective goals.

4. *Performing:* Roles and responsibilities have stabilised and the main aim of all
   individuals is group success.
It is therefore clear that the development of the team culture takes time and that the rate
of progress through the distinct phases will depend on how all the personnel involved
in the team, including the coaching staff, management and the players, interact.

Putting this kind of theory into practice, Mark Norton (see Chapter Ten) used
an athlete-centred approach to establish a quality team culture with a senior boys'
volleyball team and found the process extremely rewarding. By his own admission,
Mark initially found the process difficult to manage but gradually became more
comfortable with allowing the athletes to make their own decisions. If the team were
to own the team vision and values then an inclusive approach to developing main
mission goals was warranted.

Among the team's mission goals were: to win six out of ten of its Monday night
games (using a squad system); to win the Canterbury Championships (once an A
team was selected—incidentally, which the boys would do two weeks before the
championships); to be in the top ten teams at the National Championships; to be an
exciting team to watch; and be known as an team who never gives up, is a tight unit
and who is mentally tough. Added to these aspirations was the team's dream goal: to
make the semi-finals at the Nationals.

To achieve these aims the boys were split into small groups to prioritise strategies
(forming). Then as a whole squad they confirmed and committed to the strategies
(storming) that they felt were best suited to achieving their goals and living their values.
The strategies they finally committed to were: talk constructively at appropriate times;
take care of things outside volleyball so we can enjoy the game and our season; respect
each other at all times; attend all training sessions—physically, mentally and socially;
remain positive no matter what; always demonstrate positive winning posture; and
always be there for my teammates.

As a demonstration of their commitment to the team the boys came up with the key
statement 'Binding together to be a better team' (storming). From there, they decided
to use a symbol to represent their dedication to the team values—and chose a gluestick
to would hang around their necks and wear both to school and to volleyball practice
and competitions. The athletes introduced penalties for those who did not wear the
gluestick at required times (norming).

The team achieved all its goals apart from the dream goal. The whole process that
the team had gone through demonstrates the impact of the athletes' self-monitoring
on the success of the team. Because the athletes took responsibility for the direction
of the team, they greatly enhanced the team spirit which came to be admired by all
(performing). Further exploring how the team goals were met for the season, Mark
said:

... every other goal, and those little goals like being a tightest team, mentally 'tough', exciting team, I think we reached all those. It was those two things (being the tightest team and being mentally tough) that enabled the team to beat teams who were more athletic or more skilful. Other teams were more athletic and more skilful, but not consistently because their mental side of the game didn't allow them to be ... All this showed the depth of the team because these guys came in and managed to get us to where we were, and then in the end too, when a couple didn't play so well, still came on full force ready to play. You could count on them all.

A comment from one of the players typifies the ethos of the team:

... the team culture and just being part of the team. That's all I played for at the end. Yes, we were winning but I knew it was because the way the team was working together because we were heaps smaller than and not as athletic as the guys who we played.

Group Effectiveness

One would think that bringing the best players into a squad would ensure success but this is not always the case. A classic example comes from 2004 when unexpectedly Greece won the UEFA European Championships, a victory based on a strong team culture and hard work. As noted above, every group has a structure and individuals are expected to fulfil roles (or behaviours) for the benefit of the team. No matter how talented they are as individuals, as team members they have to work together effectively and fulfil their different roles to contribute to overall team success. It is the clarification, understanding and ensuing acceptance of the disparate roles that warrant attention within the coaching process.

Steiner's (1972) formula for group effectiveness is:

Actual productivity = Potential productivity – Faulty process losses

According to this model, actual productivity is how the team performs and how successful it is and potential productivity is the potential for success, considering the abilities of the individual team members and the resources available to the group. When individuals work in teams, interaction, communication and coordination are vital. The third component in the formula, losses due to faulty processes, normally includes two aspects:

- *Motivational factors* have a negative influence where the individuals within the team are less motivated than their teammates, affecting the team's overall productivity.
- *Coordination factors* may arise where there is a breakdown in an individual's technical attributes or timing, on which team strategies and tactics often depend.

For example, the team's ability to secure the ball in a rugby line-out depends on the precision of the throw, the concentration of the supporting players and the accuracy of the catcher.

Given the complexity of each of these different components in the formula, a coach's understanding of group dynamics and effectiveness is vital to assessing the productivity of the team.

Another crucial factor for coaches to appreciate is the phenomenon of *social loafing* within groups which has implication in regard to the individual athlete's effort in contributing to the group. Social loafing is defined as a reduction in motivation and effort when individuals work collectively, as opposed to when they work individually (Latané, 1986).

Early evidence of this phenomenon comes from the Ringelmann effect, named after a psychologist in the late nineteenth century who found that that, during a 'tug-of-war' rope-pulling activity, the more individuals there were in the team the less effort each individual put in due to motivational and coordination losses. More recently, from swimming research Latané, Williams and Harkins (1979) found that in a simulated gala, individuals in the relay swam slower than in their individual events when they knew that lap times would not be announced. The opposite occurred when they knew that their lap times would be announced.

Such examples demonstrate clearly that social loafing is detrimental to team success and that strategies are needed to counter it. In particular, it is important to have strategies to draw out the positive side of the motivational and coordinating factors to improve productivity from a practical point of view. Matt Powell (see Chapter Five) provides an example of when he noticed social loafing at training:

> I find it frustrating because there are a lot of people who can hide in these games. One of the things I started to do straight away was get cameras on individuals and just see what they are up to. I generally pick an individual who I know is as involved … maybe that has helped, I don't know, maybe the culture of the boys has changed, but now everyone is contributing, everyone is working, everyone is looking for work, we are getting lot more out of the games at the moment I think.

Team Cohesion

Carron (1982) identifies cohesion as a dynamic process that is reflected in a group's tendency to stick together and remain united in the pursuit of its goals and objectives. Carron's definition pinpoints two essential facets to team cohesion. First, it requires task cohesion or the ability of the group members to work together and remain focused to achieve a specific task. The second facet is social cohesion, meaning that the individual group members like one another and enjoy each other's company. These characteristics have clear implications for the coaching process given that a central part of the process is to maintain a clear and candid communication channel: as the team becomes more cohesive, there is more likely to be a more open expression of views relating to both task and social issues.

Both task and social aspects are evident in the two dimensions of cohesion:

1. *group integration*—how individuals feel about the group as a whole; and
2. *individual attraction to the group*—how attracted the individuals are to the group.

At different levels, an individual may be part of a team because of the social interaction it entails or alternatively just to play the game—more often than not, it is a mixture of both. For a team to be cohesive, the individuals within the group must display similar motives for being involved and subscribe to a common goal. One valid and reliable psychometric instrument that is used to investigate group cohesion in research is the Group Environment Questionnaire (GEQ) (Brawley, Carron and Widmeyer, 1987). This questionnaire comprises 18 items (questions) that measure four different scales: two scales for group integration (task and social); and two scales for individual attraction to the group (task and social). It concentrates on how attractive the group is to the individual and on the individual's perception of the group.

Coaches often refer to the importance of 'togetherness' or 'team spirit' within a squad but is there really a positive relationship between team cohesion and actual performance? A question that researchers are continually investigating is whether a cohesive team results in successful performance or whether successful performance helps to build a cohesive team. The research in this area indicates that cohesion is positively related to team success in *interactive* sports. Moreover, it appears that the influence goes in both directions: success is more likely to lead to cohesion and vice versa. To understand this relationship, however, it is important to consider how task and social cohesion (the two facets of cohesion identified above) individually have an impact on performance. In general, research studies have shown that those teams exhibiting high task cohesion tend to be successful and those teams showing high social cohesion but low task cohesion tend to be less successful. High cohesion is also less important in coactive type sports such as golf than in interactive sports such as rugby.

Lyn Gunson (see Chapter Four) discusses how important it is for a team to have a mutual task to strive for:

> Team culture to me is best established when there is common purpose and that common purpose is meaningful to the group and highly transferable.

From her own experience she relates an example of a mutual task that served as an exercise for building team cohesion :

> [We were] taking two-and-a-half to three hours to get taped before games because the one physio was doing it all … That is not a good amount of time to have the tape on. I asked for the group to do as much of their taping as possible in a half-hour period. There were moans and groans about that at first but, because we identified why and that it was a constraint, they could see what the purpose was. The interesting thing in observing that was that after a while, it became a team-building activity: players coexisted doing something that had meaning and it gave some a sense of control over themselves [which] they needed before playing. The time was cut to 27 mins. Obviously, people [who] were injured were taped by the physio, but there were others who were preventive taping and quite capable of taping themselves. I favour those types of team activities which have meaning for the whole group and in effect build team. In our efforts to support international players, we sometimes take away their sense of responsibility and ownership.

Mike Ruddock (see Chapter Three), advocates developing social cohesion, such as by staging both team and family barbecues (BBQs):

> So we can always stay united rather than just doing our work, we can stay united. Another week we have a BBQ so that the families can come along so, making the effort so it is the players on one hand, but the families as well.

He also made use of a team song in the past:

> … we got a bit of a song after we didn't perform well, after a game in the changing rooms, in the second half of the season, which is good, we could look to a team song which we sing together, representing the symbol of our tightness.

Mike acknowledges that the nature of the game has changed with professionalism and that therefore the approach to the development of social cohesion is completely different to when he first started out on his rugby career:

> I think people make assumptions in rugby, assumptions that people have good spirit. When the opportunity was around we did that, go off and have a few beers after the game and a sing song; over the years [it] might have been more difficult to do things like that because you might have lost a game and you want to make sure the guys are united and focused and together. But to fancy them drinking and singing after the game they think

they are OK, but we've still done those things to keep us united and keep us together. They might lose a bit of fitness for example, to go and have a few beers but we gain in the longer run in our team spirit, the sense of togetherness and wins and losses and ups and downs together. We come out on the other side stronger, so we become more knowledgeable because we sat and talked about it after the games and things like that.

The conceptual model of cohesion as proposed by Carron (1982) is characterised by four fundamental characteristics:

1. a *multidimensional* element, recognising that the cohesion construct has many dimensions (e.g. group integration, individual attraction, task orientation and social orientation) all of which interact;
2. a *dynamic* aspect as a group's cohesion changes over time;
3. an *instrumental* aspect, exemplified by the shared sense of purpose and reason for the group or team; and
4. an *affective* element, or the satisfaction gained from both the task and social aspects involved in the functioning of the team.

Team cohesion can be examined as a function of a variety of salient factors:

* *personal factors*—individual orientation, satisfaction, individual differences;
* *team factors*—group task, desire for group success, group ability, group stability, group productivity norm;
* *leadership factors*—behaviour, style, coach–athlete and coach–team relationships; and
* *environment factors*—contractual responsibility and organisational orientation.

Lyn Gunson refers to this multidimensional aspect of team culture in the modern era when she considers a number of individual and cultural differences within a team. She maintains that a skilful coach takes a holistic approach to channelling all the different values and behaviours in the same direction but also celebrates diversity. It is important that a coach is aware of the perceptions of team members in relation to status hierarchy and where they fit in within the team. These status differences exist because people hold different beliefs and perceptions about the importance of various attributes and which ones are deemed prestigious. In regard to her own coaching experiences Lyn reflects:

Of all the netball teams I have taken, there are sometimes five different cultures in the team. Netball seems to be a game where there are socio-economic differences, intellect differences, age differences and life experience differences. I actually believe more in the concept of community. You've got a community of people on your hands for a period of time ... The culture rises out of the group you've got. However, I strongly do believe in having some basic principles which establish a connecting forum from which to go forward and pull them together.

When it comes to developing the culture, Lyn is a strong believer in observing and analysing the different elements of the group:

For each team I have taken, the first thing I have done is look at the team and say, 'What have I got in here? Have I got older players, younger players, less mature players? Have I got people who are used to being in charge? Have I got people who need information?' and have a complete assessment of who this team is in its current form. I don't ask them, I just see them operating …

Lyn also pinpoints four principles that are fundamental to a successful team culture. The first she describes as:

… direct communication—[for example] there is no point me discussing [something] with you if the person it affects is sitting on the other side of the fence.

She is clearly of the view that general conversation or gossip undermines group productivity and is detrimental to group behaviour; if an issue is worth discussing then it should be sorted out directly and not behind the scenes as it were. She goes on to identify the other three fundamental principles:

… the second one is take responsibility for your own performance but also for the group performance. The third is [honesty, which] we can operate on [through direct communication] … and the most important one for me is to celebrate difference … when you have got people of the variety that you have in some of these groups, trying to make them be the same is not only impossible but also undesirable. It is much better to approach it in the community sense and get them at least adhering to similar principles that can then make their differences coexist rather than saying, 'You have to like each other'!

Lyn describes the activities that she has used to promote the principle of celebrating difference:

I think there are important exercises you can undertake. One is to change the discourse of the group to reflect the principles. Enlist the senior players to take leadership actions. There are functional ways to achieve [a celebration of difference] as well—for example, group meetings, individual interviews, use of outside activities in order to create situations where people can either get to know one another … and understand how each other think about something, or can demonstrate the behaviours they might display in situations of stress. Therefore, if you can get them accepting the difference and then working with that, that's much better than getting into conflict.

Seven Steps to Establish a Quality Team Culture

The following seven steps are key factors that have to be considered in shaping a specific team culture. As the following discussion indicates, the process of establishing shared operating principles and a clear course for team development is reflected in the behaviours demonstrated both on and off the field of play.

1. Team Vision

The development of an effective team culture should start with a clear vision. A shared sense of purpose which is characterised by mutually agreed team goals is critical to the strategic development and growth of a team. Team goals have been demonstrated to be more strongly associated with success than individual goals (Prapavessis and Carron, 1996). The team has to own the vision and subscribe to the aims and objectives and the individual members are then accountable to the team. It is crucial to link the team's overarching vision to its holistic development, rather than emphasising the end result alone. The athletes must understand fully and subscribe to the agreed mutual direction for the development of the team; they should be involved in the process as authors of their own destiny. Once everyone within the team is committed to changes in practice and to cooperating fully for the good of the team then the results can be startling. This vision should clearly link to the tradition of the team.

Ian Rutledge (former New Zealand Black Sticks women's hockey coach) has a creative and innovative approach to developing team vision with his team and truly believes that having a high-quality team culture is instrumental to success. He explains his methodical and analytical approach to developing such a culture:

> I think the most common thing a coach and players share is generally where we want to get to. Both parties want to be the most successful they can be. As for us, we want to be the best team in the world … that is my goal for the team. The players have the ability to do it, so now it is just a matter of them buying into it and once they have bought into the team goal, they bring their goals into it and we work out what is realistic and what is not realistic. [I ask them] is my goal too over the top for them? Can they handle the pressure I am putting on them by having such an extreme goal?

The players appreciate the coach's belief in them and also value the coach providing a general direction for the team. To achieve this direction he shares the decision making and breaks the squad up into subgroups:

... like forwards and backs, oldies and youngies ... we do it in different ways, just to break up the group thinking a little bit. It is better to have small groups so that you actually get people thinking. In big groups, the dominant people function, so we have nothing over a group of five. We run over situations, from the plays to what values they want to instil. It's more about they want to be perceived and then we make a check on reality by living up to the values that we put on ourselves.

Ian asks his athletes pertinent questions:

... how do we want to be perceived? If you are on the sideline watching the Black Sticks training or playing, what do you want observers to see? If you read a newspaper article, how do you want to be perceived or described as?

Once the information from the subgroups is collated, a draft paper is prepared and the players are sent away to reflect on what has been written. Ian explains:

I have been involved in teams in the past who have had goals and values and they look great, they take the playbook home, fantastic, and they are all happy with it. Then we put them into the back of our locker and we never see them again. We wanted the values to be something special, something that you could live and breathe and actually demonstrate. So we actually pick terms that could be demonstrated and (made) visible, something we could physically observe and measure ... they chose the direction they wanted to take, I just made sure we took the path towards the goal that we decided upon.

For the Olympic campaign the whole team took full advantage of the limited time afforded to international team camps and focused on team-building activities. In doing so, they finalised the team values, which were:

... Kaizan, a Japanese word for continual improvement; winning attitude; mental toughness; bravery; courageous communication; the ability to perform and respect ourselves and our vision.

The team's choices bring us to the next step towards establishing a quality team culture.

2. Shared Values and Behaviours

What does it mean to be part of the team and to represent such a group or organisation? How does the team wish to be perceived by external sources? A team's values symbolise its collective identity. It is the values embraced and the behaviours exhibited that really fashion the team culture. The creation of values to live by is another task that must be undertaken collectively. The resulting decisions show the team identity and brand the culture. Within an athlete-centred, humanistic coaching approach, it is vital that everyone is included in both formal and informal activities and that the shared values and behaviours are wholly inclusive.

In regard to establishing values Don Tricker explains that classic values are important:

> It's all about respect, it's about integrity ... We had three questions that we essentially asked: How are we going to deliver this? (What are) the values and how are we going to live (them)? The team went through the process which included reviewing what we did in 2000, deciding what's relevant now and what's not. Some (values) survived and some were revised or adjusted. The purpose of our culture was to create an environment that is enjoyable and meets the expectations of the team ... international sport, when you are playing in a world championship final, is incredibly stressful, therefore the environment must be enjoyable. When we built the team we made sure that it was an enjoyable process. We created competitive scenarios that challenged the team. The outcome was a series of shared experiences based on humour. It was these experiences that helped us get through difficult situations.

Don Tricker also explains that when the athletes take ownership of the core values to abide by, they also have to take responsibility for reinforcing them:

> ... they are policed by athletes as well because the athletes have built and own them. The values are ours, not mine; they were not imposed on the athletes by me. The athletes ensure that the values are lived. We have a simple expectation that we all must ... be prepared to face the consequences of every decision we make. The philosophy that we have is that we will support any poor decision once. But, if the individual chooses to repeat that poor decision, then they need to be prepared to pay the consequence. That may well be non selection. That is the ultimate consequence—an athlete explaining to family and friends that they could not be trusted.

Another who recognises the importance of shared values and behaviours is Ian Rutledge. For his team, the values were printed on laminated card and every single member had a copy to remind them of the campaign values. Ian maintains that the role of the athletes is crucial to the establishment of this quality culture:

> ... it is driven by the players, it really is. I am here just there to provide facilitation ... the values I buy into as well. Some of the values that they have, I don't agree with, or I might not agree with. I agree with them at the

moment, but if you want your players to make decisions and truly believe in empowerment, like [in] any organisation you have to walk out of the room and with compromises. There is no point in walking in and saying, I will buy into six of … [those seven values], but the seventh one I am going to do my own thing.

3. Clear Roles and Responsibilities

Fundamental to the development of an effective team culture is the identification of clear roles and responsibilities. 'A role is the pattern of behaviour expected of an individual in a social situation' (Carron and Hausenblas, 1998, p. 157). Roles within the team can be formal, such as being in a particular playing position or having the role of captain, or an informal role, such as being the team social organiser or spokesperson. According to a model set out by Beauchamp and Bray (2001), role performance is dependent on three role-related constructs:

1. role conflict, or the degree to which a player is unable to fulfil the demands of his or her established role;
2. role ambiguity, or the athlete's level of the understanding of his or her role; and
3. role efficacy, or the extent to which the player believes that the role can be fulfilled successfully.

Team members have to accept their roles and also be satisfied with them if they are to achieve optimal role performance.

Coaches often rotate roles in training sessions so as to provide opportunities for empathy and a better understanding of the role of others. If coaches wish to instil leadership values in all athletes (shared leadership) then they also need to recognise that certain positions in sport are more likely to assume leadership roles because of the behaviours required. For a quality team culture it is vital that the athletes feel ownership of the team and that all athletes, rather than just a chosen few, are part of the decision-making process.

4. Team Cohesion

The team ethic, unity and camaraderie are all important factors in the development of a team, as previously discussed. This dynamic process of bringing a team closer together from both task and social perspectives is essential in developing a quality team culture. It provides the opportunity for collective mobilisation of efforts and a shared focus of attention. Success is generally achieved when team members are willing to act as members of a group rather than as independent individuals; however it must be appreciated that there is a place for individualism within a team too.

Through becoming more cohesive the team benefits from an improvement to its collective efficacy—its perception of the team confidence at a given time and its ability to be successful. In the words of Zaccaro, Blair, Peterson and Zazanis (1995), collective efficacy is a 'sense of collective competence shared among members when allocating, coordinating and integrating their resources as a successful, concerted response to specific situational demands' (p. 308)

Another benefit of cohesion is that it helps to establish team norms. Team norms generally represent the expected standards of behaviour for a group and also establish priorities for disparate behaviours. With high task cohesion correlating with performance, research has shown high perceptions of cohesion are positively related to conformity to group norms (Prapavessis and Carron, 1997).

The dilemma for a coach wishing to instil a team culture is interesting: which approach is the most effective, for that particular team at that specific time? It is here that the coach requires an understanding of group dynamics and how the members work effectively towards a common goal. The involvement of the athletes in the decision-making process is central to the success of the team. The dynamic nature of team cohesion and development has to be taken into account while nurturing the team culture; the skilful coach will be aware of the constant changes and will act accordingly. In response to a question concerning the practicalities of implementing a team culture Mike Ruddock said:

> You asked the question whether we needed to explain culture first and we assume that everyone understands what a team culture is. But people talk about it, don't they? They write about it in the media, people comment on it and assumptions are made about it. So I was quite pleased to actually, looking back, to have done some formal work on it with specific companies.

In his current role at Worcester Warriors, Mike understands clearly that the reputation of the team and indeed the wider club is vital and is constantly under scrutiny by a wider audience, including other clubs, the media and the general public. At Worcester, Mike explains:

> We have our trademarks that we want to achieve by the group, which have been put forward by the players; those trademarks are established and very visible downstairs. They are things like physicality, every time we play, that is a trademark of our culture. We always go out there and be a physical team to play against, for example. That would be a big one that we want to hang our hat on.

The values central to the team culture have to be reviewed continually. Again involvement of the athletes is critical to this task. Mike explains that:

… basically, we have gone a little bit deeper on the rugby-specific ones. Basically, we kept the ones that we had established from last year, like being clinical and trying to play expansive [two from last year, in addition to knowledgeable, united, ruthless]. We said we could add or take away from those, but the players were quite happy with those. But in a workshop, I asked them to look into more rugby-specific trademarks. The guys were quite happy with those.

Mike is also a strong advocate of the development of professional values both on and off the field of play and an appreciation for what it means to be in that privileged position of representing the club. His club has developed the 'Worcester Way' that all the team and management subscribe to, meaning that, for example, they:

… understand that the 'Club' and 'Team' are more important than any individual, take personal responsibility for your actions, be honest, work hard to achieve your goals, have a strong sense of where the club has come from, improve the team by investing in yourself, be hungry for success, conduct yourself in a professional manner.

5. Respect and Integrity

The coach has to treat the athletes with respect and develop a meaningful rapport and trust with them. This process is crucial to establish and maintain an accomplished reciprocal relationship based on integrity. Similarly mutual respect among teammates is key for an affirmative team culture. It does not necessarily mean that teammates have to like each other or indeed spend time with each other socially. However, they do need to be willing to show regard or appreciation for themselves, their teammates, coaching staff and also consideration for the sport in general. With reference to the task cohesion element, the athletes need to show respect for the roles and responsibilities of others. Conflict is almost certain to be the outcome if there is a lack of respect in the team. Integrity and honesty are also important attributes; where they are lacking, there is a clear disparity between what is said and what is actually done. In a quality team culture, team members have to demonstrate commitment to the team, be held accountable for their actions and accept responsibility for group outcomes.

These criteria are captured in Ian Rutledge's description of the culture in his team:

We don't have curfews, we don't have late fines, or anything like that. We just expect people to understand human decency.

Likewise, respect and integrity have always been part of Mike Ruddock's value system in relation to team culture and he has researched the topic in depth. As part of a leadership achievement programme for a recruitment company, where he worked after resigning as the coach of the Welsh national rugby team, he put a module together, drawing on his international experience, that traced the history of team culture, how it evolved and the importance of how values or the value system impact upon team culture. Reflecting on this work, he says:

> That was quite an interesting learning curve for me. I used that as part of presentations. I also used some video footage to go with it as well. For example, I showed New Zealand doing the haka, that was part of it. I wanted to show that it wasn't just a challenge, the haka wasn't just a challenge to the opposition for that; it basically pre-empted an 80-minute battle; it was a way of showing their identity, their brand, their culture. [I wanted to show] what it represented and [that] it was built on an honour system and their value systems ... that the population had come together, different races, but it was built on so many things. That one action represented not just a challenge, but represented a nation in terms of their value system and their competitiveness and their—how other people perceived their brand and how they are. There were all sorts of things, 'We are proud, this is our brand, this is who we are, and here it is'. Whatever you think of the haka, what you get from the haka is an example of their tenacious fighting spirit, their honesty as a group of people, that they—you know that they are going to be physical, you know that they are going to never give up. And actually, what they do is that they are going to tally all that up by doing the haka. This is a representation of their culture and anyone who doesn't buy into that is not going to be used as a role model to represent, to show that worldwide, globally to a mass audience.

Mike also makes an important point that representing an organisation, establishment or team says something about you and, because you are associated with a certain team, others have a certain perception of you and that team. A team is very much like a brand that you associate with a certain set of values and behaviours. For example, given the observation, 'When you say the All Blacks, you immediately think that these guys are not going to walk away from a challenge, and they tell you that', it is understandable that, as well as having intense respect for each other, the All Blacks have gained respect and admiration from worldwide audiences.

6. Effective Communication

Effective communication is necessary as both a way to prevent issues arising and a way to solve those that do arise within a team. An open and honest communication channel based on support and empathy is crucial for an effective team culture to prevail and flourish. Transmitting and receiving messages efficiently, as the cornerstone of successful teamwork, can be achieved in a number of different ways. A common method is to hold regular team meetings to provide the team members with an opportunity to contribute creatively to the decision-making process.

Open and honest discussions can foster mutual respect and appreciation for the role of others within the team. Key messages for individual team members are: have humility and empathy; listen carefully to the views of other team members; appreciate individual differences; and learn how to give constructive feedback. In this environment the players can learn from the coach and, equally importantly, the coach can learn from the players. For an inclusive team culture, the coach has to be aware of task dependence within team sports and that certain playing positions interact with occupants from other playing positions on the field of play on a regular basis. Therefore careful management of the coaching process is actively encouraged so as to allow all players the opportunity to communicate effectively with each other.

Mike Ruddock appreciates that coaches require an understanding of group dynamics and of the factors that impact on team cohesion. He has certainly personalised this approach with his present club:

> So I think that we all have assumptions that just being together is enough. It's obviously deeper than that. You can have people together and they don't get on with each other, so just being together is not enough. You've got to just put those assumptions away really and try to work out something more specific things that bind us. So things like [being] committed to our rugby trademarks, our goals [which are downstairs on the back of the changing room door] and also our training goals are … We review it from time to time, you know it is quite powerful too, putting our training goals on the back of changing room doors, so every guy who comes out of the room, he is virtually looking straight at the training goals. So I think it is very powerful.

7. Social Support

A key aspect in the development of a quality team culture is an attitude of selflessness and an appreciation that the team is bigger than any individual. For such an attitude to work, the team members have to be prepared to help each other out by providing emotional and technical information, help and advice. The team members have to be committed to the team and place the welfare of the team ahead of personal ambition— they have to look out for each other. Through this dedication and self sacrifice sustained by the team network, individual team members are supported in any eventuality. As Kidman and Davis (2007, p. 132) express it:

> There is a Maori word that encompasses the notion of team spirit: wairua which literally translated means 'oneness'. It refers to a spirituality that

contributes to an individual's wellbeing. The word covers all that is positive about team culture (i.e. values and attitudes, respect and trust, caring and concern for others). Without wairua, the quality of team culture is diminished and therefore the chance of success is limited.

This team spirit is not always obvious but without it the team will not grow effectively.

As a fundamental step in establishing a quality team culture, a coach has to be content with the approach that is to be adopted. Mike Ruddock appreciates that the task of nurturing the culture of the team can indeed be formal or informal. He also acknowledges the enormity of the task:

> Such a big area, you could have a formal approach to it in that you sit down and say to them, for example to the players, 'Do you understand what a team culture is? Explain it, define it. Do you know what values are? Do you know what behaviours are?'... I have been more comfortable shaping informally ... I shape the culture in my own way ... perhaps there is some way I should have explored it a little bit more in a more formal sense.

On occasions in the past, Mike has used more formal support:

> I have used an external expert who pushed the team culture, but he came in, he didn't talk or explain culture or ask the players to explain culture or their understanding of it. He obviously adopted a strategy that increased the players' honesty in feedback, if you like, to each other and the management to each other, which I thought was a very positive thing, even though we had some trials and tribulations along the way. We came through that and that has definitely helped us. But on reflection it could have also stopped certain people. It is quite an interesting process.

> If a team is to reach its potential, each player must be willing to subordinate his personal goals to the good of the team. - Bud Wilkinson (1916-) US football coach

Conclusion

Team culture comprises the informal and formal mechanisms that drive the team towards a common agreed goal. A positive team culture is associated with successful performance. To formulate this culture, the coach needs to treat all those involved with the team with respect, include them in the decision-making process, develop a rapport with the players and ensure an open and honest communication channel based on mutual respect, trust and cooperation. This dynamic process involves the frequent use of positive and process-orientated team affirmations to develop collective efficacy. The process will only work with leadership that is fair and coherent.

The coach has to understand the players and the relationships between team members, and scrutinise the functional efficiency of the team. Yukelson (1997) proposes six methods that coaches can use to help build their team:

1. get to know your athletes as unique individuals—find out something special and personal about each one;
2. develop pride in group membership and a sense of team identity—for example, use goal boards, mission statements;
3. create team goals and team commitment—use a comprehensive goal-setting programme;
4. provide for goal evaluations—review and monitor progress through communication, performance profiling and feedback;
5. hold periodic team meetings—maintain open and honest dialogue;
6. provide player counsel—hold scheduled meetings with the coach and members of various subgroups to ensure all members of the team are represented.

Each method points to the central theme of this chapter: together everyone achieves more.

References

Bales, R.F. (1966). Task roles and social roles in problem solving groups. In B.J. Biddle and E.J. Thomas (Eds.), *Role Theory: Concepts and research*. New York, NY: John Wiley.

Beauchamp, M.R., & Bray, S.R. (2001). Role ambiguity and role conflict within interdependent teams. *Small Group Research, 32*, 133–157.

Brawley, L.R., Carron, A.V., & Widmeyer, W.N. (1987). Assessing the cohesion of teams: Validity of the Group Environment Questionnaire. *Journal of Sport Psychology, 9*, 275–294.

Carron, A.V. (1982). Cohesiveness in sport groups: Interpretations and considerations. *Journal of Sport Psychology, 4*, 123–138.

Carron, A.V., & Hausenblas, H. (1998). *Group Dynamics in Sport* (2nd ed.) Morgantown, WV: Fitness Information Technology.

Carron, A.V., Hausenblas, H., & Eys, M. (2005). *Group Dynamics in Sport* (3rd ed.) Morgantown, WV: Fitness Information Technology.

Kidman, L. (2001). *Developing Decision Makers: An empowerment approach to coaching*. Christchurch: Innovative Print Communications.

Kidman, L. & Davis, W.E. (2007). Empowerment in coaching. In W.E. Davis and G.D. Broadhead (Eds.) *Ecological Task Analysis and Movement*. Champaign, IL: Human Kinetics.

Latané, B. (1986). Responsibility and effort in organisations. In P. Goodman (Ed.), *Groups and Organisations*. San Francisco, CA: Jossey-Bass.

Latané, B., Williams, W., & Harkins, S. (1979). Many hands make light the work: The causes and consequences of social loafing. *Journal of Personality and Social Psychology, 37*, 822–832.

Martens, R. (2004). *Successful Coaching*. Champaign, IL: Human Kinetics.

Prapavessis, H., & Carron, A.V. (1996). The effect of group cohesion on competitive state anxiety. *Journal of Sport and Exercise Psychology, 18*, 64–74.

Prapavessis, H., & Carron, A.V. (1997). Sacrifice, cohesion and conformity to norms in sport teams. *Group Dynamics, 1*, 231–240.

Steiner, I.D. (1972). *Group Processes and Group Productivity.* New York, NY: Academic.

Tuckman, B.W. (1965). Developmental sequences in small groups. *Psychological Bulletin, 63*, 384–399.

Woods, B. (1998). *Applying Psychology to Sport.* London: Hodder & Stoughton.

Yukelson, D. (1997). Principles of effective team building interventions in sport: A direct services' approach at Penn State University. *Journal of Applied Sport Psychology, 9*, 73–96.

Zaccaro, S.J., Blair, V., Peterson, C., & Zazanis, M. (1995). Collective efficacy. In J.E. Maddix (Ed.) *Self-efficacy, Adaptation and Adjustment: Theory, research and application*. New York: NY: Academic.

When your values are clear to you, making decisions becomes easier. - Roy Disney, US actor, author

Your mind is what makes everything else work. - Kareem Abdul-Jabbar

One who is afraid of asking questions is ashamed of learning. - Danish Proverb

Listen to the desires of your children. Encourage them and then give them the autonomy to make their own decision. - Denis Waitley, US motivational speaker

Chapter Seven

Play and Children

Guest Author: Paul Cooper

Give Us Back Our Game (www.giveusbackourgame.co.uk)

For many people their sporting journey begins in childhood. It may simply be the thrill of throwing, kicking or hitting a ball for the first time, or running, jumping or swimming. It may be the challenge of playing an informal version of a sport in the garden, park or school playground. The circumstances, environment and experiences in these formative years can lead to a lifelong passion for sport and other forms of physical activity. Clearly, therefore, the topic of play and children is particularly pertinent to the athlete-centred coaching focus of this book.

Children's Song

We live in our own world,
A world that is too small
For you to stoop and enter
Even on hands and knees,
The adult subterfuge.
And although you probe and pry
With analytic eye,
And eavesdrop all our talk
With an amused look,
You cannot find the centre
Where we dance, where we play …

R.S. Thomas (1993)

I am a grassroots football (soccer) coach from Gloucestershire, England who with Rick Fenoglio, a senior lecturer hailing from the United States of America (USA) and lecturing in exercise and sport science at Manchester Metropolitan University, founded the children's sporting initiative Give Us Back Our Game (GUBOG) in September 2006. It was a reaction to my experiences as a youth coach and my observation that the children's game I had played for fun with my friends in the street, parks and playgrounds had been usurped by coaches who had a different agenda based on league tables, results and adult values. Although the issues that Give Us Back Our Game has tackled are mainly concerned with children's football, it also has been involved with rugby league, rugby union and golf. As Gill (2007) said in a review of our website, 'Give Us Back Our Game connects the dots between childhood, sport and play'.

On the Alliance for Childhood website the quote of the month for May 2009 dealt with the subject of children playing in the great outdoors:

> Forty thousand generations of human beings have grown up doing this. And two generation's haven't. (Moss, 2009, cited on www.allianceforchildhood. org.uk)

It has recently become fashionable in many smarter villages of England to have, underneath the main sign identifying the village you are entering, an additional one that reads, 'Slow! Children Playing'. Where? I would need to drive up the side of a house and plough through a bedroom wall to have any likelihood of endangering a child. Then I would have to explain to the local magistrate that I didn't stand a chance as the child stepped from behind his or her PlayStation and out onto the carpet.

There are a number of reasons for the steep decline in outside play for children including: the constant media attention on the subject and saturation coverage of high-profile incidents; the huge increase in traffic on our roads; the fear of 'stranger danger'; and the knowledge that, if your child needs help, many passing adults will no longer come to his or her aid. In its 2007 research, The Children's Society showed that 43% of parents in the United Kingdom (UK) thought that children should not play outside until they were at least 14 years old. In 2009 the charity Living Streets found that only half of today's 5-to 10-year-olds in the UK had ever played in their street, where nine-tenths of their grandparents had played during their own childhood. It is also clear that parents are well aware of the need for outdoor play: 87% of UK parents surveyed by the National Trust wished that their children played outside more. However, many parents feel boxed in by changes in society and an irrational fear that their children could be in danger.

A Changing Landscape

So the landscape for children's play has changed dramatically. In earlier years as a grassroots football coach, I could always rely on getting my point across about the importance of play in children's sport to parents. It was simply a matter of getting them to cast their minds back 20 or 30 years to when they themselves had played a rich variety of games outdoors. The new generation of young parents, however, often fix you with a blank stare when the subject is brought up.

Like toothpaste in an emptying tube, the creativity and invention of children's play have gradually been squeezed out of their lives, with children not allowed out for a number of reasons stated above. The opportunities for preschool and primary school play have also diminished. In countries such as the USA and UK there is a focus on measurement and results in early education at the expense of play. In the Scandinavian countries, in contrast, the educational process starts when children are seven rather than five, but they catch up very quickly with their counterparts in the USA and UK. Another notable difference in Scandinavia is the firm emphasis on play and the learning that goes with it (Palmer, 2006).

From a survey of 100 primary schools in the UK in 2008, GUBOG found that a third of schools had banned ball games in the school playground on health and safety grounds. In addition, many traditional games such as British Bulldog, which had been played for generations, had been banned for being too rough. One young lad was so perplexed that he wrote to the GUBOG football campaign to share his story:

> Although his primary school in Dundee had banned football in the playground, he could not resist the temptation to bring a tennis ball out of his pocket one December lunchtime and start an impromptu game with his friends. The kick about did not last long and his punishment for breaking school rules was to miss half of the school's Christmas party.

Children are no longer even trusted to manage their own space. I have observed in my travels that many schools are now opting to paint garish coloured zones in the playground to inform kids where to go and what to play in which zone.

The idea that children need to be shown how to play and where is laughable. Play is what children do; it is their language and their lore. No one has studied play more than Peter and Iona Opie, who have documented games, play, language, rhymes and jokes up and down the UK in a series of fascinating books. Iona Opie spent 15 minutes a week in the same primary school playground from 1960 to 1983 observing children and their play in her delightful book, *The People in the Playground* (1993). She describes succinctly why there is no need for adult lines and boundaries. Namely the playground is the domain of children and contains structure among the chaos:

> At first the playground seemed uncontrolled confusion. Balls whizzed by my head, bodies hurtled across my path, some boys were on the ground pummelling each other, and a dense black mob rushed across, apparently taking no notice of anyone else. (Opie, 1993, p. 2)

Gradually, through, she came to identify a sense of the structure:

> ... it became possible to sort out the intermingled games, the chasing games; the chasing games for instance, which was superimposed upon a diffuse game of Germans and English, both games being intersected by boys competing in running races ... I soon realised that any child with a look of concentration on his face was likely to be part of a game. (p. 2)

Moreover, when the children emerged from class at the top of the steps leading down to the playground, they would stop and cheer—drawing attention to their presence—

before catapulting down into the throng below. Agreements were also important and children took responsibility to select teams, make up the rules and organise the games. They even played pre-game games to select a chaser or team. From her observations of behaviour during the restricted time (15 minutes) of the morning break, Iona Opie notes:

> Speed is essential. If they argue about the rules they argue rapidly and agree without much delay, knowing that prolonged argument means that the game may not be played at all.

> More often 'the boss of the game' organizes it with force and authority. It is not necessarily the strongest or the oldest who become leaders, but those who have self-confidence and the ability to make decisions. (Opie, 1993, p. 4)

Liverpool football legend Tommy Smith, in his excellent autobiography *Anfield Iron*, writes a great deal about his childhood and its importance to his development as both man and footballer and his appreciation of the need for rules:

> I am sure those games instilled in me and my pals a sense of responsibility and a notion that one had to adhere to rules in life if you were not to spoil things for other people … We had no referee to apply the rules of the game. When a goal was scored we restarted the game with a kick off from what passed as a centre spot. When a foul was committed, a free kick was taken and no one took umbrage. (Smith, 2007, p. 24)

As he recalls it, he and his friends recognised that failing to play by the rules would spoil the game for everyone:

> Those games played without supervision taught us that you can't go about doing just what you wanted because there are others to think of. Of course it was not a conscious thought at the time, but these kick-abouts on the bomb site taught us the rules of society and prepared us for life. (p. 24)

What Do We Do with Talent?

We have never had such a plethora of places to learn stuff. Football, with academies devoted to the sport sprouting up around the globe, provides ample evidence of this trend. Intensive places of learning are bursting with knowledge and able to analyse everything from a player's running gait to how many successful passes he or she makes in a game. How do we accommodate our top talents into these centres of learning?

In the last 10 years academies have changed enormously with superb facilities and equipment. They also contain many specialists, not just in coaching, but in fitness, nutrition, psychology and medical care. Academies are important institutions in producing players, but dealing with the top talents is the real challenge as they may need a different approach from a squad player.

This academy culture has been borrowed from education. Yet, as Holt (1967) observes, schools and the wider public do not generally trust children to learn on the grounds that either they cannot be trusted or must learn to deal with an imperfect world. He writes of the difficulty of changing such ingrained attitudes which he believes adults cling to because:

> … it gives them a license to act like tyrants and feel like saints. 'Do what I tell you!' roars the tyrant. 'It's for your own good, and one day you'll be grateful,' says the saint. Few people, feeling themselves powerless in a world turned upside down, can or even wish to resist the temptation to play this benevolent despot. (Holt, 1967, p. 297)

A few football academies have grasped the importance of play and the essence of street football that is much more child- and game-orientated. I watched a Manchester United Academy under 10's team play a game where the opposition were generally bigger than the United boys. The opposition played well but they played more of an adult game and passed it quickly, one and two touch. They did not experiment or dribble nearly as much as the United youngsters as they were under strict instructions and were given very little freedom in the way they played.

So when do children get the chance to be creative and run with the ball and take players on? In an interview, United Academy coach Tom Statham spoke to me about this creativity:

> How are you going to create the next Christiano Ronaldo or the next Lionel Messi if you don't give them the freedom to run at people, take risks and be creative? If you can't do it at nine and ten, when can you? … They are going through the player and the ball stage, the other stuff comes later. At the end of the day we are trying to develop players for the Champions League.

The problem with natural talent is that some coaches lack a proper understanding of these players, seeing them as mavericks and a threat to 'the team' and coaching control. Yet such players need to be guided gently rather than shoehorned into a 'one size fits all' philosophy.

Arsene Wenger once said of French football star Thierry Henry that at least 20 English players in non-league football were as good as the French forward but it is easier to break a player than make one. That is the challenge that faces clubs and coaches. How can the special talents flourish in a game that is based on being part of a team? It is often these talents that can provide a moment's inspiration to change a game and win a match. To some extent they also don't fit the mould that clubs use to develop their players. They need to be left alone more frequently so their creativity can prosper.

In his thoughtful autobiography, *Soccer at the Top*, Sir Matt Busby expands on this line of thinking:

> Great players ... do not conform readily. They do the unexpected. That is also why they are great players. If they did what was expected they would be ordinary players ... It also happens that ... the individual genius aids teamwork because HE gives ordinary players a ball that makes life easier for them ... (Busby, 1973, p. 168)

He also has some insights into how coaching has changed the team environment:

> Coaching is for ordinary players. It makes them better players. That maybe is why most great coaches were themselves ordinary players. They know how to improve an ordinary player's game because they had scope for improving themselves. Great players don't understand why lesser men can't do great things. They have difficulty in explaining to others what they themselves do by instinct. (p. 168)

Birthdates

We already know that there is a serious flaw in the recruitment of players for academies as the figures in England show that the vast majority of players entering academies are born in the first four months of the football year and only a handful come from the last third of the football year. Talent is of course spread across people born throughout the year and there is an argument that the late developers eventually could become the noted talents as they have to constantly punch above their weight. In a recent study at the University of Gloucestershire, Palmer (in press) has found that the bias towards the September to December birthdates in children's grassroots football leagues follows a very similar pattern to that of the academies.

Give Us Back Our Game organises community sessions across the UK at which all children are welcome, whatever their ability. The birthdates of these children are spread evenly throughout the year, showing nothing of the birthdate bias in structured football controlled by adults.

In an interview, John Allpress, player development manager for the Football Association, came up with some possible explanations for such bias:

> It's the attitude of the people. It is certain because the facts bear it out. The statistics show that the minute adults get involved; some children

get excluded from the programme. They are seen not to be effective in matches and therefore they are left out or become sub [a substitute player]. The kids don't get a game and there is a danger in that because what is the basis for excluding kids from the programme? When the kids decide, everyone is involved. There is no bias; people don't get excluded from the programme.

It is a fact that 50% plus of players at an academy are born in September through to December and less than 10% are born in May to August. Why is that? They are exactly the same as the other children only they are a bit younger, so why does that discrepancy exist? It is not just the academies; it is all the way through football and grassroots football. The minute adults are involved, the bias kicks in … because the adults have a team and they want their team to win so they pick the stronger kids. Your team got beat 4–0 so you are crap; our team won so I feel good and I can go to the tyre factory on a Monday morning and I can say my team wins every week. That is where people get their self-esteem and it is understandable and maybe even human nature but it is only there because people want to win games. When the kids decide, it's not there and the players that could make it through are among the younger group.

If coaches took a more humanistic, child- and player-centred approach, they would put an end to such bias as the emphasis would be on long-term development and not just today's match.

Creativity and Inspiration

In attempting to explain the place of creativity and inspiration in sporting achievements, Ed Smith (2009) acknowledges that it may never be fully understood. Recognising the difficulties of analysing it rationally or integrating it into professional planning, he makes a case for not interfering in the creative process:

> There will be an element of self-awareness in all these processes—a management of talent, a regulation of originality—but also a good amount of instinct. Forces beyond rationality lead creative people to follow certain paths and not others. Like strikers with an instinct for where to be in the penalty area, something takes them into different (and better) creative territory. (p. 14)

With all that money spent on facilities, the coaching badges, the staff and wages and with all that technology at their fingertips, it is presumed coaches know all the answers.

However, that is where the problems begin. Can you teach creativity by getting kids to copy 10 tricks used by the top Brazilian players of all time? And who taught the Brazilians?

Recently teenagers have had a bad press in the UK. Moreover, the worldwide perception is that UK football lacks creative, intelligent players. Yet the country is stacked with talent, even if it is not always being found and nurtured properly.

For nearly 50 years the youth of this country has been the most creative force in popular music across the globe: starting in the 1960s with the Beatles and Rolling Stones, moving on through the age of rock with Pink Floyd and Led Zeppelin and the punk era with groups like the Clash and Sex Pistols, and coming most recently to the Libertines, Coldplay, Arctic Monkeys and other ground-breaking groups. This music culture is a playground where you can do what you want. We learn from listening and watching our heroes, learn from our friends and from trial and error. These musical talents are largely self-taught and wholly responsible for the creative process in writing and performing their songs.

So would this process of creativity and inspiration be enhanced by an Academy of Pop or would the establishment of such an institution see the dilution or even loss of spontaneity, intuition and the creative process? The environment for the young musicians is still there in the bedrooms, garages and small halls up and down the land, but the original university for football—the streets, parks and playgrounds—has all but disappeared.

The UK has never properly addressed the decline in the street football that is still played in the countries that produce the best technical players. A recent study from Liverpool John Moores University compared the outcomes of coach-centred and athlete-centred approaches in relation to the premiership academies. It found evidence that although a coach-centred approach might boost performance initially, the improvement was likely to be sustained in the long term. With athlete-centred coaching, by contrast, the emphasis:

> is on players taking responsibility for their own development, finding unique solutions to movement problems, exploration and discovery. This 'hands off' approach may be more effective in developing 'smart' learners who are able to apply their skills in a variety of performance situations (i.e. what has been termed 'adaptive' rather than 'routine' expertise. (Holyoak, 2005, p. 639)

The Games We Played

Children are creative as informal sport demonstrates clearly. As the amount of structure, equipment, and players are reduced, their opportunities for creativity increase. In global terms, such opportunities could encompass beach football in Rio de Janeiro, a pick-up game of basketball in a Chicago schoolyard or street hockey in Toronto.

My brother and I lived in the family house in an idyllic location; with a wonderful view of the river Torridge. The setting came at a price as the lane was full of elderly people who are not prime candidates to play in goal or keep wicket. With just the two of us we had to be inventive when playing cricket (an 11-a-side sport), so devised a game where each of us was joined by 10 team members—a mixture of trees, bushes, telegraph poles, jumpers (pullovers, sweatshirts) and coats laid out for a cordon of slips.

With a full team each we could play a whole test. When batting if you hit the ball in the air and it hit or landed on one of these static fielders, you were out caught. If you were batting at 9, 10 or 11; you could be out caught even if the ball went along the floor and hit a fielder. We would play a whole Ashes series, England versus Australia, and had to bat or bowl left-handed if the player we were role-playing at the time played that way. We also had to use their bowling or batting technique—for example, as a stone wall right-hander or a swashbuckling left-hander or, when bowling, a quickie or a leg break bowler. There was a lot of learning going on but, as we saw it, we were just having fun.

A friend of mine had a similar experience with his brother in their small garden where they devised more than 20 different football games for two players. They would write all the names of the games on pieces of paper and draw them out at random and play the games one after the other. Such creativity and inventiveness was duplicated in most families and gardens across the country.

Simple conditioned cricket games that everyone played—such as 'tip and run' where you had to run if you hit the ball with your bat—made for greater fun with more run-outs and a higher turnover of batsman; ideal for the playground when time was limited. Another rule was that you were out if you hit a six; this rule restrained the best shot of all, not something children would normally choose, but it had the advantage of preventing an excessive number of sixes, which could have meant too many lost balls and no game.

Testimony to children's inventiveness under constrained circumstances also comes from Holt (1967). At the school where he was teaching, most of the playground for building was lost, sport playing and instruction time was cut back and the boys were not predisposed to great athleticism. Nonetheless the school consistently was able to field a competitive school softball team. It happened, Holt explains, because the boys learned by watching and copying the older players:

> Here would be a boy in the third or fourth grade who seemed so hopelessly clumsy, unathletic, and ignorant of all the rules and skills of baseball that

> it looked as if he could never learn to play. Two years later that same boy would be a competent and often an expert player—and many of them did almost all of their playing at school. (Holt, 1967, p. 188)

The result was a far greater achievement than what a much bigger school at which he had taught had managed, despite its large playing fields and more generous amount of time for sports lessons. Part of the reason, Holt confesses, may have been related to his earlier approach to coaching, in which he spent much time explaining technique:

> I remember a couple of boys that I was trying to teach to bat and throw. I can still see their sullen but resigned faces, feel their limp, uncooperating muscles, and practically hear their thoughts. Here was school brought right out into the play yard, where they were supposed to be having fun, or at least a moment's respite from school. Small wonder we did not get far. (p. 189)

He speculates that the results might have improved considerably had the boys been given the opportunity to play with, observe and copy the older children at the school.

When we were young, for football we had practical conditioned games such as 'three and in', a football game played with one goal where every third goal brought a change in keeper. It was a simple, fair way of giving everyone had a turn given that most children would prefer to not be in goal.

The essence of these stories is that when we played such games while we were growing up, no one ever told us of their importance. It is just what we did as kids. Yet they were incredibly significant to the development of our skills.

A good example comes from a comparison of the formal game of football, with nets in the goals, with the informal 'jumpers for goalposts' game. 'Jumpers for goalposts' is an English name for an informal game of football. All you need is a ball and players. The players take off their jumpers or coats and use those as the goals.

In the formal game, if the England and Manchester United forward Wayne Rooney was on the edge of the penalty area and the ball bounced up nicely he would volley it high into the roof of the net without a second thought as he does not have to retrieve the ball and his only focus is on scoring a goal. It is a lot more complicated down the park with a pile of coats or jumpers for goalposts. If you kicked into the imaginary net where Rooney had scored, some players would say it would have gone over the bar or around the post or both! Moreover, if you blasted the ball and you had no nets, the beaten keeper, hands on hips, would extract some revenge by looking at where the ball had landed some 100 yards away and then look at you and spit out, 'You can get that!'

So you first had to bring the ball both in and down a bit. Those in the know would also give the keeper hope with the idea that he would decide that goalkeeping was fun and stay in goal for the game rather than taking your precious position out on the pitch. Therefore the perfect goal was not hit too hard so that the keeper still had a 30% chance of getting a fingertip to it and the ball remained with an easy distance for retrieval. This was an incredible skill to master—technique, psychology and diplomacy, all in one volley.

Children's Sport Today

Sport is very different today and firmly in the hands of adults. That can be a pleasurable experience, but nevertheless it is a lottery, dependent on the philosophy of the coach. The expectations are those of an adult and have very little to do with how children organise and play their own games.

In grassroots football in England most football is played in junior clubs. Leagues start at under sevens and become competitive at under nines (i.e. results and league tables are published!). There is a great deal of structure and organisation with leagues insisting on certain formats and maximum squad sizes. Too often the same children are consistently omitted from the team or are always on the bench as the coach selects what he or she considers to be the strongest team each week. In the child-directed game there are no substitutes and everyone plays.

How does a six-year-old fall in love with the beautiful game standing on the sideline on a freezing winter morning? It comes as no great surprise that, in a junior football league in Essex, only 54% of players who are signed on at clubs start a league game each week. The coaching in these leagues is often highly prescriptive with adult structures and an overemphasis on fitness and training without the ball. A short match at the end is seen as a treat.

Another negative about adult-organised children's football is the score lines that it can produce. I watched an under 10s game that finished 25–1 and the coach of the winning team berated his players for letting in a goal. On the playground, children controlling their own game would never allow such a divergent score to emerge. Usually the two best players would take turns to pick a player for their side and would go through each ability level until everyone was chosen. As a child, if I was last chosen, I still played every minute of the game. The games had to be fun and picking equal teams made it both fair and competitive. For example, if the score line went to 5–0, the children stop the game, swap over a couple of players and start back at 0–0. This is the simple logic of children at play.

A games and play approach where children are able to breathe and explore is important. Holt (1967) describes a common pattern that he observes in their learning:

> First, a great bold leap forward into exciting new territory. Then, for a short while, a retreat back into what is comfortable, familiar, and secure. But we can't predict much less control. This rhythm of advance and retreat,

exploration and consolidation, and this is one of the main reasons why the learning of children can't, or at least shouldn't, be scheduled. (p. 187)

Rick Fenoglio (2008, p. 48), co-founder of Give Us Back Our Game, gives the following pointers to youth football coaches:

- Use the Give Us Back Our Game 80/20 rule for training and match play (if possible 80% or more of the training time should be spent with the children playing adapted small-sided games. The remaining 20% can be used for warming-up, instruction and other fun non-football games that develop multilateral co-ordination).
- Small-sided games are a more effective and more match play-specific method for learning skills than drills. Drills are too far removed from actual play to be highly effective.
- Mistakes are good! Mistakes allow the player to recognise and, in time, discard unsuccessful strategies. Praise the bravery that goes into trying! Studies show that children either take no notice of criticism or play worse as a result.
- Evidence shows that the first coach a young player has is vital for instilling a love of the game by creating a safe, non-threatening and enjoyable environment in which children can learn. By giving some ownership of training to the boys and girls themselves and by letting them make some decisions, you foster empowerment, independent learning and their own personal love of the game.
- Training should be variable so that learners can explore and discover their own solutions to football problems. Remember that history shows that the best players developed *their own way* of playing skilfully and achieving success on the pitch.
- 'Instruction' from coaches can be used—but this should be in the form of 'nuggets of information' that the player can quickly and repeatedly attempt in a small-sided game.
- Demonstrate only briefly then let players experiment and try to find their own way of performing a movement or skill.
- Use guided discovery and question-and-answer techniques rather than prescriptive coaching.
- In the Give Us Back Our Game approach, coaches shape and guide rather than direct; and know that game intelligence and skill can be more quickly and more effectively developed by the use of adapted, game-related activities.

Conclusion

> Play is the universal language of children.
>
> Anon.

As society changes there is an increasing lack of unstructured outdoor play. This play once covered many different sports that were in the main organised, played and controlled by children. There are a number of reasons for today's lack of play including the huge increase in traffic on our roads and a perceived danger from strangers. Such concerns have been fuelled by the media and have become a hot topic.

The alternatives are normally adult-led and structured. Children often have very little input into what happens and who plays. Sport for children, even at an early age, can mirror a target-driven education system, with an emphasis on results, points and league tables. This culture discriminates against children born later in the sporting and academic year who have a much reduced chance of participating in this structured environment. It also makes it harder for children to learn at their own pace and to gain trial and error experiences through playing with children of different abilities and ages.

Creativity and inspiration can be lost in this structured approach for children at all levels. A games approach is recommended as a substitute for the lack of free outdoor play. This child- and player-centred environment allows for more exploration, for decision making and for mistakes, which are a key part of learning. Games, both free play and conditioned, can make up to 80% of a session to allow for a more holistic approach to children's sport. We really need to stop imposing our will on children and instead give them the opportunity to just play and have fun.

Our children are watching us live, and what we
ARE shouts louder than anything we can say. - Wilferd A. Peterson

I have found the best way to give advice to your
children is to find out what they want and then
advise them to do it - Harry S. Truman

References:

Busby, M. (1973). *Soccer at the Top*. London: Sphere.

Fenoglio, R. (2008). Developing skilful players (a neuro-physiological basis for developing future skilful players): Why the Give Us Back Our Game approach is THE best way to produce young gifted players. *Total Youth Football Magazine, 3,* 43–49.

Gill, T. (2007). *No Fear: Growing up in a risk averse society*. London: Calouste Gulbenkian Foundation.

Holt, J. (1967). *How Children Learn*. Washington DC: Penguin.

Holyoak, D. (2005). Practice, instruction and skill acquisition. *Journal of Sport Sciences, 23*(6): 637–650.

Moss, S. (2009). *The Bumper Book of Nature*. London: Random House.

Opie, I. (1993). *The People in the Playground*. Oxford: Oxford University.

Palmer, D. (in press). The relative age effect: Are we wasting potential? *Give Us Back Our Game*.

Palmer, S. (2006). *Toxic Childhood*. Arkansas: Orion Books.

Smith, E. (2009). *What Sport Tells Us About Life*. London: Penguin.

Smith, T. (2007). *Anfield Iron*. London: Transworld.

Thomas, R.S. (1993). *Children's Song: Collected Poems 1945–1990*. Arkansas: Orion Books.

Those who educate children well are more to be honored than they who produce them; for these only gave them life, those the art of living well. - Aristotle.

I believe that children are our future. Teach them well and let them lead the way. Show them all the beauty they possess inside. -Whitney Houston

For success, attitude is equally as important as ability. - Harry F. Banks

Chapter Eight

A Constraints-led Approach to Talent Development in Cricket

Guest Author: Ian Renshaw with Greg Chappell

Queensland University of Technology with AIS-Cricket Australia's Centre of Excellence

The aim of this chapter is to increase understanding of how a sound theoretical model of the learner and learning processes informs the organisation of learning environments and effective and efficient use of practice time. Drawing on an in-depth interview with Greg Chappell, the head coach at the Centre of Excellence—the Brisbane-based centre for training and development in cricket of the Australian Institute of Sport (AIS) and Cricket Australia—it describes and explains many of the key features of non-linear pedagogy. Specifically, after backgrounding the constraints-led approach, it deals with environmental constraints; the focus of the individual and the implications of self-organisation for coaching strategies; implications for the coach–athlete relationship; manipulating constraints; representative practice; developing decision-makers and learning design including discovery and implicit learning. It then moves on to a discussion of more global issues such as the reactions of coaches and players when a constraints-led approach is introduced, before finally considering the widely held belief among coaches that approaches such as Teaching Games for Understanding (TGfU) 'take longer' than traditional coaching methods.

Background

Sports coaches are constantly looking for new and innovative ways to improve their athletes. At times, this search leads them to coach by a 'recipe book' or to unquestioningly adopt the latest fad or fancy. Currently it has led many coaches to take up a 'back to the future' approach to coaching games by playing games. Correspondingly many coaches are moving away from a technique to a tactic approach and exploring more game-based approaches such as Teaching Games for Understanding (TGfU) (Bunker and Thorpe, 1982), Game Sense or Play Practice (Launder, 2001).

Despite the intuitive appeal of TGfU and related approaches to many coaches, however, empirical research is somewhat inconclusive as to whether a games teaching methodology is superior to more 'traditional' technique-based teaching approaches (see Chow, Davids, Shuttleworth, Button, Renshaw and Araújo, 2007). Questions remain as to why coaches are increasingly adopting TGfU when the empirical data on its efficacy are limited. Although motivational factors (Griffin, Mitchell and Oslin, 1997) and greater enjoyment (Kirk and MacPhail, 2002) have been cited as valid reasons for adopting it, how TGfU might support learners in the acquisition of game skills or game understanding is still uncertain. For example, questions remain about the effectiveness of the approach when working with advance-level athletes.

Undoubtedly, variations in research designs used to empirically investigate the effectiveness of TGfU approaches have made it challenging to interpret data from research (Chow et al., 2007). Some researchers (e.g. Hopper, 2002) have recognised that it is fruitless to attempt to make a dichotomy between technique and tactical approaches to skill acquisition. Instead, they argue that research should focus on gaining a theoretical understanding of the teaching/learning processes underlying different pedagogical approaches (e.g. Holt, Strean and Bengoechea, 2002; Rink, 2001). This may be problematic as TGfU has been criticised for lacking a theoretical basis (Davids, Button and Bennett, 2008). However, in recent work we have suggested that '… a valid conceptual foundation for the function of TGfU is the constraints-led approach which underpins Nonlinear Pedagogy' (Chow et al., 2009, p. 133).

Non-linear pedagogy

Given the aims of the book and that we have written extensively about the theory behind non-linear pedagogy elsewhere (e.g. Chow et al, 2006; 2007), here we provide only a very brief overview. Non-linear pedagogy is 'based on application of the concepts and tools of non-linear dynamics' to coaching practice (Chow et al., 2006, p.72) and, as such, it is predicated on a view of the learner as an 'open-dynamic system'. Put simply, this approach identifies that the 'system' (e.g. an individual performer, a team, or a competition event) should be seen as complex and made up of many interacting parts (Davids et al., 2008). Because they are open and are sensitive to changes in their surroundings, dynamic systems are able to adopt many different states of organisation.

This is an important concept for coaches because it highlights that (i) performers have the potential to solve performance problems in a number of ways and as such rejects the concept of one optimal movement solution and (ii) deliberately manipulating the surroundings of athletes makes it easier to change organisation states. For example, an athletics (track and field) coach could manipulate the distance between hurdles to encourage novice hurdlers to take three steps between each hurdle.

In summary, in adopting a dynamic systems approach coaches use athlete-centred approaches in response to behaviour through a process of self-organisation questions under constraints.

Constraints

Constraints are boundaries that shape a learner's self-organising movement patterns, cognitions and decision-making processes (Passos, Araújo, Davids and Shuttleworth, 2008). Newell (1986) has proposed three categories of constraints:

1. Performer constraints cover physique and mental skills such as self efficacy, emotional control and motivation, technical skills and fitness level, all of which can influence decision-making behaviours.
2. Environmental constraints include: physical environmental constraints such as weather conditions, practice facilities and perhaps the structure of the backyard or locality in which a player was raised; and cultural constraints such as family, peer groups, the culture of a sport club and access to high-quality, developmentally appropriate coaching.
3. Task constraints include the goal of the task, rules of the game, equipment available and the relative state of the game.

As movement skills emerge from the interactions of key constraints in learning situations, coaches need to consider the dynamic interactions that are also taking place. It is essential to have a well-developed understanding of the key constraints underpinning skilled performance in specific sporting contexts in order to implement non-linear pedagogy because then the coach can deliberately manipulate the key constraints on learners with the aim of developing functional movement patterns and decision-making behaviours (Chow et al., 2006).

A coach's choice of which constraints to manipulate is determined by his or her understanding of the key factors that are acting as 'rate limiters' on the emergence of higher levels of performance of individuals and teams. Traditionally the term 'rate limiter' is associated with motor development and is typically used to describe how the relatively slower rate of development of a specific subsystem can act to prevent a new behaviour from emerging. For example, a lack of strength can delay the onset of walking in babies (Thelen and Smith, 1994).

These ideas can be applied in sport coaching. In this context, rate limiters may include environmental constraints such as limited opportunities to practise in specific conditions and exposure to a high-level coach as well as task constraints such as limited opportunities to use new equipment or to practise against highly skilled opponents.

What this discussion highlights is that, in adopting a non-linear pedagogy, coaches should implement a holistic approach to skill acquisition. This approach acknowledges that a change in one component of the system can change the whole system spontaneously and substantially. Perhaps coaches intuitively concur with this view when they talk about looking after the small, apparently inconsequential factors—factors that many coaches describe as 'looking after the so-called 1 percenters'.

Coaches' Views

When exposed to the constraints-led approach, coaches often express the view that the ideas are very interesting but too difficult to comprehend. Nonetheless, recently (particularly in Australia) interest in the approach has gradually increased. There may be a number of reasons for this greater level of interest, including: the appointment of skill acquisition specialists who have a background in dynamic systems theory to sport science support positions; redoubled efforts to enhance practitioners' understanding via publication of a series of 'coach friendly' papers and a book chapter; and the determination of proponents of the constraints-led approach to take every opportunity to present the ideas at physical education conferences and coaching forums as a way of demonstrating how 'theory' can be relevant to inform 'practice' (e.g. Chow, Button, Renshaw, Shuttleworth and Davids, 2008; Chow et al, 2009; Renshaw and Clancy, 2009; Renshaw, Davids, Chow and Shuttleworth, 2009; Renshaw, Davids, Chow and Hammond, in press). Our aim throughout has been to facilitate the design of evidence-based practice across the physical education and sports coaching professions.

Demonstrating the increasing interest in the ideas of the constraints-led approach in the sport community, influential bodies such as the Australian Institute of Sport and Cricket Australia have embraced the approach. However, the ongoing challenge is to provide coaches with appropriate resources that enhance their knowledge and understanding of this new approach so that they have the knowledge, skills and confidence to implement the approach in their own practice.

Greg Chappell and the AIS–Cricket Australia Centre of Excellence

In 2008 Greg Chappell was appointed as head coach at the Brisbane-based AIS–Cricket Australia Centre of Excellence. The Centre was launched in 2004 and replaced the Commonwealth Bank Cricket Academy that had been based in Adelaide for 15 years. As a former test 'legend' and experienced coach, Greg was ideally placed to take over this crucial role. From 1970–1984 he played 87 Test matches for Australia (48 as captain), scoring 24 centuries and averaging 53.86 runs, before embarking on a coaching career that included extensive coaching experience at state (South Australia) and international (India) level. Greg's role as head coach includes overseeing the implementation of all Centre of Excellence programmes, providing leadership to the men's and women's programmes and the continued professional development of the Centre's coaching staff.

My involvement with Greg and the staff at the Centre of Excellence came about as a result of a presentation I gave describing the constraints-led approach to staff at the Centre's annual review in November 2008. From subsequent observation and discussion it became apparent that through experiential knowledge Greg based his approach to coaching on similar principles as those advocated by non-linear pedagogy. Greg was very keen to develop a programme that was more deliberately aligned to TGfU (Games Sense) at the Centre and the ideas and philosophy of the constraints-led approach appeared to fit naturally with Greg's own thoughts on coaching. It was felt that underpinning game and practice design with a set of guiding principles could enhance the quality of the programme and consistently provide relevant and realistic learning opportunities for the Centre's scholars.

The Chappell Philosophy of Coaching

Greg's coaching philosophy is grounded in his experiences as a player (from the backyard to the Test arena) and as a coach of his son and international players, as well as in his own intensive research into learning and the common features of great players (see Chappell, 2004). Although many might say that coaching children is a very different task from coaching internationals, Greg explains that in his initial attempts to 'teach' his son to bat he learned a great deal about how all individuals develop skills. He also realised very quickly that traditional coaching does not work:

> From my point of view the thing that I've learned over the years from personal experience, first of all as a player trying to learn and then as a coach trying to teach, is that you can't teach it. You know, it's something that you learn.

As a child Greg was fortunate that his father seemed to have a natural understanding of learning. Given that Greg and his two brothers played cricket for Australia it might be fair to say that his father got a few things right! Interestingly the Chappell brothers were not the first generation of the family to play Test cricket: their grandfather, Victor Richardson, played in the infamous Bodyline series of 1932–33. It is interesting to speculate how his achievements might have shaped the thinking of his son, Greg's father. Greg recalls:

> Whilst he [Dad] had us coached formally for a few years, in my case with a friend of his who was a very good country cricketer and taught us the basics of forward defence, back defence, cover drive and so on … for every one of those sessions, dad would spend five or six sessions throwing half volleys, long hops, full tosses and teaching us to score runs. So that was … well … creating the environment in which we learnt to score runs. I mean he wasn't sitting there and lecturing us about it, but just by what he did he ingrained in us that we were looking to score runs.

In addition to the valuable time they spent working with their father, the Chappell boys found that their cricket skills were constantly being tested in their own early version of the cricket academy—namely, the training they gained from playing cricket in the backyard. In Australia, playing informal 'pick-up' games in backyards, streets or parks is known as *backyard cricket.*

Various commentators have seen backyard cricket as a significant cultural constraint (see further discussion below) that assists the emergence of many of the great Australian players from Trumper to Hussey (Cannane, 2009). Likewise Greg strongly believes that these early experiences are a significant factor in providing a foundation upon which expertise can develop:

> I mean those early years of where we played our make-believe Test matches in the backyard or whether we were an older brother or younger brother or whether it was just me throwing the ball against the wall, the imagination was a really important part of it as well and I think many years later I used that experience in visualisation sessions and so on.

Unstructured play opportunities may be a major part of the development process as they provide a base for potential champions, establishing many of the conditions that have been identified as essential for ultimate high achievement. Perhaps the key factor is that, in playing in backyards without pressure from overbearing adults, children can learn in a fun environment that helps to develop a lifelong love of the game. Only by the cultivation of this 'romance' with cricket (see Bloom, 1985) will players develop the intrinsic motivation necessary to sustain them through the vast amounts of play and practice necessary to develop high-level performance skills. Moreover, backyard cricket has far more to offer than fun alone: it provides holistic development of physical, technical, tactical and mental skills. As Greg notes, after playing backyard cricket against his older brother (Ian), the mental demands of Test cricket were 'a breeze' (Cannane, 2009).

Cultural constraints are important factors in talent development. A key component in this regard is the importance of having heroes to emulate, which appears to be a constant in the early development of future champions (Phillips, Davids, Renshaw and Portus, in press). A hero from the locality of the young player is even more powerful as the youngster will identify with the player: 'if he/she can come from my club/town and play for Australia then so can I' (Coyle, 2009).

Imagination in play seems to be another important component in developing excellence. Many young Australians have 'played' many times for their country a long time before they are awarded the 'baggy green' (a cap awarded to debutant Australian representative players). Many share the experience of playing in 'big games' in the backyard, which may have value well beyond being 'fun'. Australian rugby legend John Eales, for example, spent many hours as a youngster in his backyard kicking goals in 'Bledisloe Cup matches'. So in 2000, when he was faced with the challenge of kicking a penalty goal to win the Cup in injury time in a real-life game against the All Blacks, Eales had been there before as 'he had kicked a 100 of those goals as a youngster' (he did kick it!). The challenge for coaches is that many of the parks and backyards that have nurtured future champions are disappearing and that modern parents are reluctant to let children play in unsupervised environments (see also Chapter Seven).

Practical Implications of a Constraints-led Approach for Coaches

As one of the key foundations of a constraints-led approach is that the individual's unique interaction with the environment and task constraints underpins performance, programme design needs to be founded on the specific needs of each individual. Constraints-led coaching is therefore an athlete-centred process. Although individualising coaching programmes does not necessarily change the way coaches actually interact with their athletes, underpinning practice using non-linear pedagogy means that coaches have a more hands-off role and are able to act as a facilitator in the process of players improving their performance.

Another key concept tightly linked to the idea of constraints is that one of the fundamental attributes of dynamic systems such as learners is their capacity to achieve stable (and unstable) patterns through the process of self-organisation. Self-organisation occurs because the subcomponents of a system are able to spontaneously adjust and adapt to each other (Davids et al., 2008). In sport, some coaches have intuitively understood that performers have the ability to self-organise. For example, Gallwey (1979) rejected the idea of teaching by providing explicit instructions to performers and developed strategies that 'quietened the mind' allowing 'the body' to solve the problem by self-organisation. This approach makes sense because typically movements are not controlled by higher levels of the central nervous system and draw heavily on subconscious control of movements (Bernstein, 1967).

Moreover, once a coach has a good grasp of the strengths and weaknesses of individual performers, he or she is in a position to manipulate constraints to facilitate the 'removal' of factors that are acting as rate limiters. Crucial to the potential emergence of *improved* performance is the design of the learning environment. As Greg discusses, designing effective learning environments means that players are able to explore the task constraints and find solutions that match their own unique intrinsic dynamics:

> … really it's in creating the environment where they can learn and rather than 'telling them'—as [legendary cricketer Don] Bradman said in his book *The Art of Cricket*, tell them what you want them to do, not how to do it and let them work it out for themselves. And I believe very strongly that that's the most efficient way to do it.

In cricket batting, an often overlooked rate limiter is footwork which underpins balance. Greg addresses this issue by designing a task that facilitates the development of these generic factors that underpin batting per se. The task does not focus on developing balance in isolation (i.e. by viewing batting as a summation of subcomponents that can be broken down and then put back together) but is developed via a holistic approach where task success requires the development of good balance. Greg explains:

> … footwork is something that I just don't see being trained in cricket. And it's such an important part of batting. I mean footwork is about getting yourself into the best possible position for that particular delivery to play the shot that you've decided to play. Yet I see so many players minimising footwork and trying to catch up with their hands which doesn't work very well, consistently anyway. I mean it can work well on given days but it's not efficient over the long term. So we've sort of worked on two sets of drills which is basically about improving the footwork; which is a standing drive on the front foot, driving on both sides of the wicket but keeping the ball on the offside of the front leg so that you actually taking the head to the line rather than the leg to the line. So from a balance point of view the player is better positioned. And then the sort of extrapolation from there is to do down the wicket drills with the same intent to get as close to the ball as possible, but keeping the ball on the offside of the front leg again so that the head is going to the line and therefore the balance is improved. What I see with that is if you use the legs well, then the bottom half and the upper half of the body actually work quite well in sync. If you cheat with the legs, then you can see the disconnection between the upper half and the lower half.

One further issue for coaches undertaking a constraints-led approach is that, because individuals have the capacity to self-organise under constraints, the design of the practice environment needs to be carefully considered because it will have a major impact on the movements that are produced. For example, it is important to have practice tasks that lead to transfer of skills to the competitive environment. In creating realistic practice environments, coaches need to ensure that information present in the competition environment is likewise present in practice because it is only by performing representative practice tasks that players can become attuned to key information sources.

For example, expert cricketers are able to identify ball type from observing the bowlers' movements as they deliver the ball (Müller, Abernethy and Farrow, 2006; Renshaw and Fairweather, 2000). As such, developing young players can only develop this perceptual skill by practising against real bowlers. However, because many coaches believe that actions (or technique) can be developed in isolation from the perceptual skill, they provide lots of opportunities for batters to practise against bowling machines. This approach not only reduces the batters' opportunities to develop their perceptual skills to the level required but additionally, as demonstrated in recent research, changes the timing and coordination of batting strokes (Pinder, Renshaw and Davids, 2009; Renshaw et al, 2007). Perhaps this research is nothing new to the top coaches, as Greg's response indicates:

> ... what my intuition told me for years was that the bowling machine was a totally different exercise from batting against the bowler. From my own personal experience of batting against the bowling machine, it wasn't a great experience because once I've done it a few times I decided that it wasn't going to help me with batting. I was better off not to bat at all than to go and bat on a bowling machine because the activity is so different. [In an actual cricket match] you know the bowler's preparation to bowl; you know everything—all of the cues and clues that you're getting from the bowler is really important to get into the rhythm of the bowler and to get the timing of your movements. You take the bowler out of the equation, you stick a machine there that spits balls out at you and you've lost all those cues and clues. What I've subsequently found is that research is telling us what my intuition and my experience was telling me. The other thing is that the research into expertise tells you that experts are better at picking up the cues and clues then the average player. So why take it away from everyone and stop them from developing the things that will help them get better?

So what does Greg use to develop skill if the bowling machine is locked away in the shed? Although he is a strong advocate of games play (which is strongly supported by those coaches who adopt a constraints-led approach), he is not opposed to the idea of getting players to develop skills in tasks outside of games. However, given the principles of coupling perception with action as discussed above, skills should not be practised in a context that is decomposed, irrelevant and unrealistic (e.g. part–whole learning), as Greg recognises:

> Breaking things down to single components and trying to drill that component in isolation from everything else, just doesn't seem to make sense and I haven't really seen it work for anyone. The thing that works most efficiently is to train the whole process, the thinking and the physical all together.

One of the key practice activities that Greg advocates is the use of *task simplification* rather than *task decomposition* (see Davids et al., 2008). Specifically he favours the use of *slow* deliveries as opposed to *fast* throw-downs highly favoured by many cricketers:

> So basically the drills are done with slow throws. Again, even the fast throw-downs are not much better than a bowling machine. You've got slightly more cues as far as the information you're getting from the thrower but if the throws are fast, you know, a talented player can just stand there again without using the feet very efficiently and throw the hands at the ball and have reasonable success at it and think they're doing well. But actually they're training themselves to get out ... So the slower throw-downs cause two things. It causes them to get into the rhythm because if they get into position too early or too late it has a negative impact. But also with the slower throws it actually forces them to have to move to the ball rather than just stand there and throw their hands at them. We're finding that it works, works quite well ... what I see with that is if you use the legs well, then ... the bottom half and the upper half of the body actually work quite well in sync.

As highlighted above, it is important to understand how coaches can manipulate task constraints that can *shape* new behaviours. Even when practising skills the link between perception and action should always be maintained.

Developing Decision Makers

A common problem in many sports is that opportunities to develop decision-making skills are limited to actual competition because training has tended to overemphasise the development of technical skills. For coaches in a traditional sport like cricket, where there is a history of training by *net practice*, the challenge is to design learning opportunities that are as close as possible to the competition environment. A games-based focus is fundamental to the approach Greg adopts in his coaching in order to develop decision-making skills:

> The one thing that I have learned is that if you want them to be able to compete and play successfully then the decision-making process has to be trained as much if not more than the physical process, and—you know what—most cricket sessions are very much about the physical aspects of it, but very little about the mental aspects in the context of the way it would be in a game situation. So if you want players to improve in those areas then you've got to put them in those situations and for me the only way you can do that is to make it in a game scenario, a game environment where the whole process is trained, the decision making as well as the physical.

Non-linear pedagogy's emphasis on the mutual relationship between the individual and the environment highlights that, because 'animals' become attuned to their 'habitats', the only appropriate way to assess performance is by observation and analysis in the *real world*. That is, cricketers (and their coaches) should not use non-representative tasks such as batting against a bowling machine to assess performance in cricket matches. Similarly the concept of nested tasks advocated by ecological psychologists has important implications for assessing decision making (Gibson, 1986). In effect, an episode (e.g. one delivery) is nested in the whole event (an innings, a match, a series). When assessing a player's decision-making abilities, the player and coach have to carefully consider the specific decision in the context of previous events. For example, when analysing a batter's dismissal in an actual match, it is necessary to consider the previous balls faced, the state of the game and environmental conditions, as Greg elaborates:

> The video replays [of the dismissal] only tell you part of the story. They tell you it's a snapshot of that instant … the wicket may have come from something that happened two balls, three balls, six balls, eighteen balls before. [For example,] a fast bowler [might have] bowled a bouncer that all of a sudden shakes [the batter's] confidence and all of a sudden therefore the footwork fails/breaks down and the decision making breaks down because they might be expecting a short ball when they get a full ball and they're in trouble. So again, I'm very conscious of the fact that what the player thinks about, what they expect, what their intent is, has a very big bearing on what their physical activity, physical actions are.

Greg's reflections highlight the importance of providing contextual information when training to develop decision making. Players should be given detailed information that they can use to mentally immerse themselves in the task, providing opportunities to make decisions in game contexts that are as close as possible to the 'real thing'. Thus practice that provides the interacting constraints typical of games (i.e. managing mental skills, coping with fatigue, adapting to changing task demands) enables the holistic development of performance.

The application of the principles of dynamic systems theory and ecological psychology discussed above has some important implications for the way coaches provide instruction and feedback. Coaches can adopt a constraints-led approach to underpin instruction, feedback and the design of practice as a means of providing discovery learning opportunities that minimise potential disruption to performance by unnatural explicit instruction. Proponents of non-linear pedagogy would argue that coaches should promote natural implicit learning by creating environments that enable exploratory behaviour of players who can then learn movement skills without recourse to verbal instruction.

The Importance of Discovery Learning

According to the principle of self-organisation under constraints, coaching must be more hands-off than it would be under a traditional approach. Providing learners with opportunities to discover solutions rather than 'prescribing' answers is a basic tenet of non-linear pedagogy. This approach creates a learning environment that facilitates exploratory behaviour and self-discovery via natural subconscious learning of movements (see Renshaw et al., in press) rather than using explicit instructions that would encourage players to analyse their own internal movement. As Greg highlights in the following discussion, for batters in cricket this kind of learning environment can be achieved by asking them to hit balls into target areas, thus requiring them to focus their attention externally.

> Basically let them get out there and discover for themselves. I know with young batters, the best way to let them learn to bat is to get them batting, but you obviously control the environment … give them target areas to hit that encourage them to play the shots that you want them to learn. It's so much more efficient. I have seen it just work so well with young cricketers, where if you stood there and tried to teach them—'Get the left foot here and your left elbows up here and do this and do that'—they just can't do it, it's highly inefficient.

Implicit Learning

A standard component of many coach education courses is Fitts and Posner's (1967) model of the learning process. In this approach the performer is said to move through a continuum from a cognitive phase to an associative phase and finally to an autonomous phase. By implication, beginners need to 'think' their way through the early stages of learning and it is only experts who are autonomous and able to perform at a 'subconscious' level. This generally accepted premise of skill acquisition leads to standardised approaches to coaching based on providing performers with lots of explicit instructions and feedback. However, for some coaches—such as Greg—this approach is problematic. The perils of relying on explicit learning and encouraging the player to think too much were brought home to Greg when he himself tried to learn a new sport:

> The one thing that I learned not only from playing cricket, but it's probably come home to me more in trying to learn golf since I finished playing cricket, was that if you think about what you're doing, you can't do it … so [for the coach] it's [about using] all that distraction stuff, anything that stops them thinking about it and lets them just get on and do it.

As highlighted above, because most basic movement patterns are under subconscious control it is no surprise that forcing learners to switch to higher levels of control through providing explicit instructions and feedback will disrupt their performance and make it more difficult for them to automatise their skills (Beek, 2000). Greg extends his thoughts to encompass the impact of explicit learning on cricket coaching:

> You certainly can't stand there and try and explain it to them and expect them to be able to do it because then they stop watching the ball ... if you are in any way thinking about what's happening at your end [when batting], you physically can't see the ball. For a bowler, if he's physically worried about what's happening with his action at his end, he's got no control over where the balls going to go at the other end.

The approach Greg uses emphasises that feedback should be intrinsic to the task and does not need to be augmented by coaches:

> The feedback [from] the player is that they more often hit the ball in the middle of the bat. It's got a sweeter feel, it's got a sweeter sound, so we're trying to train them to use that biofeedback as their measure of the success of that particular activity. We're seeing some quite marked improvement in the more efficient use of the body and I don't know any other way of doing it.

Variability

From the discussion above it is clear that games players have to deal with constantly changing individual, task and environmental constraints. It seems logical therefore that players need a range of solutions available so that they can cope effectively in competition. Despite this logic, many coaches consider that it is important to develop the perfect technique that is 'repeatable' on the assumption that with such a 'perfect technique' players can cope more effectively with the pressure of competition. However, research evidence shows that human movement systems cannot repeat movements exactly (see Schöllhorn and Bauer, 1998) and that a key characteristic of experts is that they are able to adapt movement sub-systems to achieve success through 'functional compensatory variability'. For example, to shoot accurately, experienced basketball players are able to adjust the wrist movement to compensate for differences in elbow or shoulder movements (Button, MacLeod, Sanders and Coleman, 2003). More generally, the concept of functional variability emphasises that each *successful* individual will have developed a 'range' of unique optimal movement solutions that enable him or her to deal with the requirements of any specific performance.

A constraints-led approach to skill acquisition emphasises the importance of functional variability within individuals and has implications for the way practice is structured. Consequently an important feature of practice is to provide opportunities for players to develop adaptability by creating learning environments with high levels of variability. This is a fundamental aim in Greg's coaching. Adaptability is essential for modern elite cricketers as they can be required to play three different forms of the game, on different surfaces, in different climates—with these conditions often changing daily. Additionally international touring teams have minimal 'lead-in time' before major games meaning that they must be able to adapt very quickly to new physical, emotional and cultural environments. Greg constantly challenges players by adding variability into learning tasks:

> I'm very much of the opinion that putting them into environments where ... they're challenged to do things differently [is critical]. So it might be different pitch conditions, different ball conditions [and] different parameters in a session to encourage them to have to do things a little bit differently than the way they've done them before. So, just putting them into those situations, whether it's in game-based training [or in skill development activities] that we're trying to bring into the centre of excellence, [it] is more than just net sessions.

We have found that designing games to facilitate opportunities for players to work on all aspects of their game can be very challenging and requires coaches to be innovative and creative. For example, in one small-sided game I observed a key constraint was that the players were not allowed to throw over-arm as they had completed a high volume of throwing the day before the session. Changing this one apparently minor factor changed the game demands substantially. Specifically the intensity in performance was lost as running singles became too easy because fielders had to throw the ball in under-arm to distant targets. The coaches quickly picked up on this problem and changed the task constraints. The fielding team was given five 'single' stumps that it could position wherever it chose in the outfield. Hitting any of these stumps by an under-arm throw could result in a run-out. This change in the task constraints led to a much more realistic game with match-level intensity and the added benefit of increasing the decision-making challenges for batters and fielders alike.

Some After-thoughts

The interview with Greg brought up a number of points that are worth exploring by anyone considering adopting a non-linear pedagogy or games-based approach to coaching. An interesting issue is how the approach can change the coach–athlete relationship. This section addresses common criticisms of the approach—namely, that it draws resistance from players and assistant coaches and that it is only useful if you have plenty of time.

The Impact of Adopting a Constraints-led Perspective on the Coach–Athlete Relationship

The individualised nature of the constraints-led approach, allied with the more hands-off approach to coaching advocated by the principle of self-organisation under constraints, has important implications for the coach–athlete relationship. I asked Greg how he thought the approach affects his relationship with the players. He felt that on the whole it improves the relationship as it changes the overall role of the coach from someone who prescribes solutions to one who has more of an advisory or 'mentoring' role:

> I think … it lessens the danger of the breakdown in relationship that comes from lecturing, lecturing someone about what they should do or what they're not doing. I think it lessens the impact, it increases the responsibility of the athlete to his improvement or her improvement and I think that brings the responsibility back fairly squarely where it belongs—with the athlete. I mean the coach at the end of the day is a resource. I think coaching in cricket is … there's an expectation and it's unrealistic, that a coach can come in and wave a magic wand and make somebody better. It can't happen. It won't happen and if you try and wave that magic wand it will usually turn to dust and, as I say, the individual will go backwards. It's more of a mentoring role, it's more of a resource provider that you can set up the structure of sessions that will lead towards certain outcomes and then it's up to the individual to get out of it what they're capable of getting out of it.

In contrast to a traditional approach, when coaches create an athlete-focused environment they share the responsibility for programme design based on the needs of the athlete. Conversely failing to adopt an athlete-centred approach hinders the development of an athlete's confidence, as Greg observes:

> All that the individual hears [in a traditional approach] is that 'I'm no good' and it actually reinforces what they already think anyway; that 'I'm no good, I can't do this', you know—'I'm not good enough, I'm a failure'; all of the negative impacts that we're trying to avoid. I think the best thing that you can do as a coach generally is to try and boost confidence and put them in situations where they can have some success. Equally you've got to put them in some situations where they'll have some failure as well so they understand the difference between the two … you know …

punishing somebody who's struggling by making it harder for them is not going to help them get better. In fact you've got to wind it back a bit and try and lower the standard of competition or whatever to give them a chance to drill some new activities if that's what they're going to do and as they become better at it, ratchet up the challenge and try and drag them a little bit further. But do it in a way that they perhaps don't see it as, 'Oh hang on, this is all of a sudden getting tougher'. Just gradual[ly] change the environments so that the challenge is greater and drag them forward that way, rather than telling them they're no good.

It is worth noting the power of the last two quotes from Greg in terms of creating highly motivating coaching environments. By providing an environment that encourages personal responsibility and ownership of performance development, along with learning tasks pitched at levels that facilitate feelings of competence, a coach helps to develop more intrinsically motivated players by enhancing feelings of relatedness, competence and autonomy—essential factors in self-determination theory (Ryan and Deci, 2000).

The Reaction of Players and Coaches

One of the key advantages put forward in support of approaches like TGfU is that most games players find such an approach highly motivating. Yet how do developing professional players react to a training environment in which significant proportion of their time is spent 'only playing games'? Do they see it as appropriate to their stage of development? Similarly what is the reaction of coaches who have had less exposure to games-based training? A key part of introducing the new approach, in my experience, is to first educate the coaches and players as to why it is being introduced. At the Centre of Excellence such education is provided to staff before the scholars arrive and then to the new scholars themselves. Greg feels that once the programme has commenced, positive feedback is likely to come through improved performance.

From the point of view of the coaches, he observes:

I think there's been across the board I'd say a general reluctance; some have been more ready to have a go at least and let's have a look at it and see. Others, well ... this is not what we know. I think a certain amount of scepticism was out there but I think within a short space of time most of the coaches have come on board.

As for the players, Greg discusses the feedback he has gained from their involvement in this games approach:

And the players certainly, the feedback that I'm getting from the players is that they notice the difference ... the initial feedback [from the players] was 'Ooohhh, where are we going to get our volume from; where are we going to get to hit a lot of balls because this is going to be less volume?' The big thing that we've had to convince them is that if you have quality, that it will be actually better for you than lots of inefficient practice. The volume can actually be bad for you, if you're training the wrong things [e.g. bowling machine practice]. Better off to train the right things, do it efficiently and once it's working, stop. More is not necessarily better. Often less is better. Do it, do it well and get the quality and then get out of there and then go and do something else. It is better for the mind because if you're not doing it with intensity; with sort of game-like intensity then it's not going to be overly efficient. Better off to try and get it as intense as possible; do it for a shorter time but with quality [then] you'll get better outcomes. As the programme has progressed and the guys have actually realised that we're actually hitting the ball quite well, [they have realised] maybe we don't need the volume.

This Approach Takes Longer

An interesting point Greg brought up is that before cricket in Australia became professional, training times were much shorter because players had 'day jobs'. Since professionalism has come in, training sessions have tended to become longer, seemingly on the assumption that because they have the time players should do more. The quantity versus quality debate is ongoing in the sports coaching and motor learning community (see Davids, 2000). Greg offers his perspective on it in this way:

> You know, just because you've got 24 hours a day and you're a professional [it] doesn't mean you have to spend 24 hours a day at training. From personal experience of having played in an era where we didn't play full-time cricket and being restricted in the time that we had to train, [lack of time] actually forced us to be more efficient with the way we trained and we didn't have any negative effects from not hitting a thousand balls a week. In fact I think we had some positive effects from not dulling ourselves down, wearing ourselves out mentally and physically doing dull things. We were off doing other things and I think that's something that I would certainly like to see change [over training] in Australian cricket. Yet I think if we're to get back or maintain our position at the top of all formats of the game, we're going to have to train smarter not harder. I just don't see that that training harder works if you're not doing it the right way.

The quantity versus quality debate links to the common criticism of games-based coaching strategies from traditional coaches who suggest that these approaches are all very well, but they take longer to work. If the task for performers never changed and one organisational state could be used to solve the tasks, then drilling players using blocked practice to develop the optimal movement solution would be time effective. However, as the discussions in this chapter have indicated a clear message for coaches is that a key to skilled performance is the ability to adapt to changing individual, environmental and task constraints. In developing this ability, players need to be exposed to high levels of variability of practice by using repetition without repetition. The term 'repetition' is used here in the sense that learners should not be required to repeat an identical movement pattern from situation to situation, but instead should be encouraged to repeatedly construct subtly differing, but successful, coordination solutions during learning (Renshaw et al., 2009). In making their contribution to this end, coaches should create practice tasks where the learner doesn't repeatedly practise the same solution to a problem but instead is continually forced to search for new solutions to the same problem (see Renshaw et al., 2009). From his experiences, Greg provides some evidence to support non-linear pedagogy:

> Well I know that with the experience that we've had here and previously working in other environments in India and in Australia that where we've done this sort of training, we've actually seen some really good results quite quickly. Whereas generally when you're trying to explain it to someone and do the traditional sort of training, you actually see them go backwards more then you see them go forwards … and it's not going backwards and then getting better, they just go backwards and then they start to lose confidence, they [then] lose confidence in you as a coach and I would be as guilty as anyone. I mean, most human beings won't look as themselves as being the problem, it's always someone else is the problem and as a coach that's a huge danger—that by talking too much and doing too much and trying to lecture them, and not putting them in situations where they're training the whole process, the mental as well as the physical you're really limiting their chance of getting better.

Conclusion

In conclusion it is worth noting Greg's response to the common criticism levelled at TGfU or games-centred approaches that 'it's just playing games'. I asked:

> So your approach comes across as very simple in terms of what it is and one criticism of the approach is that it's just playing games and it's not coaching. How would you answer that?

Greg responded:

> Well I think that's what coaching is, to be quite honest. I think it's creating environments, setting the environment where somebody can learn rather

than standing there and just hearing yourself talk for the sake of talking and the one thing that I have learnt over the last 10 years of coaching at first class and international level is that the less you say, the better. In fact, often the best thing you can do is to say nothing. Observation is a very big part of coaching and I think you've got to create opportunities where you as a coach can observe and see what is actually happening in certain situations so that you can then hopefully design a session that can give them a chance to improve in the areas where they need to improve. Standing there giving them a lecture is not going to do that. And as a parent I probably learnt more than as a coach ...

Although those of us who adopt non-linear pedagogy are strong advocates of games-based approaches such as TGfU, it is worth making clear that a constraints-led approach is not the same thing as TGfU, despite the use of many similar processes and similarities in philosophy. In fact, a constraints-led perspective can be used to support the design of learning tasks across the learning styles (e.g. Mosston and Ashworth, 2002).

Critics of the games-based approaches have stated or implied that coaches are abdicating responsibility by simply allowing players to play games. In response to such criticisms, this chapter has demonstrated that underpinning programme design with a strong set of theoretical principles can enhance learning design. Adopting a more hands-off approach to coaching does not imply a hands-free approach and in fact designing representative games and practice tasks can be more time consuming in the initial preparation. I would argue that this extra time is more than worthwhile if it produces more effective, quality learning environments that holistically develop highly motivated, confident, autonomous, highly skilled and adaptable games players.

It's really impossible for athletes to grow up.
On the one hand, you're a child, still playing a game.
But on the other hand, you're a superhuman hero that
everyone dreams of being. No wonder we have such
a hard time understanding who we are. - Billie Jean King

References

Beek, P. J. (2000). Toward a theory of implicit learning in the perceptual motor domain. *International Journal of Sport Psychology, 31*, 547–554.

Bernstein, N. A. (1967). *The Control and Regulation of Movements*. London: Pergamon.

Bloom, B. S. (1985). *Developing Talent in Young People*. New York: Ballentine.

Bunker, D., & Thorpe, R. (1982). A model for the teaching of games in the secondary schools. *The Bulletin of Physical Education*, 5–8.

Button, C., MacLeod, M., Sanders, R., & Coleman, S. (2003). Examining movement variability in the basketball free-throw action at different levels. *Research Quarterly for Exercise & Sport, 74*(3), 257–269.

Cannane, S. (2009). *First Tests: Great Australian cricketers and the backyards that made them*. Sydney: ABC.

Chappell, G. (2004). *Cricket: The making of champions*. Melbourne: Lothian.

Chow, J., Davids, K., Button, C., Renshaw, I., Shuttleworth, R., & Uehara, L. (2009). Nonlinear pedagogy: Implications for teaching games for understanding (TGfU). In T. Hopper, J. Butler & B. Storey (Eds.), *TGfU ... .Simply Good Pedagogy: Understanding a Complex Challenge*. Ottawa Physical Health Education Association (Canada).

Chow, J.Y., Button, C., Renshaw, I., Shuttleworth, R., & Davids, K. (2008). *Nonlinear Pedagogy: Implications for TGfU*. Paper presented at the Teaching games for understanding: celebrations and cautions.

Chow, J.Y., Davids, K., Button, C., Shuttleworth, R., Renshaw, I., & Araújo, D. (2006). Nonlinear pedagogy: A constraints-led framework to understanding emergence of game play and skills. *Nonlinear Dynamics, Psychology, and Life Sciences, 10*(1), 71–103.

Chow, J.Y., Davids, K., Shuttleworth, R., Button, C., Renshaw, I., & Araújo, D. (2007). From processes to principles: A constraints-led approach to Teaching Games for Understanding (TGFU). *Review of Educational Research, 77*, 251–278.

Coyle, D. (2009). *The Talent Code*. London: Random House.

Davids, K. (2000). Skill acquisition and the theory of deliberate practice: It aint what you do it's the way that you do it! *International Journal of Sport Psychology, 31*, 461–466.

Davids, K., Button, C., & Bennett, S. J. (2008). *Dynamics of Skill Acquisition: A constraints-led approach*. Champaign, IL: Human Kinetics.

Fitts, P.M., & Posner, M.I. (1967). *Human Performance*. Belmont: Brooks/Cole.

Gallwey, T.W. (1979). *The Inner Game of Golf*. London: Jonathan Cape.

Gibson, J.J. (1986). *The Ecological Approach to Visual Perception*. Boston: Houghton Mifflin.

Griffin, L.L., Mitchell, S.A., & Oslin, J.L. (1997). *Teaching Sport Concepts and Skills: A tactical games approach*. Champaign, IL: Human Kinetics.

Holt, N.L., Strean, W.B., & Bengoechea, E.G. (2002). Expanding the Teaching Games for Understanding model: New avenues for future research and practice. *Journal of Teaching in Physical Education, 21*, 162–176.

Hopper, T. (2002). Teaching games for understanding: The importance of student emphasis over content emphasis. *Journal of Physical Education, Recreation & Dance 73*(7), 44–49.

Launder, A.G. (2001). *Play Practice: The games approach to teaching and coaching sports*. Champaign, IL: Human Kinetics.

Kirk, D., & McPhail, A. (2002). Teaching Games for Understanding and situated learning: Rethinking the Bunker-Thorpe Model. *Journal of Teaching in Physical Education, 21*, 177–192.

Mosston, M., & Ashworth, S. (2002). *Teaching Physical Education*. London: Benjamin Cummings.

Müller, S., Abernethy, B., & Farrow, D. (2006). How do world class cricket batsmen anticipate a bowler's intention? *Quarterly Journal of Experimental Psychology, 59*(12), 2162–2168.

Newell, K.M. (1986). Constraints on the development of co-ordination. In M.G. Wade & H.T.A. Whiting (Eds.), *Motor Development in Children: Aspects of co-ordination and control* (pp. 341–360). Dodrecht: Martinus Nijhoff.

Newell, K.M., & Rovegno, I. (1990). Commentary—Motor learning: Theory and practice. *Quest, 42*, 184–192.

Passos, P., Araújo, D., Davids, K., & Shuttleworth, R. (2008). Manipulating constraints to train decision making in rugby union. *International Journal of Sport Science & Coaching, 3*(1), 125–140.

Phillips, E., Davids, K., Renshaw, I., & Portus, M. (in press). Expert performance in sport and the dynamics of talent development. *Sports Medicine*.

Pinder, R., Renshaw, I., & Davids, K. (in press). Information-movement coupling in developing cricketers under changing ecological practice constraints. *Human Movement Science, 28*, 468-479.

Renshaw, I., & Clancy, J. (2009). Developing intelligent games performers. *Active Education (7)*, 50–52.

Renshaw, I., & Davids, K. (2008). *Implications of Nonlinear Pedagogy for Instruction, Practice, Organization, and Feedback*. Paper presented at the Fourth International Teaching Games for Understanding (TGfU) Conference.

Renshaw, I., Davids, K., Chow, J., & Shuttleworth, R. (2009). Insights from ecological psychology and dynamical systems theory can underpin a philosophy of coaching. *International Journal of Sport Psychology, 40*, 580–602.

Renshaw, I., Davids, K., Chow, J.W., & Hammond, J. (in press). A constraints-led perspective to understanding skill acquisition and game play: A basis for integration of motor learning theory and physical education praxis? *P.E. & Sport Pedagogy.*

Renshaw, I., & Fairweather, M.M. (2000). Cricket bowling deliveries and the discrimination ability of professional and amateur batters. *Journal of Sports Sciences, 18*, 951–957.

Renshaw, I., Oldham, A. R. H., Davids, K., & Golds, T. (2007). Changing ecological constraints of practice alters coordination of dynamic interceptive actions. *European Journal of Sport Science, 7*, 157–167.

Rink, J.E. (2001). Investigating the assumptions of pedagogy. *Journal of Teaching in Physical Education 20*, 112–128.

Ryan, R.M., & Deci, E.L. (2000). Self-determination theory and the facilitation of intrinsic motivation, social development, and well-being. *American Psychologist, 55,* 68–78.

Schöllhorn, W.I., & Bauer, H.U. (1998). *Identifying Individual Movement Styles in High Performance Sport by Means of Self-organizing Kohenen Maps.* Paper presented at the Proceedings of the XVI Annual Conference of the International Society of Biomechanics in Sport, Konstanz, Germany, 7–12 July.

Thelen, E., & Smith, L.B. (1994). *A Dynamic Systems Approach to the Development of Cognition and Action.* Cambridge, MA: MIT.

It is not only by the questions we have answered that progress may be measured, but also by those we are still asking. - Freda Adler, US educator, criminal justice specialist

I can do something else besides stuff a ball through a hoop. My biggest resource is my mind. - Kareem Abdul-Jabbar

Everybody wants to be somebody. The thing you have to do is give them confidence they can. You have to give a kid a dream. - George Foreman

Chapter Nine

Guy Evans: the Challenges of Change

Guest Author: **Christian Edwards with Guy Evans**
University of Worcester

This chapter is a result of an analysis I completed as part of a leadership class for a Master of Science degree at the University of Worcester. The assignment asked me to look holistically at a coach and his or her leadership abilities and approaches. I chose Guy Evans as he was taking a class on philosophy and practice of sports coaching for his Master's degree where he was required to complete a self-reflection of his coaching as an assignment. We both thought that we would benefit mutually from analysing Guy's coaching.

Sharing an office with Guy for four months allowed for daily informal conversations and observation of coach–athlete consultations which formed the primary method of data collection. To gain an in-depth understanding of the basketball team's culture and of the personal opinions and experiences of both coaches and athletes, I used an action research process to follow Guy's development as a coach in his desired attempt to take on an athlete-centred approach for the season. Guy was interviewed at length on seven occasions and we talked informally throughout the season. Field notes were taken of training sessions and matches, and players were interviewed through individual and group interviews during the season, with discussion surrounding player development and success. The assistant coach of the national league team and the director of coaching were also interviewed. Audio recordings of interviews, along with focus group data and field notes, were transcribed verbatim, and players and coaches were asked to re-read and affirm statements.

During the project Guy actually coached two teams: a national league team where he was the head coach and had an assistant and a university team where he was a player-coach and had a different assistant. I observed him working mostly with the university team, but the national league team also has some influence in this analysis as many of the university players played for the national league side. Guy was new to the university side and thought that the process of change would be more challenging in this environment due to players' unfamiliarity with his approach:

> More feedback was desired for the university side specifically, as I was the fourth coach in four seasons and therefore was attempting to change the culture. With the national league side, I was going into my second season

and therefore my own philosophy and values were already present within the culture of that particular team. Players possessing a higher playing ability generally played on both teams.

Guy's interest in participating in this project was sparked by his desire to learn more about the athlete-centred coaching approach. It was only during his studies for a Masters degree in Sports Coaching that he had become aware of athlete-centred approaches; previously he had always been exposed to and tended to use autocratic ways of coaching. Thus when I asked Guy, following the completion of this project, why he had decided to change his coaching approach, he responded:

> I was interested in trying some new things as a coach because it is my belief that in order to progress in any field, you need to move away from what you are comfortable with, to a certain extent, without forgetting or neglecting what your strengths are. Therefore, we attempted to foster a team culture and environment where players had responsibility over the goals, values, and overall vision of the team. However, I remained the primary decision maker in most areas, so I would describe the approach that was taken as being more 'cooperative' than anything else, incorporating many of the values of athlete-centred coaching.

At the end of the project, I became a player manager and was able to continue to follow the development of both Guy and the team. As part of this latter role, I was able, with Guy, to work on some players' mental skills once the project was completed.

Guy's primary focus for this project was to work on establishing a quality team culture, though he also attempted to increase his questioning, improve athletes' mental skills and use a bit of Teaching Games for Understanding (TGfU). He was interested in strengthening his rapport with the players to gain their support and trust. To this end, with varied success, he and the players mutually established goals and values throughout the season. The intention behind this process was to enable the athletes to take ownership of and responsibility for their learning, decision making and team goals. However, as Guy reflects later, he did not feel that he monitored the goals and values as much as he should have done to get players' buy in. This reflective process that Guy used all the way through the season was a highlight in his coach development.

In this chapter, Guy's philosophy of coaching, his process of establishing the team culture and a range of his coaching practices are presented. His techniques for attempting to enable athlete learning and his struggle with some external factors are also discussed.

Guy's Development as a Coach

Guy recalls that he started to develop as a coach from an early age:

> I have always been someone that steps to the forefront, so to speak, someone that will make their voice heard. My parents always taught me to stand out from the crowd and be myself, and to me that meant being a leader. Anything and everything I did as a youngster involved me taking some kind of leadership role, whether it be sport, school, friendships, or otherwise.

Although football was Guy's first love, at the age of eight his interest in basketball was sparked through seeing the game on television:

> I had no coach or any means to play the game except for a toy hoop in my bedroom. Based on where I grew up in Mid Wales, there was very little opportunity as a youngster to get seriously involved at the time in any sport apart from football, rugby and perhaps athletics. For years I would mimic what I saw on television and re-create the games in my bedroom, and then my parents bought me a real hoop. Once my dad nailed that to the side of my house, that's all I did after school.

While at high school, Guy managed to set up a basketball club with the support of a physical education teacher, and gradually his responsibilities progressed to coaching and helping to organise both training and matches. This club eventually developed from a school club into a town club with the aim of developing basketball in the local area. He reflects:

> The thing I am most proud about is the fact that now every weekend back home there are young people playing basketball, which was not the case 10 years ago.

As a player, Guy has represented Wales at under 18 and senior levels. As he sees it, his desire to coach as well relates to the need to promote more basketball coaches and his involvement has developed as part of a natural process:

> When I started to play, I had very little help, apart from my PE teacher Mr Walby, and my friends. The closest basketball club was 50 miles away, and although once I got older and improved (and I had the amazing support of my dad to take me there, for many years), I had to be my own coach. Once I got a team together locally, I naturally became the leader of the group and therefore took over coaching responsibilities. I was told by my teachers, friends and other coaches that coaching would be something I should consider to pursue.

After leaving sixth form at 18 years of age, Guy was accepted to the University of Worcester to complete a Bachelor of Sports Coaching Science (Hons), from which he graduated in 2008. During his undergraduate studies, he continued to coach in Wales for the summer and be a player-coach for the university. In 2007 the university's Director of Basketball also appointed him to coach the national league team. At this point, he was the youngest coach in the national league and still an undergraduate. The Director of Basketball identifies a number of reasons for Guy's selection including his:

> ... incentive to set up basketball in his local area ... his professional attitude and honesty with players.

Team focus group responses indicate that the team expected Guy to emerge as a leader:

> [Guy] was put in place by the [Director of Basketball]; however he took on this role himself, and players expected him to take on this role. Leaders emerge naturally; they should be selected when they show themselves ... players should have a say in who is coaching them ...

As part of this leadership project, the first step I took to analyse Guy's coaching was to complete a strengths, weaknesses, opportunities and threats (SWOT) analysis based on speaking with him and the players, and through observing his coaching. From this analysis, Guy identified that he would like to work on:

* putting more effort into constructing an overall team vision;
* including everyone in the team, and particularly younger players, in discussions and decision making where appropriate; and
* being flexible in planning.

From the SWOT analysis, too, it was evident that Guy aims to be a transformational leader (one who inspires and enthuses followers (Rowold, 2006)) and aims to empower players. However, implementing this athlete-centred process is difficult, as David Hadfield (2005, p.38) points out:

> Many coaches with whom I have worked find it difficult to become an athlete-centred coach. Why? The prescriptive coach-centred approach is how they were coached and it is how they learned how to coach; now it has become a habit and, like all habits, it is hard to change—especially under coaching pressure. When things are getting tough, prescriptive coaches who are trying to become empowering tend to revert to a 'do this, do that' approach. It is what they know, it is easier, it is quicker and it shows anyone who may be in doubt who is the boss around here and who owns the knowledge. But is it the most effective approach? I would argue that in many cases it is not.

So, as Guy was keen to develop his self-awareness—awareness that there is an issue and that change is needed—and as part of my role in the action research process, it was important that Guy had an understanding of this situation. In a sense Guy needed be convinced that the benefits of change outweigh the costs of which he became aware through his studies and the feedback provided through my observation. Guy developed this understanding superbly. Through our continued discussions about his coaching, his self-awareness blossomed. Part of the process was to clearly discriminate between the current way and a different way of doing things, which represents another step coaches can take to enable buy in. Without effective self-analysis (either proprioceptive/ kinaesthetic or cognitive), coaches cannot develop the self-understanding required to change and improve (see Chapter Twelve for further discussion on coach self-development).

Guy's Philosophy of Coaching

Guy's major aim in his basketball coaching has always been to develop players to be the best they can be. During one of the first interviews, Guy spoke about his philosophy of coaching:

> My philosophy is to achieve our goals by any means possible. I have to do everything in my power to get the team to where they need to go.

Guy also alluded to promoting the team's success:

> My personal outcome of success is to say I did the best I could; I want the first years to say they have learned a lot and the third years to say this is the best year of basketball they have had. Both teams are development sides and I aim to develop players.

An interesting influence on the development of Guy's philosophy is that the 'assigned' assistant coach of the national league side had a markedly different philosophy— that the team is a 'performance side not a development side'. Their philosophical differences may have been due to a lack of an overall clear vision for the team within the basketball programme. According to Schroeder (2007), the effective administration of a programme requires leaders and followers to understand and be able to express the programme's underlying purpose and its reason for being. About the differences he experienced with his assistant coach, Guy says:

> We don't have a clear statement [for the overall basketball programme] that really backs up our values; I think we have all the components of a vision we just don't have a statement. The team has goals and values [on the university side] that were co-constructed by the coach, assistant coach

and players. What we lack is a clear and coherent [overall] statement, and we could look more into using symbolism to reinforce our vision.

Speaking about the assistant of the university side, Guy suggests that, though there wasn't an overall vision for the club, this assistant was open to change and they developed a good working relationship:

For the university team for which I was in charge of, I was lucky enough to have an assistant with a high level of emotional intelligence … someone who would listen, be approachable from a player's perspective, but also someone who had the confidence to make his own suggestions and have input.

As other coaches in this book and the first edition suggest, it is important for the coach to have some say in selecting the right people around him or her, people who have the same philosophy and a similar vision, to better help the players' learning.

Guy tries to develop ownership and establish 'mutual trust, team culture, group goals, values, and rules'. He allows players to lead three individual sessions a week on their own, and his role, as he perceives it, is to 'guide players rather than instruct them'. However, in practice just as Hadfield (2005) points out, the wider pressures of winning may have influenced Guy in his attempt to focus on player development:

I always want to win, partly for my own satisfaction, but also as a way of repaying those who have put their time and effort into giving me opportunities to coach and have assisted with my development. Last season, a loss would have a profound effect on me for a couple of days.

These overarching pressures (ones that he has no control over) can impact on a young coach like Guy, especially as he tries to institute change. Those who he perceived to have influenced his career and how he assesses himself as a coach have taken the traditional approach to coaching, which in turn would have influenced Guy's perspective on change. In his efforts to change, he adopted a more task-focused transactional approach. Nonetheless the external pressures related to winning still influenced his actions. His players identified that Guy uses a traditional style saying that he is 'very prescriptive in training and that they should get more of a say'. Recognising that a dominant, traditional approach may constrain the learning, motivation and enjoyment of the players, Guy continues to reflect on this issue.

Guy's overall goal of 'player development' may not fit with the 'win at all costs attitude' that is so often part of our culture and wider society. However, I observed that he made some real attempts to develop players. For example, during a game when the team was winning by 20 points, he was shouting at the team to carry on pushing for more baskets. He explains:

There were guys just running up and down the court. What is the point in being here? To improve! We are trying to improve, so all the minutes count.

In this match he played all bench players and the starting line-up apart from himself. In justifying his actions he says:

Why do I need to be on the court if we have the depth that we have? I have achieved at this, my aim is to improve these players. I would rather give other players the minutes to develop them.

It is true that, in games that were close and in some practices, I observed that players who were bench players either did not get minutes or did not get time on court. Yet here the nature of basketball needs to be taken into account: most teams commit to a nine-player rotation, leaving at least three players without significant court time.

Despite such features implicit in the game, Guy was keen to implement this athlete-centred approach to develop players. Here he perceives his own role:

… is to guide players rather than instruct them … leading a group your overall goal is to develop that group so much that they can function at their best without you being directly involved in the process.

Guy also believes in developing 'some leadership within the group and some decision making and ownership'. This idea supports an athlete-centred coaching approach as it encourages independence in athletes and provides social and cognitive benefits. He explains his attitude:

It is easy to coach in a style that promotes athletes becoming dependent but really I think what you want is a shift towards them becoming independent. They need to think for themselves. My approach became 'I may not have all the answers, but I believe I do have all the questions'.

One of the external influences was the expectation that the team would be promoted to a higher division based on league results. Ultimately this primary goal was not achieved. However, with Guy's philosophy, he felt that the team was successful in terms of realising their potential and coming together as a unit. The type of reflection that Guy used all the way through the season was a highlight in his coach development:

I am extremely competitive as a person and a coach … I want to win at everything. As you mature, get older, and gain more experience, you realise that the only person you should compete against is yourself. Whether you win or lose is subject to so many external factors, and it cannot easily be controlled … we knew … what we could control, however [the success] was our shared effort in working towards our goals.

Following the feedback from this action research project and Guy's own development throughout this period, his philosophy has changed:

> My personal philosophy of coaching is that it is my job to assist the athletes in reaching their goals. Because I have been on the other side of the fence, I recognise the importance of being a help rather than a hindrance. I don't believe in ruling by fear or trying to put myself on a pedestal above the players. I think it's my duty to represent the players but also attempt to impart some positive lessons about life along the way, not just basketball.

The Process of Establishing a Quality Team Culture

One of Guy's major objectives in applying an athlete-centred approach to coaching was to co-construct a team culture and gain mutual understanding. Indeed, Yukelson (1997) refers to the following core components as necessary to build a successful team and develop a quality team culture: shared vision and unity of purpose; collaborative and synergistic teamwork; individual and mutual accountability; cohesive group atmosphere; team identity; open and honest communication; and peer helping and social support (also see Chapter Six). This collective approach is effective as it allows shared decision making and individuals are more likely to buy in to values. Sport team culture is viewed as learned shared team 'experiences, practices, routines, meanings, values, and understandings that players express and communicate' (Kao and Cheng, 2005, p. 23). Kidman and Davis (2007, p.12) suggest that without quality team culture, 'success, learning, and often winning are difficult' as the team culture addresses both the psychological and the social needs of athletes (Liu, 2001). It was evident that Guy attempted to support the collective approach in his focus on team culture. As Guy suggests:

> Team culture develops throughout a particular season or timeframe. It is not something that can be simply conjured up in the space of a two- or three-hour meeting.

According to Gross (2004), successful coaches make their expectations clear at the beginning of the season and, with their assistant coaches and players, establish team culture. Research suggests that if coaches are to establish a quality team culture and to get athletes to buy in to the culture, they need to involve athletes in creating these shared values (Kao and Cheng, 2005).

So, as a primary step to establish a *mutual* team culture with the university team, Guy decided that the squad should be involved in creating the goals, values and the strategies:

> ... to get the best out of the team, we set team goals and all players signed it.

To start the process of establishing this quality team culture, Guy gathered the university team together for an initial meeting at the start of the season. During this session the team and coaches co-constructed team goals, values, strategies for living up to those values, and rules and responsibilities. Players were then to sign the resulting co-constructed document to indicate their agreement to follow it for the season.

The process of co-construction began by splitting the team in to small discussion groups in which they considered a series of questions. First, to establish team goals, Guy asked what they aimed to achieve from the season. After the small groups of players provided numerous suggestions, Guy asked players to vote on the six areas they thought were most important to progress this season. These six areas then became the teams' goals for the season.

Team Goals

- Gain promotion from Midlands Conference 2A.
- Get to the final of our university competition.
- Incorporate and develop a team atmosphere through training and games.
- End the season with a sense of team and self-achievement.
- Have fun.
- Have individual training sessions for a minimum of three times per week.

Although many coaches co-construct or set goals for the team, often these goals are put into place with minimal consideration as to how they will be achieved and what values are required for the team to fulfil these goals. On the process of setting goals Guy indicates the importance of setting values simultaneously with goals as he suggests setting goals without values is:

> ... blind labour ... values are required to underpin the behaviour necessary to achieve the goals. The importance of establishing values, in my eyes, is for the purpose of underpinning and supporting the team's goals with a collective, shared point of reference for what our team hopes to incarnate. What makes a mere group of people a team is both a shared vision and interdependency, but establishing goals alone is not enough. Constructing a list of values acts almost as an informal morals and beliefs system, with the hope that the behaviour exhibited in our particular social world of basketball has a domino effect on how we conduct ourselves when not directly in the presence of the team. It is desired that their basketball experience is simply a microcosm for their actions in wider society.

Thus to create and prioritise team values and strategies for living up to these values, the team went through the same process for the team goals and came up with the following.

Team Values

- Inclusion – value everyone's role.
- Work hard and give maximum effort.
- Show respect.
- Have trust in and loyalty to the team.
- Have a winning mentality.
- Show dedication/commitment.

Strategies

- Be on time.
- Use positive reinforcement
- One person talks at a time.
- Always ask for help if needed.
- Mentally and physically prepare for each training session and games.
- Listen and learn.

Guy thought this was a useful process for the team, as players were empowered to develop mutual directions for the team. On the other hand, the assistant coach of the university team argues about the value of the time it took to develop these formal cornerstones of team culture:

> I don't always think these culture sessions are the best idea; sometimes you just need to play. It takes away actual playing time.

This incongruity became an additional factor in Guy's reflection and highlights the difference in coaching approaches as Guy thought these sessions were 'very beneficial'. However, Guy responds to the assistant coach's concerns:

> I was very careful in my planning to ensure that these sessions did not take away from physical practice time … in fact, they actually added to what we did on the court, and took place on days we did not have access to our training facility.

In Guy's continued self-reflection of his coaching, he highlights one of his concerns in implementing and maintaining the values the team had identified:

> Clearly in order for these values to be effective, frequent reinforcement and reminder of the team culture is required so everyone can be accountable but, more importantly, so that the athletes feel like the exercise in constructing it was not a worthless one. Upon reflection, I definitely could

have done more to strengthen the impact of these values via both subtle and direct reference to them. We also did not define exactly what the values *mean*—we only came up with buzz words such as 'inclusion', 'dedication' and 'respect' to name a few. But these words are likely to have different connotations for different people.

The final part of the co-construction process involved identifying a set rules and responsibilities that the team should live by to govern their behaviour. These rules and responsibilities were to action the values and strategies and aim towards the team goals. Two external, quite controversial responsibilities from the previous year were kept: that is, the freshers (rookies) were responsible for washing and distributing both the 'kit' (uniform) and 'medibag' (first aid kit). The other rules and responsibilities were created by the team as follows.

Rules and Responsibilities

- Any player late for practice gets 16 sidelines for every minute late. Cut-off point is five minutes.
- Any player who misses practice with no prior reason misses the following game.
- Table officials—a free-throw shoot-out will be held at training to decide the table officials for the ladies' basketball home fixtures. The last two players in the competition will have this responsibility.
- Referees are elected for each game.
- Players pay £2 per game—home and away.
- Everyone will chip in with after-game responsibilities before getting changed.

Players believed that through the process of developing goals, values, strategies and rules and responsibilities they had developed a 'strong team culture'. The values and strategies helped them to:

> … know how they should act and that means there is no problem with discipline in the team.

Players were observed to be living up to the set rules and values for the season. For example, when a player arrived late for training he, without talking to anyone, started his sidelines. He was observed at the following practice to be 15 minutes early. Players also spoke about sayings they had created together, such as '1, 2, 3, defence, huddles, clapping in drills', and behaviours that they thought were a strong part of their team culture (based on the values of *respect* and *inclusion*). However, players who were new to the team felt that team members were not living up to the value of *inclusion*. The external factors affecting the structure of the team, namely that this team shared players with other university teams, may have made it more difficult to live up to this value and Guy struggled to deal with this. I observed that in general players struggled to understand their role within the bigger club system due to this exchange of players. It is difficult to form a team culture when players come and go as they are selected or deselected from other club teams.

However, with both of Guy's teams, players who played for the national league side alongside the university team (largely the older players in the university team) collectively established team player roles. Such roles were determined in the national league side through focus groups where player roles were discussed using the same method as was used for establishing team values. Clearly, then, in implementing his athlete-centred approach Guy encouraged athlete input, in contrast to many coaches who continue to define players' roles and take ownership and responsibility away from them. I observed Guy enabling the players to define each of their roles. The following example shows how the team determined players' roles; players signed these role sheets to demonstrate that they accepted their role in the team.

Player Roles (Determined by the Team)
- Energy
- Rebound
- Get out and run on the fast break
- Hustle
- Knock down open shots
- Spark defensive stops
- Penetration
- Calm attitude
- Be positive
- Defensive leader

All players within focus groups from the national league side indicated that they understood their role. For example, one player comments:

> I feel very much part of the team with large role; I shoot rebound and play a big guy's spot.

However the men who played solely for the university (largely the younger players, freshers) had not gone through the process of establishing team roles; therefore they felt their role was ambiguous. Observing their response, Guy notes:

> Based on feedback that the guys submit each week the national league players wanted more clarity of their role; other more pressing issues came out of the university side feedback, therefore players' roles have not yet been addressed.

Bray, Beauchamp, Eys and Carron (2005) suggest players who do not understand their role will be less satisfied, whereas players with clear roles experience less competitive state anxiety and are more cohesive. Interestingly I noted evidence of a lack of attention to the value *respect*, in a club whose culture has been that the rookies need to *earn* their right to play on the team. So despite the roles being established, the senior players had a stronger influence on decisions. When asked about this issue in the focus group, the university first years (freshers) said:

> I don't feel like a player on the team ... my role in this team is to wash the 'kit'.
> I am a bench player; I don't have a clear team role.

Guy reflects on these comments:

> Greater clarity was needed in differentiating between *roles* and *responsibilities*. Perhaps due to time constraints or possibly due to some of our players not feeling as [much] part of the team as others, I believe that some of our athletes misinterpreted these terms and felt as if their role was simply to 'wash the kit'.

According to Maslow's hierarchy of needs, individuals must feel a sense of belonging to a team and have self-esteem (Whitmore, 2002). If players who are new to the programme within the university team are to progress to this point in the hierarchy, clear roles must be collectively established for them. These players must also be provided the opportunity to openly express their views (Andrews, 2000) so that senior players do not dominate team discussions. Providing such opportunity may involve more than Guy saying in team culture sessions, 'Has anyone got suggestions?' Instead, an approach identified in educational literature (Biggs, 2006) as effective in gaining feedback is to use more group discussions, allowing all group members to discuss ideas then give feedback as a group.

As Guy says about the process he followed with his team:

> During the process of putting the values together, there was little conflict as I don't think they had experienced anything quite like it before. In particular, two of the more senior players commented afterwards that they really did not know what to expect and didn't question the process. Therefore conflict probably would have been beneficial—it would have strengthened and clarified the statement that we made.

From my observations the value of 'one person talks at a time' worked most of the time. However, the person speaking was often the head coach, the assistant coach or a senior player. This tendency may point to the perceived power and leadership of these roles.

To enable team values to be practised it is important to discuss the leadership amongst the team. Leadership is an ongoing process where all members have the opportunity to assist the team to adapt to changing situations. Theoretically every team member may be a leader (Kogler, 2001). Teams have both formal leaders (i.e. the coach or team captain) and informal leaders (Heifetz and Laurie, 1997; Loughead and Hardy, 2004). As Neubert (1999) explains it, informal leaders are individuals who are not designated as leaders within the organisation hierarchy but influence others around them. According to Loughead, Hardy and Eys (2005), both formal and informal leaders play two important functions: task functions (i.e. aiding the group to achieve its goals) and social functions (i.e. satisfying group needs). Individuals on Guy's team with longer tenure within the teams were viewed by players as taking leadership roles, consistent with the findings of previous studies (e.g. Loughead et al., 2005; Rees and Segal, 1984; Yukelson, Weinberg, Richardson and Jackson, 1983). The reason players gave for senior players holding leadership roles was that they were more 'experienced'. However, that experience need not translate into stronger leadership qualities as Guy recognises:

> The [senior players] have only taken a leadership role and they are only more vocal on court because they have been here for longer ... there are players coming through with much better leadership skills and that are much better players but they don't get a say because they are in the first year and are less confident to speak up.

Putting aside these somewhat controversial issues, interestingly the players appreciated the purpose of the values and extended their application to player selection. They suggested in the interviews that the 'team should be selected by who is working hardest in training'. Some players thought that 'this does not always happen' and 'they should get a say in team selection'. First years within the programme thought they were not given a fair chance, both 'to voice their views and in selection'. To give players a say in team selection, a mutually agreed team selection policy may be adopted in future. This way of practising *inclusion* would enhance the true intention of the values and enable the team to develop in mutually agreed directions. Initially such a shared approach to selection could be primarily adopted in training and then, if it proved successful, it could be adapted to operate in competitive games as well. Such a concept is quite controversial amongst coaches in general, with many feeling that selection is the coaches' responsibility. In a true athlete-centred, humanistic coaching environment, however, players and coaches together should decide on selection.

In summary, it was evident that once the team values were established, Guy met with some teething problems in monitoring and implementing them, making it difficult to further develop his changed approach as he had intended. According to Andrews (2000) if a successful team is to be developed, individuals need to be able to speak their minds freely. Players who were new to the programme felt 'overlooked' because the coach:

> ... knows how older players play already therefore picks them and new players haven't had [a] chance to prove themselves.

So, as Guy attempts to implement his desired philosophy, his previous experience has superseded his ability to make that change, perhaps because he reverted back to old habits (Hadfield, 2005). Guy reflected on this observation, as he always did, and appreciates the feedback that can contribute to his continuing work to develop his culture. The power constructs had never really been considered prior to this project. Coaches' power relationships will be addressed further in the next section (also see Chapter Twelve).

The Process of Enabling Athletes

Traditional (coach-centred) coaching has not really focused on the athlete, environment or task. Coaches have been known to simply tell athletes what goal to achieve and which game plan to run. Thus athlete-centred, humanistic coaching is an evolving paradigm that challenges the traditional practices in coaching where coaches hold total power and control over the athletic environment. Athlete-centred coaching utilises steps similar to those of the Ecological Task Analysis model (Burton and Davis, 1996):

1. establishing mutual goals and directions (e.g. coach and athletes);
2. allowing athlete choice and control in the sporting environment;
3. manipulating variables within the sport environment to facilitate athlete performance; and
4. providing instruction (Kidman and Davis, 2007).

Guy has begun to include most of these steps in his coaching.

To follow these steps, a successful leader needs an understanding of the power dynamic between the influencer and the follower (Crust and Lawrence, 2006; van Kippenberg and Hogg, 2003). One of my passions is the power constructs that are displayed and influence others. Power is described as the ability to influence the behaviours of others and is considered to be group centred, as it rarely belongs to one person. A coach's power can often supersede what the athlete wants (Laios, Theodorakis and Garlianos, 2003). In relation to this perceived power, I asked the players within focus groups about Guy's power relation in the team. They justified his power because they perceived him to have expert knowledge:

> He is very knowledgeable ... he has won a BUSA [British Universities Sport Association] championship.

This expert power can assist or hinder the relationships in the team as the players say:

> [Guy] has power over [our assistant coach] and controls what he does.

Guy was observed using reward power as described by Laios et al. (2003). He frequently told players, 'You want to make the team, [player name], show me how much you want to make the team', or would reward players with minutes of court time if they were living up to the values and putting the effort in. It is quite common for the traditional, coach-centred coaches to use reward power, which fits within their punishment and reward systems. As Guy was a product of a culture with such coaches, it is no surprise that he has fallen into using a reward approach. However, it also should be acknowledged that there is a time and a place to use rewards to enhance a goal that has been set, as long as it has been established as a mutual goal or encourages athlete success.

It seems (as mentioned in a discussion on team culture above) that the senior players on the university team were perceived to have positional power, as it is described by Laios et al. (2003), over less experienced players in the team. This perceived positional power may have contributed to the first year players' additional duties such as 'taking the kit to be washed', their lack of a clear team role and their own view that 'experienced players don't have duties, whereas I have to take the kit to be washed'. Such perceptions put the first years in a position of lower power from the start, despite Guy's suggestion that 'some of these players have better leadership skills than some more experienced players'. In this position they experienced a form of intimidation based on the traditional positions on the team. For example, some first year players felt '... talked down to by senior players'.

To overcome such tensions, it may help to share additional duties among team members rather than allocating them solely to first year players. Don Tricker in Chapter Eleven provides an example of how he dealt with the senior players on his national softball team, the Black Sox:

> We have always viewed our bus trips as learning environments. However, this was tested on our first tour when some of the senior players decided that they were going to introduce a ranking system when sitting on the bus. They decided that because of their status they would sit at the back of the bus as they understood [the senior players of] the All Blacks did. We let it go for a couple of days, then we sat down with the senior players and talked to them about it. 'Okay, why are we doing this?' 'Oh, because the All Blacks do it.' 'So, we are followers are we, we are just doing this because someone else does it? I thought we wanted to be trendsetters, why are we following everyone else?' We then asked how we could win

without the younger members of the team who were sitting at the front of the bus. It was acknowledged that we couldn't. Then I asked why then were they treated differently? How were we going to leverage off each other's knowledge and experience when we did not sit together? The following day the ranking system was removed by the athletes and the bus trips returned to the required learning environment.

So in the interests of making the values of *inclusion* and *respect* an active part of the team culture, an understanding of these perceived 'power plays' occurring on the team would have benefited Guy's coaching. Since Guy's participation in this project, I have seen evidence of his understanding of these various roles and he continues to reflect on how to overcome the related issues and enable shared power. It is a difficult construct, but Guy has suggested that he values the challenge of implementing it in his future teams.

It is important for Guy and players to mutually agree on a way forward. Guy states he aims 'to build leaders'; however, to achieve this, the coach has to enable athlete independence (Hinkson, 2000). To this end, in training, instead of being prescriptive (i.e. previously 'what I say goes'), the coach might adopt more small-group player-led drills, with players providing feedback to other team members. This shared leadership may also be adopted to fulfil athletes' perceived need for individuals to take a social leadership role (Burke et al., 2006).

Some Other Coaching Practices

As part of this action research project, Guy became aware of the games approach of TGfU. As his particular concern for this project was with team culture, he made the deliberate decision to focus less on TGfU. However, he reasons that TGfU has a place in his coaching as one way to deal with the continued need for players to begin to make their own decisions:

Attempting to integrate TGfU into training was a challenging task, but one that I feel was necessary due to what I observed during our games. It appeared to me that on the practice floor, working individually, we had players with a relatively good level of skill in certain areas, but the application of this skill, and particularly the decision making, left a bit to be desired. For example, I noticed that players had a tendency to look [in] my direction in games when they faced a dilemma, which is a counterproductive habit which shows a severe over-reliance. It is a players' game, not a coaches' one, and players need to learn to think for themselves.

Another important tool to help decision making and organise a team culture is questioning. About his attempts to question, Guy says:

> My use of questioning has evolved over time. At first I used questioning simply for interaction purposes, to ensure that I had the athletes' attention and to gauge their responsiveness to my overall approach. With experience and learning, I'm now better at asking more open questions that promote higher order thinking and do not simply ask the athlete to make a 'yes' or 'no' distinction. For example, I find asking questions such as 'So what could we do defensively when the ball is in the corner, if we are in a 2–3 zone?' effective in stimulating some possible strategies and solutions that perhaps I haven't even thought of. Furthermore, when athletes are probed and approached in this way, it reinforces the ownership aspect that is important.

Interestingly the players did not perceive Guy as using questioning a great deal:

> [Guy] dictates what they do [and] uses little questioning.

Certainly questioning or TGfU practices was minimal during the training under observation, yet perhaps the players did not notice the extensive use of questioning and athlete-centred practices I observed during coach–athlete individual consultations. During these times, Guy examined player requirements above the needs of basketball. For example, he asked players:

> How is your work going?
> How is everything going this year?
> Are you finding time to fit everything in?
> Are you content with everything at the moment?

Such questions demonstrated Guy's intended holistic approach to player development. In this area, I observed interesting and humanistic communication with the players.

Athlete-centred, humanistic coaching revolves around sound communication. Based on his experience, Guy rates communication as one of the most important coaching strategies:

> I have had coaches who were tactically excellent; however they could not communicate it. The best coaches are good communicators.

Guy reflects on his communication, as he really wants to work on developing rapport with the players:

> I have learned a lot this year. I have an assistant coach [on the University side]—he is a really good listener, he has been really useful for the team: if you speak to him, if it's not his time to speak he will listen, it's a two way

thing. I felt one of my biggest mistakes last year was I didn't develop that rapport with individual players until really halfway through the season and by that point you know they had formed opinions on me and I had formed opinions on them. Although a mistake is not a mistake if you learn from it, it is just something that happens. I went to the [Director of Basketball] this year and said, 'I need more time with the guys. We need more than one session a week to develop a relationship we as coaches have to become accustomed to players and players have to become accustomed to us as coaches.'

Although Guy feels he has developed interpersonal relationships and feels that he has built rapport with players, the players themselves wanted a bit more:

[Guy] needs to develop and encourage team cohesion outside of games more, the social side, and not be so against going socialising as a team.

On socialising, Guy felt that it was inappropriate to go out with the team and that players would be distracted from working on their basketball. In contrast, some players thought the team would be stronger if members 'socialised together'. Burke et al. (2006) suggest the coach need not be the one who takes on a social leadership role: either a formal social leader can be elected or it could be an informal role taken by an emergent leader.

Implementing a More Athlete-centred Approach

In this action research project, there was a difference between Guy's observed leadership behaviour and players' perceived needs. Therefore, it was suggested that Guy needs to collectively define his role within the team based on player needs. The process of doing so might involve team culture sessions that follow the same method as was used in defining player roles.

I also observed a difference between Guy's perceived leadership behaviour and his actual leadership behaviour. Many coaches fail to self-reflect on their coaching behaviour and how it might affect their athletes. A beneficial method to aid self-reflection is to visually record the coach's match and training behaviour (see Chapter Fourteen), thereby providing the coach with a visual record to use in self-reflecting on adopted behaviours and the athletes' responses.

When asked whose needs were being served during training and whether the needs of winning were overshadowing the needs of players, including their needs for development and growth, he responded:

We need to recognise that development and growth comes first, and winning should be viewed as the byproduct of these things.

Such ongoing dilemmas prompt Guy to self-reflect on his philosophy while coaching. It was evident from his continued attempt to be self-aware that Guy demonstrates strong emotional intelligence (see Chapter Twelve), which is needed to make changes. Frequently coaches behave based on how they have been coached and do not see how their behaviour is affecting their players' development. A critical friend may aid in any self-reflection, as Guy states on the basis of his engagement in the action research process:

> I think any coach would benefit from having an objective observer cast a critical eye on their coaching process. It's interesting to look back to the time of the study and reflect on how some things have changed. However, if there wasn't the opportunity for someone to come in, it wouldn't be possible for that type of retrospection.

From the players I also gathered some evidence regarding how they adapted to a more athlete-centred approach. They were highly satisfied with Guy's more holistic focus, preferring it over the solely physical focus that they had experienced in the past. Comments on this topic include:

> I learned fundamentals, identified weaknesses, coaches push us to develop.
> I have developed under [Guy] more mentally and emotionally than physically.
> I enjoy having [Guy] as our coach, sessions are of a high intensity and are enjoyable.
> We feel we are achieving our goals and we are on track.
> I have matured mentally, emotionally and physically.
> He dictates, but if someone has an idea he will listen and may take it into consideration.

The players also identify some strategies for Guy to work on to enhance team cohesion and an athlete-centred environment:

> There have been times when people haven't contributed to the team and there have maybe been times when they could have helped out but weren't given the chance, but that's basketball. Coaches need to make sure that everyone is equal.

After I finished the assignment and became player manager, he requested the opportunity to work with me on mental skills with the players, still as part of the action research project to implement his athlete-centred approach. Through Guy's various learnings, he became more aware of how important the psychological edge is for players to develop. He also aimed to develop players holistically and recognised the importance of integrating psychological skills into his players' preparation and game:

> There were two primary reasons behind our willingness to recognise the importance of mental skills in our overall approach towards development. Firstly, it is my philosophy that athletes must be developed holistically, that they must be challenged and stimulated intellectually, and that improvement must be looked at from more than just one perspective. Secondly, the emerging theme in our season was an inability to close out close games, which we suggested was linked to psychological factors such as coping with pressure and playing with confidence in the fourth quarter. This consideration was based on athlete feedback, and their responsiveness to the sessions informed how they were progressed.

Many coaches associate poor or inconsistent performances with mental weakness or a lack of mental skills, failing to consider players' lifestyle demands (e.g. home life, work demands), and dive in with the suggestion that players need to work on the mental side of their game. In doing this coaches sometimes miss the real issues that are affecting players' performances. Through his individual meetings (as mentioned above), Guy built a strong rapport with players. In speaking with players in these sessions about issues over and above the realms of basketball, Guy demonstrated a sound holistic understanding of their needs. From my own role of observing and feeding into these discussions I was also able to build rapport with players. Along with lifestyle issues, a recurring theme was that players perceived a need to develop greater mental toughness. In addition, Guy identified players during games and in training who were using negative self-talk out loud, with statements such as 'That's rubbish' and 'What the hell'. He was keen to help players deal with stresses of the game and reduce their negative self-talk.

To address these issues a series of mental skills sessions was integrated into training and pre-match preparation. First, Guy and I gathered information about players' mental game by meeting the team and asking players about what they felt the issues were—when they felt stressed and what they might do to deal with these stresses. The players came up with issues similar to those Guy had highlighted such as negative self-talk, their routines and lucky items of clothing, and their need to leave negative thoughts in the changing rooms.

We gave all the players notebooks in which they were to record their reflections—both positive and negative—on games and training, and set weekly goals. Over the next four weeks a number of mental skills were integrated into physical practice including: imagery, pre-performance routines, cognitive restructuring (rephrasing negative thoughts) and parking negative thoughts (some players using the physical signal of removing their warm-up shirt and leaving it in their bag and zipping it up, with the suggestion that all negative thoughts were left behind before they went on to the court). Mental skills were also worked on in training through conditioning practices with different playing scenarios (e.g. we are in the last five minutes of the game, we are down on score and we need these free throws to be in with a chance).

Symbolism was another factor that Guy thought important for players to develop mental strength and for creating a team vision. He asked all players to bring something that was really significant to them to a training session. Players brought items such as photos, newspaper cuttings and CDs. These items went into a box, which became a symbol of 'what, who and why we play basketball' and was taken to every game. This box reinforced the quality team culture and Guy thought that it unified the purpose for the team: 'We are playing for everything and everyone in the box'. Players were allowed to add items to the box throughout the season, and it was referred to throughout the campaign.

Finally Guy transcribed all the positive statements that players had said within training and mental skills sessions and stuck them up in the changing room. These statements were then used in pre-game pep talks, adding to the team culture and empowering all players as they were all involved at some point in creating these statements.

Some Challenges of an Athlete-centred Approach

Effective leadership is not so much about the way the power is applied but about the style that is adopted (Barnes, 2002). In regard to whether his own coaching style is autocratic or democratic, Guy states:

> ... due to the situation-specific nature of coaching it is a continuum; I cannot say I am one or the other.

A largely autocratic style was observed during training, which according to Barnes (2002), does not allow for personal growth as it reduces initiative and creativity. To enhance personal growth, a more democratic style is required. Interestingly, contrary to Lam's (2007) research finding that basketball players prefer an autocratic style, the university players within Guy's team preferred a democratic style. It is therefore important for a coach to establish what particular athletes' needs are and adopt a leadership style in line with those needs.

As Rick Humm identifies (Chapter Twelve), knowing how to read people is a key to athlete-centred coaching. Achieving such *empathy* is something that Guy wants to continue to work on. Lombardo (1987) suggests leaders who are empathetic never lose sight of the experience their athletes are undergoing. Providing additional evidence for Guy's good use of empathy, his players say:

[Guy] is always there if we need to talk to him, and he respects our education and knows our individual needs.

It is possible that Guy has developed this empathy from his own similar experiences in reaching his current coaching position, as he reflects:

I have been through it so I want them to get the most they can. I have been through all the stages: as a first year I played for the second team, then went on to play university first team and played for the national league side, was training with the BBL [British Basketball League] squad; I have also co-coached the first team. Now I am teaching some of the players in class and coaching the national league and university seconds so I know what the guys are experiencing as I have seen it from all angles.

Another challenge that Guy raises is that:

... players do not like to be put out of their comfort zone as there is a period of time when they are disillusioned ... however they need to work through this period to get back to a state of equilibrium.

According to Piaget, being taken out of our comfort zone is a major influence on our development (Egan and Kauchak, 2004). It takes the developmental stage from equilibrium to disequilibrium which ultimately assists our understanding and development and ability to adapt to different situations—qualities that are vital in the sporting context.

The challenge for Guy is his perception that he cannot afford the time required for players' experience of disequilibrium. Nonetheless if a coach is to implement the philosophy of player development, he or she must allow players time to adapt. For Guy, influences against the inclusion of such adaptation time include the external factors and the players' culture that impacted on his understanding and practice of sport coaching in regard to 'winning' over 'development'. His approach becomes more difficult in the context of the 'winning at all cost' attitudes of many sports teams.

When the main focus is winning, Loughead and Hardy (2004) suggest, the development of athletes' leadership is largely ignored. According to Weiss and Friedrichs (1986) and Cannella and Rowe (1995), institutional issues often affect the coach's leadership behaviours. Where coaches value winning above all in coaching their teams, they sometimes promote this value at the expense of their own ethical behaviour and moral development of athletes (Dodge and Robertson, 2004). Moreover, the adoption of a 'winning at all costs attitude', with its associated neglect of athletes' needs and sabotaging of the pursuit of excellence, leads sport participation to degenerate into a means to an end (Boxill, 2003, p. 45). On this issue, Guys says:

I think most coaches would be more comfortable being accountable for themselves, without external pressures. However, it is the reality of sport that we are judged against measures that we cannot always control. At every club there will be institutional pressures and part of a coach's development is to learn to deal with these and make sure everyone is on the same page.

About his own struggle with the developmental philosophy, Guy says:

Coaching in an athlete-centred way makes sense; however, it's not always possible. The reason I say that is most people have been coached in a coach-centred way so they are not used to that approach but the pay-off can be huge. Individuals are also assessing my performance; if I am just sitting around and the players are leading everything, they are going to think, 'Who the hell is this guy?' With this approach you are sacrificing short-term results for long-term gains, although we cannot afford these losses. I mean, I would let the team select the team and play and develop everyone if winning was not such a big issue. When the game is on the line you need your best five, and this is how we have to do it. Anyway if you are going to empower athletes, should you not ask them how they want to be lead?

Lim and Cromartie (2001) suggest that, due to the situational demands of coaching, sport coaches have to be flexible to lead effectively. On the subject of the extent of Guy's flexibility, a typical response from the players is:

... that sometimes [Guy] needed to put the plan down and just play.

Guy's response to this feedback is:

... structured is the way I am and you should not present yourself as something you are not. At times I think I am a bit too laid back.

In his view, a major challenge in athlete-centred coaching is that 'being self-assured' is a key element to being a successful leader and that, without self-knowledge, the coach cannot really put himself or herself in any situation. Guy exhibits the essence of self-assurance in saying, 'If I am annoyed I will show I am'. That is, controlling emotions is important but being human is also part of being a coach. This self-knowledge and knowledge of emotion may relate to emotional intelligence (Mayer, Salovey and Caruso, 2004), which I have already noted was a strength of Guy's reflections on his various emotions experienced while coaching.

It has been suggested that leaders with high emotional intelligence deal with potentially difficult situations more effectively (Hayashi, 2005; Thelwell, Lane, Weston and Greenlees, 2008). Players thought that they dealt with conflict in the team and it was not really an issue; perhaps the lack of conflict was due to the clear team values and rules created at the start of the season. However, an example of an observed conflict arose when a player swore at Guy during practice. The assistant coach suggested his own approach in a similar situation would have been:

> ... a no nonsense policy; I would say, 'If you are acting like that you are out'.

Guy, on the other hand, asked the player to think about his actions following training, and later in the day the player came and apologised to the coach and they discussed his actions. In regard to this issue Guy relates:

> I won't yank someone out of the gym and tell them to go home. I find that sitting someone down and having a firm but compassionate word for me always does the trick ... when you sit them down and talk to them you see the real person.

Guy's response, as well as again indicating how his philosophy, values and vision differ from those of his assistant, highlights his emotional intelligence and self-assurance. It also provides a valuable example of how humanistic, athlete-centred coaching is always a challenge. Every situation, every person needs to be dealt with equally and fairly, but differently according to their needs.

Conclusion

The purpose of the original project was to conduct a critical analysis and provide feedback to a basketball head coach, examining his leadership styles and practices in relation to his followers. However, it evolved into taking a player manager role for the team and following and aiding the team's progress throughout the season. It was a great learning experience for both Guy and me. The changes he made and his reflections on his coaching were rewarding. In considering what he experienced through this project, Guy states:

> I found being asked to these type of self-reflective exercises increased my awareness of what I was doing, and actually made me aware of a number of other important factors involved within leadership.

Guy managed to implement a team culture with values and goals that the athletes bought into and practised. As discussed in this chapter, Guy continues to work on a number of aspects of coaching—just as every coach has areas that need further work, indicating why the need for continued development is universal. The highlight of the research project, though, was seeing Guy's open-mindedness and his ability to reflect on issues, accept them or pose a sound argument for why he chooses to be his sort of coach. Although he came across a number of challenges when implementing an athlete-centred approach, he always kept the needs of the players at the forefront. As Guy concludes:

> ... if you want to coach a group or a team successfully, should you not ask them how they want to be coached?

References

Andrews, A. (2000). *Finding the Square Root of a Banana: A team story*. Auckland: Yellow Brick Road.

Barnes, P. (2002). *Leadership with Young People*. Wiltshire, UK: Russell House.

Biggs, J. (2006). *Teaching for Quality Learning at University*. New York: McGraw-Hill Education.

Boxill, J. (2003). Introduction: The moral significance of sport. In J. Boxill (Ed.) *Sport Ethics: An anthology*. Malden, MA: Blackwell.

Bray, S.R., Beauchamp, M.R., Eys, M.A., & Carron, A.V. (2005). Does the need for role clarity moderate the relationship between role ambiguity and athlete satisfaction? *Journal of Applied Sport Psychology, 17*, 306–318.

Burke, C.S., Stagal, K.C., Klein, C., Goodwin, G.F., Salas, E., & Halpin, S.M. (2006). What type of leadership behaviors are functional in teams? A meta-analysis. *The Leadership Quarterly, 17*, 288–307.

Burton, A.W., & Davis, W.E. (1996). Ecological task analysis utilizing intrinsic measures in research and practice. *Human Movement Science, 15*, 285–314.

Cannella, A.M., & Rowe, W.G. (1995). Leader capabilities, succession and competitive context: A study of professional baseball teams. *Leadership Quarterly, 6*, 69–88.

Crust, L., & Lawrence, I. (2006). A review of leadership in sport: Implications for football management. *Athletic Insight, 8*, 4.

Dodge, A., & Robertson, B. (2004). Justifications for unethical behavior in sport: The role of the coach. *Canadian Journal for Women in Coaching, 4*, 4.

Egan, P., & Kauchak, D. (2004). *Educational Psychology: Windows on classrooms*. Upper Saddle River, NJ: Pearson Merrill Prentice Hall.

Gross, R.H. (2004). The coaching model for educational leadership principals. *The Journal of Joint and Bone Surgery, 86*, 2082–2084.

Hadfield, D. (2005). The change challenge: Facilitating self-awareness and improvement in your athletes. In L. Kidman (Ed) *Athlete-centred Coaching: Developing inspired and inspiring people*. Christchurch: Innovative Print Communications.

Hayashi, A. (2005). Emotional intelligence and outdoor leadership. *Journal of Experimental Education, 27*, 333–335.

Heifetz, R.A., & Laurie, D.L. (1997). The work of leadership. *Harvard Business Review*, *46*, 124–134.

Hinkson, J. (2000). *The Art of Team Coaching*. Toronto: Warwick.

Kao, S.F., & Cheng, B.S. (2005). Assessing sport team culture: Quantitative and qualitative approaches. *International Journal of Sport Psychology*, *36*, 22–38.

Kidman, L., & Davis, W. (2007). Empowerment in coaching. In W. Davis & G.D. Broadhead (Eds), *An Ecological Approach to Human Movement: Linking theory, research and practice* (pp121-139). Champaign, IL: Human Kinetics.

Kogler, S.E. (2001). Team leadership. In P.G. Northouse (Ed.), *Leadership: Theory and practice* (2nd ed.), pp. 161–187. Thousand Oaks, CA: Sage.

Laios, A., Theodorakis, N., & Garlianos, D. (2003). Leadership and power: Two important factors for effective coaching. *International Sports Journal*, *7*, 150–155.

Lam, E.T.C. (2007). Preferred and perceived leadership styles by NCAA basketball players. *Research Quarterly for Exercise and Sport, 78*, 107–114.

Lim, Y.J., & Cromartie, F. (2001). Transformational leadership, organizational culture and organizational effectiveness in sport organizations. *Sport Journal*, *4*, 2.

Liu, Y.M. (2001). Discussion on team culture. *Journal of Capital College of Physical Education*, *13*, 28-33, 60.

Lombardo, B.J. (1987). *The Humanistic Coach: From theory to practice*. Springfield, IL: Charles C. Thomas.

Loughead, T.M., Hardy, J., & Eys, M.A. (2005). The nature of athlete leadership. *Journal of Sport Behavior*, *29*, 142–158.

Loughead, T.M., & Hardy, J. (2004). An examination of coach and peer leader behaviours in sport. *Psychology of Sport and Exercise, 6,* 303–312.

Mayer, J.D., Salovey, P., & Caruso, D.R. (2004). Emotional intelligence: Theory, findings, and implications. *Psychological Inquiry*, *15*, 197–215.

Neubert, M.J. (1999). Too much of a good thing or the more the merrier? Exploring the dispersion and gender composition of informal leadership in manufacturing teams. *Small Group Research*, *30*, 635–646.

Rees, C.R., & Segal, M.W. (1984). Role differentiation in groups: A test of leadership role difference theory. *Journal of Sport Behavior*, *6*, 17–27.

Rowold, J. (2006). Transformational and transactional leadership in martial arts. *Journal of Applied Sport Psychology*, *18*, 312–325.

Schroeder, J.E. (2007). Aesthetic leadership. In J. Gosling and A. Marturano (Eds) *Key Concepts in Leadership Studies*, pp. 23–55. London: Routledge.

Thelwell, R.C., Lane, A.M., Weston, J.V., & Greenlees, I.A. (2008). Examining relationships between emotional intelligence and coaching efficacy. *International Journal of Sport Psychology*, *6*, 224–235.

van Kippenberg, D., & Hogg, M.A. (2003). *Leadership and Power: Identify processes in groups and organizations*. London: Sage.

Weiss, M.R., & Friedrichs, W.D. (1986). The influence of leader behaviors, coach attributes, and institutional variables on performance and satisfaction of collegiate basketball teams. *Journal of Sport Psychology, 8*, 332–346.

Whitmore, J. (2002) *Coaching for Performance: GROWing people, performance and purpose* (4th ed.). London: Nicholas Beardsley.

Yukelson, D. (1997). Principles of effective team building. *Journal of Applied Sport Psychology 9*(1): 73–96.

Yukelson, D., Weinberg, R., Richardson, P., & Jackson, A. (1983). Interpersonal attraction and leadership within collegiate sport teams. *Journal of Sport Behavior, 6*, 28–36.

And the trouble is, if you don't risk anything,
you risk even more. - Erica Jong

Truthfulness is the main element
of character. - Brian Tracy

When you make a mistake, don't look back at it long.
Take the reason of the thing into your mind and
then look forward. Mistakes are lessons of wisdom.
The past cannot be changed. The future is yet in
your power. - Hugh White

To be able to look back upon one's past life with
satisfaction is to live twice. - John Dalberg Actor,
English historian

Innovation is the one weapon
that can't be defended
against.—Sun Tzu

Chapter Ten

Mark Norton

Riccarton High School Boys' Senior Volleyball Team

The coaches featured in this book are using or have used a successful athlete-centred approach. This chapter focuses on one of them—a development coach, Mark Norton, who for this particular project coached the Boys' Senior Volleyball team at Riccarton High School in Christchurch, New Zealand. Mark Norton has coached various volleyball teams at the school, using what he saw as an athlete-centred approach to differing degrees. His interest in participating in this project was sparked by his desire to learn more about this coaching approach. My aims were to observe the evolution of both his approach to coaching and his team from the beginning of the season to the time of the National Championships.

To follow the evolution of Mark's coaching approach, I used an action research model by contributing to and managing this boys' secondary school volleyball team. Before the season started, Mark and I met to discuss the process of working together and my role as a researcher. I acted as a 'player manager', attended training sessions and games for the season and was a manager at the National Championships. The role of dealing with volleyball specifics was entirely Mark's. I noted that throughout the season, he used questioning and Teaching Games for Understanding (TGfU) to work on the boys' decision making skills. One further factor shaping the research was Mark's belief that gaining feedback is important to help him learn more about and improve his coaching and to strengthen his focus on making better players, consistent with his commitment to developing each person as a whole. Therefore my role was to observe and provide advice to Mark on the team culture and psychological aspects of the training and game for the athletes. Mark acted or did not act on my advice according to what he determined was appropriate. It was an extremely enjoyable time and a great research experience.

To collect data for Mark's process of implementing an athlete-centred approach, I interviewed him at length twice and we also chatted informally throughout the season. Two of the athletes, Luke Russell and Simon Kidman, were also interviewed. In addition, I held group interviews with the players during two different barbecues, during which the boys spoke about the team culture and the season in general. Audio recordings of interviews were transcribed verbatim and participant observation field notes were collected throughout the season.

When asked at the end of the season why he had decided to improve his coaching approach, Mark says:

> I have always wanted to have players who were empowered and could run themselves, but through doing this process I think I have learned that there is much more in it than what I was doing previously.

Along with his athlete-centred coaching repertoire of questioning and TGfU, Mark focused on ensuring a quality team culture (wairua). To this end, he mutually (i.e. together with the players) established, reinforced and revisited goals and values throughout the season. Promoting goals and values in these three ways was excellent in helping the boys to take ownership of and responsibility for their learning, decision making and team goals. Mark shared leadership to the extent of establishing a couple of mini groups but did not focus on this strategy extensively in developing his coaching repertoire. The other aspect of athlete-centred coaching practice that I observed Mark using was role rotation. Again he made only limited use of this strategy. It is important to note that, just as an athlete is encouraged to learn one new skill at a time, a coach who is learning new coaching skills should focus on mastering one before moving on to the next one.

In this chapter, Mark's philosophy of coaching, his process of establishing the team culture and a range of his coaching practices are presented. His techniques for empowering athletes are also discussed.

Mark's Philosophy of Coaching

During our interviews, Mark spoke about his philosophy for and his role in the volleyball team. The boys and their type of experience are his central focus, as he highlights:

> I want to create a positive, enjoyable and meaningful experience for the kids to be involved in. I want the team and the team mission to become a focus in the boys' lives. I also want to create good volleyballers and a team that plays quality volleyball. I suppose I like to use volleyball and physical activity as a vehicle to teach the kids about themselves, other people and how to effectively interact and function with others. That's how I treat my teaching of physical education also. Volleyball, a game hugely reliant on teamwork and one's teammates, lends itself to do this superbly. At the end of the day, if the kids have developed into better people, then I've been successful.

For this particular team, Mark decided that long-term development was important. To enable the boys to learn as much as possible from each other, he used a squad system, which meant creating two teams of even ability for the pre-season competitions on Monday nights. Mark believed the squad system would be the most effective way to develop the Riccarton High School volleyball programme. His ultimate goal was 'to have a really high quality top team and a team that would probably develop into a top team the following year'. After himself deciding to put the players into a squad arrangement, Mark gave the boys the responsibility for deciding how to run it and what direction to take. Although he contributed ideas, he regarded what the boys wanted as more important because 'They were the ones who had to do it'.

Once the squad system had been implemented for the pre-season, I asked Mark whether he thought his philosophy of formulating the squad system was working. He believed that the progress achieved to date indicated solid foundations had been laid for the future:

> They are playing some good volleyball, the consistency is not quite there yet, but they are showing signs of doing some really brilliant things ... we have not even looked at specific team systems or individual roles in terms of developing setters or hitters, we are just really working on all around skills at the moment. I think that everyone's all around skill level is improving ... my setters can hit the ball, can set the ball and everyone can do a bit of everything.

His philosophy of focusing on the boys and ensuring a good team environment was also working, Mark suggested, in that 'We are consistently getting all [team members] attending and the atmosphere they create in their trainings is great'.

Mark's Development as a Coach

Mark holds the position of physical education teacher at Riccarton High School. During his teacher training at the Christchurch College of Education, he was exposed to and influenced by the New Zealand Health and Physical Education curriculum (NZHPE). This curriculum has a philosophy of hauora (holistic well-being), which Mark has transferred into his physical education teaching and coaching philosophy.

Mark has a passion for volleyball and has been a New Zealand volleyball squad member on a number of occasions. He says that his coaching before this project was based on a similar coaching philosophy to the one outlined in the previous section but he had never explicitly thought about it or written it down. The very nature of his holistic, athlete-centred approach is in accordance with the notion of empowerment in coaching.

Mark suggests that his playing experience influenced his desire to try the athlete-centred style of coaching: 'I had some pretty clear goals of what I wanted to happen based on my own playing experience'. As his 'serious' volleyball playing days dwindled, he wanted to put more energy into volleyball coaching:

> I have always enjoyed coaching, but I have really enjoyed this team. This recent coaching experience is motivating me to put more of my energy into coaching volleyball rather than playing myself.

One of the real coaching skills in using an athlete-centred approach is the ability to 'read' people and situations. In Mark's view, one of his weaknesses lies in his limitations in this ability; for example, he finds it difficult to determine when to change a situation, when to address athletes' needs, when to discuss and when to be quiet. To learn how to 'read' people in the way that he wishes to, Mark suggests:

> I probably have to put myself in other people's shoes, and try to think from their perspective more. When listening I need to actually listen. There are all these road blocks to listening … for example, judging or thinking of a response rather than actually listening to the message they are giving and listen for meaning. That's part of listening too, reading [people].

When asked what he still needs to learn about his coaching, Mark says:

> … that's a hard question because you know what you know, you don't know what you don't know. Then there are things that you don't know that you don't know that you don't know them … I suppose it is endless. I experience more and more things and discover more things I need to learn.

The Process of Establishing a Quality Team Culture[1]

Quality team culture can be defined using Yukelson's (1997) components of team culture—namely, unity of purpose, individual and team accountability, teamwork, open and honest communication, positive atmosphere, and mutual trust. These components were trialled, maintained and reinforced with the team through Mark's athlete-centred approach. As noted above, he was already using many practices of an athlete-centred approach, but for this season his aim was to take it further by establishing and maintaining a quality team culture. Although the process of establishing the vision and values was lengthy, it was well worth the exercise. Mark believes that the team's wairua (a Maori word meaning oneness) contributed significantly to their success.

As a first step in establishing this quality team culture, Mark decided that the full

---

1 Much of this section has been used first in: Kidman, L. (2005) Athlete centred Coaching, and then later adapted into: Kidman, L. & Davis, W. (2007). Empowerment in coaching. In G.D. Broadhead & W.E. Davis (Eds), *Ecological Task Analysis: Understanding movement in context,* Champaign, IL: Human Kinetics.

squad should create the values to live by and the strategies to deliver the vision and values because:

> … I was disappointed with last year with the lack of development the boys achieved. They were a quality junior side but didn't make the required jump into senior volleyball very well. The development of a team culture was out of need. We needed to make more progress with their playing ability but also to re-create the motivation and passion for the game. That had disappeared. I am certain the latter was responsible [for the lack of development] and this was because of my neglect.

To start the process, Mark met with all interested boys who wanted to play volleyball. Eighteen boys, aged 15–18 years, trialled for the team. They formed a squad of two equal teams for the first term. Mark explains the rationale in this way:

> We wanted to have all the boys playing in the top grade because I thought to improve at all, they needed to be playing the top volleyball, even if they were out of their depth a little. So I split up what I thought was the leadership and ability and I tried to make two even teams, so they both would be able to hold their own, not necessarily win, but hold their own.

After the first term with the squad system, 'A' and 'B' teams were chosen in the second half of the season, but Mark indicated that those in the B team could still make the A team up until two weeks before the Canterbury Championships. The boys and Mark decided that the criteria for selection for the A team should be based equally on a player's skills and how they lived the values.

Initially the players were sceptical about the squad system. As Luke says, 'I think the older guys didn't respect the younger guys that much because we thought that they sort of just mucked around all the time'. Luke changed his mind after he saw how hard everyone on the squad worked. He reflects:

> I think it was really good keeping that huge squad and all training together. I think it brought everyone's level up quite a lot. That made it better when we did split up because we played the Bs and they actually challenged us. If we just split up into As and Bs, then the As would waste the Bs every time we played them and it wouldn't do them or us any good. But having close games made the Bs positive about things because they were beating us. It makes us all step back and see that we had to work a bit harder.

Simon also suggests that being part of a squad made him work harder:

> … it gives you more of [a] chance to get into the top teams …the teams are better so if you want to be challenged then you can train for the A

team and get more experience, but if you want just want to play socially; you can just play for the B team.

At the end of the season, Simon still valued the squad system. In his view, 'it makes you work harder because you want to get to the top team and have more fun trying to do that. It makes you attend training.'

As the team was compiled of two teams, a vision and team goals were established with the full squad. First, Mark gave each boy a homework book for writing decisions made during team trainings. To get them thinking about both dream and performance goals, Mark then asked, 'If you were at the end of season dinner and had to make a speech and talk to everyone about the sort of team that we are, what would be the things that you would like to be able to say?'

At first, because of the size of the squad, there was little evidence of interaction. It was obvious that due to comfort and confidence, the seniors had more to say than the junior members, who were hesitant and waited to see what their role in the whole process would be. The squad was curious about the input being asked of them as, even when Mark had been their coach previously, they had never contributed to the direction of a team in this way. Initially they did not understand or know their roles. As this was Mark's first attempt at developing an athlete-centred vision and values, there seemed to be a fair amount of experimenting and 'going with the flow' (which in itself fits an athlete-centred philosophy).

As would be expected of someone new to this process, Mark found it difficult to allow athletes to make their own decisions. However, he was conscious that he had to let the athletes speak and make these decisions if they were going to own the team vision and values. I noted that he made quite a few leading questions and statements but ultimately it was a team decision that the main mission goals were to:
- win six out of 10 Monday night games (with squad system);
- win the Canterbury Championships (once A team was selected, which the boys decided would occur two weeks before the championships);
- be in the top 10 teams at the Nationals;
- achieve a semi-final spot at the Nationals (a dream goal);
- be an exciting team to watch; and
- become known as a team who: never gives up; is the tightest; is mentally tough.

As the next step in this process, Mark explained that the boys needed to establish some values to live by. Providing them with a list of 30 values from Jeff Janssen's *Championship team building* (2002), he asked them to pick six values they considered to be important for the team, write down why they were important, and provide a definition of the value so that everyone would understand it in the same way.

At the next training session, Mark divided the 18 boys into groups of three (one senior player and two junior players) and asked each group to collate all of the values identified by the individual athletes and to pick out the six that they felt were the top priority. He then wrote the prioritised values of each small group on a whiteboard and the whole group discussed their meaning. Mark facilitated the discussion and contributed his ideas too. After much discussion and some debate, the team came up with six values for the volleyball team: respect, communication, cohesion, enjoyment, invulnerable and commitment (all worded and defined by the boys).

I thought this process was particularly difficult for Mark as he came to the discussion with his own preferred values for the team. Even though his views were included in the discussion, he seemed to 'bite his tongue' several times to ensure that the values finally chosen were the boys' decision. In this way Mark concentrated on enabling the athletes to contribute to major decisions rather than allowing the coach's power to supersede what the athletes want, as often happens. He also had to be careful not to exploit his social power as physical education teacher for many of the players. Just as the boys had to come to a consensus and go with the majority, so did Mark. He realised that his role was to facilitate the process and follow through with the consensus reached. His intentions are reflected in the views of both athletes interviewed, who identify the goals and values as the players' and regard them as stronger because of that. Luke says:

> We were the ones that made the values. Because they came from us, we respected them a bit more than if they were just given to us and someone says, 'This is how you've got to act'. It wouldn't have been the same.

Simon takes a similar view: 'The coach was in on it, but the kids did most of it. It's better because the coaches just don't make rules and the kids have things to say, so it's better to listen to everyone'.

The next step in establishing a vision and values was to come up with strategies to meet the goals. This time, Mark asked the boys to think about what strategies would ensure the values were practised. The same process was followed; in small groups the boys discussed and prioritised the strategies identified, and then made the final choice of strategies as a whole group. As a result, they committed to the following strategies to achieve their goals and live their values:

- talk constructively at appropriate times;
- take care of things outside volleyball so we can enjoy the game and our season;
- respect each other at all times;
- attend all trainings, physically, mentally and socially (be intense);
- remain positive no matter what;

- always demonstrate positive winning posture; and
- always be there for my teammates.

By about the fifth training session, the team had established the goals, values and strategies for the season. The whole process was enjoyable to watch. I had often wondered how this age group would react to such a process, but the enthusiasm of the boys (once they knew that Mark was going to follow through and monitor their decisions) highlighted to me that these young adults revelled in it. Because they were part of the decisions, they accepted their responsibilities to ensure that each item was followed.

Once the values, goals and strategies were established, the team decided that the they needed one short, precise vision statement to represent it. After much discussion and about two training sessions later, the team came up with 'Binding Together to be Better (B3)'. The boys also decided they needed a symbol of the team's vision, goals and values; to this end they chose a gluestick because it helps to bind things together. Mark bought three-sided gluesticks to match the B3 vision statement. Each boy wrote his name and the team values on the gluestick and carried it everywhere as the symbol of his team's volleyball campaign.

As a result of this process the boys created a tight group (one of their goals) that was well known within their school. To show their commitment (one of the values), they hung the gluesticks around their necks so that they could wear them around school and to volleyball.

The gluesticks became a significant element in the development of the quality team culture. Mark tells the story of the growing importance of this symbol:

> When they developed the values, it was really important for them to say how they were going to show the values, not only at volleyball and our training, but at school as well and in life in general. So, one of the things we ensured they do is not only bring their gluesticks to anything volleyball, but we want them to carry it on at all times in school, so after the first game with their gluesticks, I made sure I had mine in my pocket the whole time and then, I was like a cowboy, I would draw it on them and have them draw it back. If they didn't draw theirs, I would give them a bit of a hard time. They started catching on to that and they were then drawing it on me by the end. They were all trying to catch me out. One of the really cool things was that they decided that they would take them into their exams. So, they walked into their end-of-year exams, one of the first things they did was to sit down at the desk draw out their gluesticks and they put it on their desk in front of them … the others would look around and they would see each other pulling out their gluesticks and I guess they get that

sense of 'we are in this together'. I am sure it stems from it, I don't know, it is spiritual, but ...

A more widespread effect was that teachers and other students came to 'idolise' the gluesticks, as Simon explains:

> In a way, the year 9s respected us because we were wearing these gluesticks. An example was that last term we were sitting in the hall and a member of the team had a Stage Challenge Practice and they put all their gear down, including the gluestick. The year 9 kid went up and grabbed his gluestick and put it on and was walking around during lunchtime and thought he was cool. The gluestick really helped us. It wasn't just at volleyball, but at school everyone respected [us] and thought we were awesome.

Similarly Luke points to the schoolwide respect that the gluesticks brought them, as well as to their impact on team values:

> [The gluestick] was good, that was a way to reinforce the values. It brought all the values together. It was the way for our season and stuff. It reinforced it a bit more. It was really cool to see people wearing them at school. Everyone knew we were a team as well. Everyone knew that we are a pretty good team and that we were pretty close.

As the above accounts indicate, the boys were soon carrying the gluesticks everywhere, including into classes and external exams. The boys then decided that if someone was caught without the gluestick, then that player or coach would get a slit in the eyebrow (i.e. a shaved line through the hair of the eyebrow) as another symbol of the team values. The boys also decided that failing to tell the coach if they couldn't make it to training would also earn them a slit. Most boys were happy to take the slit for the team. Some, however, had some cultural issues about it and, after Mark held a team discussion, the boys changed the system. By this time, the coach's monitoring of the system was minimal because the boys owned the values so firmly.

Another part of this process was the creation of a poster that included all of the boys' photos, along with the vision, goals, strategies and values. At an official sign-off ceremony, all members of the team signed the poster as a type of contract that committed them to striving for the team's goals and adhering to its values. This 'contract' proved to be another binding element as, when issues arose, the boys and Mark would always remind individuals of what it committed them to: 'you signed that you agreed to these values'. As a coach, Mark feels that the boys took responsibility for the vision, values and strategies, with the poster.

From a player's perspective, Luke reaches similar conclusions about the role of the poster:

> … having the values there in place in writing everywhere, and saying them at trainings and stuff and yelling them out, you couldn't hide away from them. You just had to do them. I think that was different. Other coaches sort of say those things, but [in our team] you've got to do these things …

That the team saw signing the poster as binding in nature became evident after an incident where one of the boys did not live up to the values. This incident was raised in front of the team, which led to a discussion that demonstrated athlete decision making. The team expressed their concern about the boy's well-being because they thought that volleyball was good for his growth and development.

In reflecting on the process of reaching a decision, Mark notes first the team's concern for the boy's well-being:

> I thought this was an amazing moment: the boys recognising the work that being a member of the team was towards well-being and saying that they needed to let him stay with the team. On the other side there were the staunch protectors of the value commitment and decided that he had to be let go. This highlighted for me how important the team was to them personally.

Ultimately, however, they decided that by signing the poster he had agreed to the contract but he was not living the values so he must be asked to leave. Mark was given the responsibility of informing the boy of the team's decision, which proved to be another learning experience. In informing the boy, Mark had to remind himself of using the poster as a tool of accountability:

> … kind of sealing the deal. The other thing was that they could be held accountable to that if they weren't living up to it. I could say, well hang on, you developed this yourself, plus you just signed it. You signed it and said you were going to do this, what's the problem?

By this time the athletes were managing the direction of the team themselves, with his role largely comprising of instructing and focusing on the values.

For the season, the boys achieved all but their dream goal. They won Canterbury Championships and placed fifth at the Nationals. At the Nationals it was evident not only to the boys and the coach but also to opposing and observing teams that the wairua practised by the boys enhanced their play. The athleticism of the team was considered lower than that of many others yet they managed to beat more athletic teams. The boys, the coach and outsiders put their success down to the wairua they had created, symbolised by the gluestick they carried. Many a player and coach from other organisations wanted to know about the gluesticks. It became a talking point at the Nationals as well as back at school after the Nationals.

The initial squad system helped the team to formulate a mutual trust and practise the values, which were tested throughout the season through different situations. Some situations were simulated, as organised by Mark. Other situations arose spontaneously and Mark used them too to get the athletes to reflect on the values. For the boys to take ownership of the team culture, they had to live the values. Mark notes how the gluestick helped the team to achieve this objective:

> Well, having the gluesticks keeps alive the values for sure. It keeps the values out there the whole time so that we don't forget about them. Part of the coaching also is to make sure that the values are always reinforced. Through reinforcing them, the players took on and lived their values and reinforced their commitment to the values by having the gluesticks on them the whole time, on show. It's almost like the ultimate crime is not to have it because if you can't organise yourself to bring your gluestick, then you are just not fulfilling the values, you are letting the team down. If that is our number one representation of what we are about, and you don't have it with you or you are not respecting it, then that is kind of the ultimate [transgression].

In reflecting on the volleyball season, Mark, Luke and Simon comment that it was one of the most successful sport seasons in which they had participated. They indicate that the success came not from winning (as they did in the Canterbury Championships) but from meeting all their goals except their dream goal and exceeding their expectations. Thus Luke states that success lay in 'bringing the team together, having [everyone] on the team contributing and everyone knowing that they are useful and being positive about it'. Likewise, Simon notes, 'because we knew each other, we knew how we played, we worked out a good game plan and we knocked off bigger teams because we didn't get down and we just played as a team.' They believe that the team achieved the value of cohesiveness, which made the team experience enjoyable (another of the values).

Enabling athletes to make decisions reinforces the natural expectations of any team. Because the athletes chose the direction of the team, they took on the role of self-monitoring which in turn enhanced wairua. With respect to reinforcing the values through the symbol of the gluestick, Mark states, 'I think it gave them complete ownership and I think when they had that sense of ownership, they were prepared to do more, were prepared to work harder and were prepared to sacrifice other things'.

This sense of responsibility led the athletes to take ownership of their preparation and performance, a foundation to an athlete-centred approach.

The whole squad was involved with this decision making process of establishing the vision, values and goals, which took about three hours outside of training as a group, plus homework that the boys had to complete in times outside of meetings and training sessions. Simon gives the probable explanation as to why most of the squad seemed quite keen to participate in this kind of decision making:

> ... it's better because the coaches just don't make rules and the kids have things to say, so it's better to listen to everyone. I hated being shouted at in other teams. It makes you want to stop trying.

Although they did not meet their dream goal of achieving a semi-final spot at National Championships, they did come in fifth place. Mark assesses this outcome in this way:

> I think you have got to look at success. What is your measure of success? Obviously, one measure could be their results and the level to which they played, which was successful ... I think another measure could be, and I suppose is the social benefits they experienced from it. This is the other side to my coaching philosophy. I think just in that alone it was really successful. I thought it taught kids about values and I think it taught them the importance of them and I think they learned a lot socially. They learned how to get on with each other. At the start, there were some rifts. There were some guys who couldn't handle one another, some personality clashes and they learned how to get over those. But for the last game [at the Nationals], it was being tired and having reached your goals and then having this last game to play that was sort of a consolation game.

Simon takes a similar view of the last game at the Nationals, suggesting it was difficult for the team to play because they had already met their goals for the season and it was a consolation game. Yet even in these circumstances the team culture seemed to prevail again and Riccarton won the game. The sets had been tied 1-1, with the last set score at 13-9 in favour of the opposing team. Then John Gibbs blocked a tough spike and Riccarton came back to win the set 16-14. In response to my question as to why the team managed to pull out this win, Simon states, 'We had a belief in ourselves. We just knew we were going to win because we were close as a team'.

When further exploring how the team goals were met for the season, Mark says:

> ... every other goal, and those little goals like being a tightest team, mentally [tough], exciting team, I think we reached all those. It was those two things [being the tightest team and mentally tough] that enabled the team to beat teams who were more athletic or more skilful. Other teams

were more athletic and were more skilful, but not consistently because their mental side of their game didn't allow them to be … All this showed the depth of the team because these guys came in and managed to get us to where we were, and then in the end too, when a couple didn't play so well, still came on full force ready to play. You could count on all of them.

The trust that the coach had in his team, and that all players had in each other, was one of the key characteristics of the quality team culture that developed over the season. Luke notes the motivation that came from:

… the team culture and just being part of the team. That's all I played for at the end. Yes, we were winning but I knew it was because the way the team was working together because we were heaps smaller than and not as athletic as the guys who we played.

Like Luke, Simon believes that:

… because of the team culture and because we knew each other, we knew how we played, we worked out a good game plan and we knocked off bigger teams because we never got down and we just played as a team, we kept together … For an example, we played a team, that through the net, they were telling us that we suck and they were going to smack us, but we kept to our own game. We didn't stoop to their level by doing anything stupid and we ended up beating them three-zip. They were fourth or third ranked team in the tournament … our team, compared to the rest of the teams in the top seven, we didn't have very much skill. We had one or two good hitters and one or two good passers and a good setter, but the rest of the teams were good at everything. They could probably beat us in skill level any day, but we beat them at volleyball because we stuck together and we communicated well.

Mark's Use of Questioning

As all the coaches featured in this book reinforce, questioning is one of the most important coaching skills to promote athlete decision making and problem solving. Mark used questioning adeptly. He found it to be a fantastic coaching tool for getting the athletes to think for themselves, to solve problems during games, to take ownership of their learning and to understand volleyball better. After putting the team in problem solving situations 'where certain team cohesiveness and tactical strategies were required', Mark would follow up with questioning that:

… [the questioning I used] allowed them to discover the strategies that would work in similar future situations. When the same or similar situations arose in the game context, they identified them as problems they had already faced and knew ways of solving them. I don't think I had to call a time out and say, 'You have to do this and this'. Often I would call the time out because they needed a break, but they more often than not did all the talking and problem solving.

One of the highlights of using questioning with his players was:

I think personally I have challenged the players more. Previously, I didn't have those [team] values set as such, they didn't decide them, and so I had fewer things to challenge them on. I have been able to challenge kids more and more. That's been good for me because … I think I've become a more assertive coach.

For their part, the players seemed to feel really challenged by questioning. On questioning, Simon says, 'it gets us thinking; instead of just doing things he explains to us why we are doing it, so it helps'. Simon also really liked having to solve problems, and having Mark pose questions rather than tell the boys the answers:

… he doesn't just tell us what to do, but then if he asks us questions, we realise what we should do in different situations. It just comes natural, so if we get in a situation in a real game, that we have practised over and over, it becomes automatic. So, he just kept on doing that and by the time the games came up, we were good at the important skills and we read the game way better.

As someone new to some aspects of the athlete-centred approach, in some cases Mark did ask leading questions. Although leading questions are necessary in some circumstances, in Mark's case their main purpose was to communicate his point to the boys in order to get the answer he wanted. Throughout the season, he worked on decreasing his use of leading questions:

Perhaps I did ask them leading questions … Sometimes I think I am just trying to give them examples, but maybe the examples might lead them a little bit.

By the end of the season, Mark was asking fewer leading questions. He admits that he needs to keep focusing on this skill.

Mark and Teaching Games for Understanding

TGfU (see Chapter Eight) is a favourite coaching strategy of Mark's. Consistent with his belief in athlete learning, he uses games as a major part of his repertoire to help athletes understand the tactics in volleyball. He says:

> I've always tried to do game-like stuff but I am really using a lot of actual games and scrimmages which the kids are enjoying. I think they enjoy them heaps more. I am just really enjoying the atmosphere in the gym.

When Mark first decided to focus on athlete-centred coaching, he specifically stated that one of his main goals was to use TGfU to help the boys to make decisions. This technique enabled the boys to make informed decisions in the games. It also responded to the boys' choice of enjoyment as one of their most important values. Given the importance that the boys attached to enjoyment, Mark felt he had to have fewer drill-type activities and more game-like activities:

> Traditionally, I have tried to train them through game-like drills but also felt it important to spend some time practising certain skills to hone techniques. But when the kids decided on the enjoyment value, I decided that game-like scrimmages would have to make up the majority of the practice so I was forced to develop some more fun games. These games had to highlight specific tactics and techniques which are required on the volleyball court and then emphasise them by making them the focus. So the game design required they work on certain key things and not the whole game.

Through the focus on game-like activities, Mark himself could develop his coaching further as he designed games to suit specific situations. One of the challenges of using TGfU has always been having confidence to try a different strategy, to find the game most suited to the situation at hand. In relation to this confidence, Mark says his experience with the technique has:

> … been really good for me because now I've got a bigger bank of games. I developed a system in which I go through to design a game. It's much, much easier for me to design them now. At first, trainings took me much longer to plan as they required much more thinking. So I suppose the time issue was a challenge but, for me, feeling like I am actually putting in a really solid effort and putting in the time makes me feel better about what I am doing.

On deciding when to use games and when to break down techniques and skills specific to volleyball, Mark says:

I think there is a time and a place for the games approach, especially in volleyball, where sometimes I think you do need just some continuous repetitions of things just to nail technique because, in volleyball, technique is so important because often they are completely brand-new skills. So there is very little transfer from other sports into volleyball because you can't just catch the ball. You are just deflecting it and you have to have the angle of your arms just right, which means you have to have your feet in certain places, and it is kind of hard to learn that if there are a lot of other things going on at once. Sometimes it's good just to teach that with some blocked practice or drill training. However, in saying that, you can still make blocked practice into a game! You've got [to] get into your Game Sense [TGfU] and your game-like drills. That's not to say [that during training you are] playing the whole game all the time, but [rather you are] practising situations at training, within your games where you can target certain aspects of the game, where they have to make certain decisions … [We played lots of] King of the Court and the kids loved it. We had good intensity. The key to King of the Court was that we were able to attempt to teach the kids about intensity, but we were also able to create scoring systems where we could reinforce the values they decided at the start of the campaign.

Using TGfU is compatible with many features of skill acquisition theory, as Ian Renshaw suggests in Chapter Eight. Mark highlights the way that games helped the boys to understand and make decisions of tactical play through game-like situations:

… it was a novel situation and they had to try, from that novel situation, to create a good enough offence to put some pressure on the six who were on the other side. That's something that I don't think a lot of coaches do. I think they train situations that are supposed to happen in volleyball. But, much of the time, things don't work the way they are supposed to work and they are novel … We played the whole game better. Other teams practise getting the perfect situation by closing the environment perhaps by throwing the ball to the setter or by other controlling means. They become good at that situation and it looks impressive, but they haven't had the experience of getting the ball that's not great or dealing with novel situations, which are going to happen most of the time in volleyball.

From the boys' perspective, they really enjoyed playing games. Most athletes who are training love game play, become more intense with it and therefore work hard on specific fitness. The intrinsic motivation they gain from playing purposeful games, means that they learn more from the different situations. Luke's observations support these ideas:

There was a lot of game-like drills which was really good. It made it more fun as well. We all played because we wanted to play the game. If we play at games at training, then it is sort of like playing the game at training. If you are having fun, you work a bit harder and the level is higher as well. Other coaches, like at cricket, they throw a thousand balls at you or something and they play this shot over and over and over again. But it is not really helping because if you are in a game then you are not going to get that ball that was thrown.

When asked if he thought that playing the game in training made a difference to how the team played at the Nationals, Luke responds:

I think it helped us when to play together and be more intense … it taught us to be intense. It didn't necessarily improve our ability a hell of a lot because we had already done that when we were younger. We already had the skills. Doing those game drills taught us how to be intense all the time.

He also considers that using the game situations in practice helped their understanding of volleyball under pressure:

I think that came from training as well. Like during drills or during game drills, sometimes he [the coach] stops and explains things, explains why we are doing these things. He does that often enough that we know it and can see it by ourselves. I guess other teams don't do that. I think they just say, do this drill and really don't know why they are doing it.

Simon sees both positive and negative sides to using games like King of the Court:

… the best thing I see that gets us controlled better will probably be pepper [a drill type activity] with two people, you get heaps of reps doing that and you get to control the ball better. King of the Court, you also stand around a lot, one stuff-up and you are off for ages. On a positive, on the sideline you can encourage your teammates and you can also learn from their mistakes.

His concern about the long waiting time for a team once it is eliminated reflects the importance of considering the 'time on task' component when designing any game for a given situation. On the other hand, the prospect of sitting out provided motivation for the players to try harder in this drill. The game also provided a pressured situation for athletes to practise in.

Simon saw some real benefits in using games to practise novel situations that might occur in competitions. The team's practice in novel situations could then be applied to novel situations that they then met in competitions:

... our defence was good. We picked up the good hitters. Maybe because we did those drills, we could read the offence from the other teams better. When we were on offence, we knew where to hit the ball or [how to hit] around the blockers. So maybe that did help. It didn't feel like it because we did drills that helped, but now that you look at it, you could probably say, a few things helped us which gave us [practice] in situations.

Simon suggests that Mark allowed the players to take risks. Rather than jumping in when he did not like the risk, the coach left it to the boys to make the choice. They learned through trial and error in games. Simon appreciated the opportunity for athlete decision making, which he compares favourably with more prescriptive coaching styles in the following anecdote:

When I was on duty at the Nationals tournament, I heard a coach say to a player, 'Don't you dare jump serve', because the game was close. The player then served and missed the serve, looked back at the coach with a sour face. The players need to make more decisions for themselves during the games. The coach can say where to serve, but not change how to serve during a game.

Implementing an Athlete-centred Approach

Mark was highly motivated to implement the athlete-centred approach and it was a pleasure to watch his process. His experience as a physical education teacher, I believe, made it easier for him to move to trialling the approach. As he had used questioning in his teaching for many years, he began with an advantage over other coaches who are starting to implement an empowerment style.

One of Mark's motivations to take up the athlete-centred approach was his belief that volleyball is a great tool to influence students to do well at school:

I've always had a real mixture and some of the kids who play volleyball tend to be some of the ones who are finding it difficult to achieve in school. I don't know whether because volleyball is an explosive game and hard hitting and it's aggressive and it appeals to that type of student ... But maybe it's the team camaraderie that volleyball can create ... [With previous teams], them getting into trouble at school has gotten in the way a little bit, because we had trainings where they haven't been able to attend because they've had their homework detentions, kids who couldn't travel because they had not been performing in the classroom or behaving well ... I think it is pretty important to do well in the classroom ... using volleyball as a wee bit of leverage to try and convince them to [try hard] in class. [Using an athlete-centred approach] enabled the boys to decide that they had to organise their lives outside of volleyball, so things didn't get in the way of volleyball.

One aspect of Mark's athlete-centred focus was to hand over several areas of responsibility to the athletes, while his own role became to facilitate. As he describes it:

> I tried giving the players decisions to make about things like punishments and trainings; pretty much everything. I think it gave them complete ownership and I think when they had that sense of ownership, they were prepared to do more, were prepared to work harder, were prepared to sacrifice other things … It really was their campaign. That was actually one of the things to draw the lines [distinguish the athlete-centred approach]. This isn't mine, this is your campaign, and this is what you [have] decided. I am just the person to help you get there.

He found the process so different from his past involvement in coaching, where 'it has been my goals and my vision and [the players] generally bought into those'. By asking for athletes' input and giving them ownership of the team, Mark feels he helped to make a more cohesive, intense and motivated team. In his previous coaching, he had thought the boys bought into the culture that he created, but he now sees that their sense of ownership was:

> … not to the same extent as when they create it themselves … [These days] often other coaches ask me in the staffroom, 'How do you find [various players] not turning up to training?'. We really didn't have any big issues with that. We had the odd one and once that was addressed through the values, we had no problems.

Mark feels he was ready to implement an athlete-centred approach, having used aspects of it for several years already. By formally practising it, he feels that he has improved but still needs to learn more:

> … it's more involved, there is more to it. It's the approach I wanted to do but I didn't know enough about it. So, now that I have learned these things, it is the way I want to coach so I'll continue to do it. No doubt I won't get it perfect, there are still lots of things that [have been] pointed out to me that I had to do … There are always going to be things that you don't get, and you don't get it altogether perfect every time. It's like anything. So, if you let those things worry you, then you will never do anything. You have to be confident with what you do know and what you are going to do.

One of the implementation issues that some coaches have raised is the potential difficulty of introducing athletes to the 'different' coaching approach. On the question of how the boys would react to a slight change to his approach, given that he had coached all of them previously, Mark responds:

> ... they are a good bunch of kids anyway so they were going to be respectful of what we were trying to do to begin with and they were going to go along with it ... I still think they needed some proof of its worth before they fully bought into what they were actually creating. I think for a while they were going, 'Yeah, we'll create this because Mr Norton said this is what we are doing and we'll do it.' But once they started to see some benefits of it and ... it really snowballed. It got bigger and bigger and bigger.

To find out the boys' views of how Mark implemented this 'new' approach, I asked them to compare his current coaching to previous years. Luke reflects:

> Well, I think the style that he used this year is a lot better than the style he's used in the past. He seems like he was a little bit more organised this year with the things that he did and that helped. It was a lot more enjoyable as well, really enjoyable to coach in that style because we all know what we are working for and stuff. We all worked together to do it. It showed at trainings, it was fun as well.

Simon makes the comparison in this way:

> It's better [this year] because he lets us talk among the group instead of making all the decisions, instead of yelling at us around the court. He lets us choose what we want to do sometimes. We can have fun doing it.

Responding to my request for him to describe what he thinks that Mark did as a coach, what was different or what his style was, Luke says:

> I don't know how to describe it. He put a whole lot of things into one. He is tough when he wants to be but he's not tough all the time. He puts an emphasis on having a good time. I think that makes everyone work harder. He is a unique coach; I have never had a coach as enthusiastic as him before. In his eyes, he was always happy and stuff. He was enthusiastic about the drills and that gets everyone into it as well ... you always turn around and he always has a smile on his face, it is really reassuring when you are playing, even though he might not be smiling on the inside.

Luke's comments reiterate that using an athlete-centred style with questioning, TGfU and athlete decision making is fun. This observation is significant alongside research data showing that players drop out when they find that their sport is no longer fun.

A further observation of Mark's approach comes from Simon when he says, 'He still helps us when we need it. He doesn't tell you much; he's just there to help us when we need it'.

What were Mark's perceptions of how the boys reacted to his focus on their learning? I wondered if they realised what approach he was trying to implement. Mark sees it this way:

> My impression is that they will think it was the values that created the success as they were very much in their face! However, the Games for Understanding were [a] huge [factor] in their success also. We never talked about the games as being key to their development, however we did discuss what each game was for and what we should learn from it. I didn't know how crucial this game-centred approach would be either until I saw how well it had come together at the end of the season. That was another thing they talked about in the initial ... they do enjoy those games and it is easier to achieve commitment and intensity when you are playing in a game, then it is in a drill training. I don't know how many Kiwi people are committed enough to pass 200 balls on the left side in a row and then pass 200 balls on your right side in a row, which is what I believe they do in Japan.

One of the unique aspects of Mark's approach, which he had introduced to his coaching the previous year, was that after he calls a time out during a competition he allows the boys to run it themselves. In regard to this system, Simon says:

> It's good because if we are down on court, we sort of know what we are doing wrong, so we don't need someone telling us what we are doing wrong. So we sort it out as a team ... a few positive suggestions [are good], not what we are doing wrong, but what we can do to improve our situation. Then we try and improve it, then if it is not working, then he will talk to us on the court and say what we need to do. We sometimes need him to get us back up after we are down.

Luke agrees that Mark's unique time out system:

> ... was good. It was good not having a coach in your ear all the time and just letting us do it. [With coaches who are directive], it always feels like you are being watched. You don't get out of it. With Mr Norton, if you made a mistake, it was really good ...you didn't get scared that he was going to yell at you, like you do with some of the coaches, you are too scared to make a mistake or if you do make a mistake it's all doom.

When asked if he would like to be coached in the same way next year, Simon says:

> I would've thought that it would be essential. I thought it would be automatic after the way that we went this time. Everyone agreed on it, so why can't we do it again? We can only get better.

The Process of Empowering Players

As part of the process of being an empowered player, Simon says he felt 'valued and important'. Mark makes similar observations from a coach's perspective:

> I think the process has helped them understand the importance of the values I used to put into place. But because they have ownership, these values have made it more meaningful for them. Players feel listened to, considered, valued and respected. With their head in a good space, the commitment, passion and dedication were outstanding. Not surprisingly their effort was never in question and their game improved as could be expected. They showed these things at training and games with lots of talk and yahoo which created fun. Then the fun created the good play.

One of the processes that Mark used initially to empower the athletes was to form small groups with the roles of providing leadership and taking ownership and responsibility for aspects of the team environment. As he explains it:

> Within the overall squad, we created smaller groups, which were responsible for different aspects that we were trying to do. I empowered each student to have some leadership or have some responsibility. Without responsibility, you can't learn how to use it, learn how to develop it. When we talk about cooperation and teamwork, they are terms that have just been drummed into the kids. You ask them the question about 'What do we need to do now?' ... the kids can always come up with the words *cooperate* and *teamwork*, but they don't actually know what they mean and they don't know how to do them in a lot of cases ... once you have said that you wanted to develop that, then you've got to teach them what they are and then give them the opportunity to practise them.

As mentioned at the outset of this chapter, this aspect of Mark's empowerment approach was not a strong focus this year. Though he talked about using small groups, it was a potential strategy that never really developed. A senior group, which was one of the two groups that Mark formed, met only once. The second group, however, had responsibility for running a parents' meeting and gave some positive indications of what might be achieved with a more general use of small groups. This group designed a great meeting, informing parents of the season, focusing on fundraising and showing the parents what they had learned thus far. The parents were impressed with the evening. The boys showed that, given this responsibility in the quality team culture that had been created, they were motivated to do this extra work for the benefit of the team.

Now that Mark knows the best way to establish a vision and values for the team, perhaps he will form more small groups with responsibilities with future teams. Other coaches in this book highlight how forming small groups for certain responsibilities helps to create leaders on the team. Many suggest that they want all athletes to be leaders. In a successful team, everyone is responsible for making decisions.

Role rotation is another aspect of an athlete-centred approach that gives athletes great learning experiences. The squad system, which is athlete-centred in nature, is a form of role rotation. To improve their ability to work together smoothly, the boys played in several different positions. Consistent with a squad expectation that all boys played equal time in the games, Mark continued to rotate players equally up to the local championships, which increased trust among the team. He reflects on the result:

> I think it came together in the Canterbury Champs, we were still trying to get people on, we were still rotating players on and off trying to get them all playing, even though I'd said and the guys had said, when it comes to Canterbury Champs side, we would play our top six and people playing didn't matter so much, but even then I still tried to get people on.

By this means all boys contributed equally and were trusted to do the job throughout the season until just before the National Championships, where the tournament required an A and a B team. An incident occurred during the tournament where Mark strayed from the wishes of the boys. He made a decision, without letting the boys know of his philosophy of role rotation. Sticking to his plan of role rotation and to demonstrate his trust in the players, he used several players who had had little playing time in a game in which the outcome did not really matter. Luke was upset at this:

> ... that's the game that we had a debrief, I remember him asking what we were annoyed about because he knew we were annoyed. I think he knew what we were annoyed about but he just wanted us to say it. But I didn't want to say anything because it would put a negative spin on things because we had the final in the afternoon. I think he should've left the rotation as it was and put the foot on the floor with all the Canterbury teams, which they were not going to bag us for giving up a game.

Mark also used role rotation well in relation to King of the Court. All three players in this game have to take on every position on the volleyball court, thus they work out the role of each player on their team. In this way they gain empathy for a setter, for example, through experiencing what this player might experience in the full game.

One of the highlights for me as a researcher of adolescents was to observe at the National Championships just how close knit the A team had become, with resulting benefits for the team. Adolescent boys sang in the warm-up and even danced to their positions in front of the crowds. They did not worry about what they looked like; they were doing it to help the team environment. To me, it was true wairua. To my question about how such shy boys managed to sing 'Row, row, row your boat' in the middle of the Nationals, Luke responds:

> We decided that we shouldn't be taking ourselves too seriously because it made us uptight on the court and we wouldn't talk as much and, so at trainings, we started acting the goat a bit and yelling out our values. It was something we weren't used to doing, but when we started doing it, it was heaps of fun and then we started, we did it in the stadium and we just didn't worry about anyone, it was quite cool. It was cool, I liked it, I didn't care what people think and …I didn't think they laughed at us or anything, they thought it was all right.

Some Challenges of an Athlete-centred Approach

As noted by other coaches in this book, one of the major challenges of an athlete-centred approach is that it takes time to empower players effectively. Yet the focus on long-term learning means that it is worth taking the time to get athletes to problem solve. On the time required to create the team vision and values, Mark says:

> It took way more time than I thought … From the start to the end, it probably took three weeks of maybe half an hour [each training session]. I didn't want to cut too much into their playing time because the boys had come to play and there were some grizzles to start with, so we had a couple of sessions at other times. [Therefore] we didn't feel like we were cutting into their playing time too much.

Luke is positive in regard to the lengthy process of setting up the values specifically:

> Well, I liked deciding the values. I think that was good, even though it was a long time. It was quite painful sitting there for that long and I think it was worth us doing it. I don't think it would have had the same impact if it was put upon us.

Interestingly, Simon perceives the time devoted to make a quality team culture as acceptable: 'Time is fine, it is part of volleyball practice'.

As a coach, too, Mark has found that he must give more of his personal time to the process of implementing his athlete-centred approach:

> … I'll tell you, I have learned some good things, important things, like I can't just rock up to training. I can't just get in my car and drive to training like perhaps I would have done, thinking about the drills I am going to do in my head before I get there on the way. I actually have to do a lot more thinking about the training and how I am going to run it.

In response to my question about other challenges related to an athlete-centred approach, Mark identifies the great depth of the learning and commitment involved:

> I have always wanted to have players who were empowered and could run themselves and, through doing this process, I think what I have learned is that there is much more to it than what I was doing. I always thought I had some pretty good teams going in terms of [empowering players]. I can now see that [my previous teams] were only touching the surface of what is actually possible. By going through this [season's process], I think what the kids are achieving now is huge compared to what I was previously. It is more holistic. So it's been a big learning curve for me for what is possible and how we go about it.

The process of listening to other people and taking on their points of view is an aspect of the athlete-centred approach that he sees as a challenge but also as a definite advantage:

> You've just got to keep checking where you are at personally and keep reminding yourself what you are doing it for and whose campaign it actually is. I think as soon as you start to think that it is yours, then you don't want to give bits away and that is not an empowering approach. So, if you keep reminding yourself why you are doing it and whose campaign it is, then I don't think there are any problems there. I think when I first started out coaching I think the reason why I was doing it was to win for myself. I wanted to have a winning team.

Another challenge that Mark identifies is having trust in the players, as he was giving them power to take ownership of the team. He says:

> I didn't entirely trust all of them; there was one or two of them where I would cringe when they hit the ball, especially serving. Having had the experience that they had in Canterbury Champs and lead-up tournaments, made them less likely to make the error. I think that was important.

A major challenge was the fallout following Mark's choice of the team to play in the Nationals as the A team, based on criteria the squad had identified. Unfortunately, once the A team (of which Mark was the coach) was chosen, the B team's culture faded and was clearly weaker than the A team's culture at the Nationals. Although Mark continued to reinforce the values with the A team, the other coach for the B team was not as strong in reinforcing the values. Without that facilitation factor, the B team, though they had a good time, experienced a decrease in the quality of their culture. Other factors, such as injuries, contributed to this deteriorating quality as well.

The nature of the high school volleyball season added a difficult barrier to the establishment of a team culture. The volleyball season covers two terms, term 4 of one year and term 1 of the following year. At the end of each year (after term 4), the juniors move into senior divisions. Mark's team did not cater well for the inclusion of the 'new' juniors, which added to the numerous learning experiences involved in implementing such an approach. Because the juniors had not been through the process of establishing the team vision and values, when they arrived in the established squad Mark asked them to decide how they wanted to be involved in the squad. The decision the boys made did not work well: they formed their own team, had their own coach and left the squad to its own devices. As Mark says:

> Those guys decided that that was what they wanted to do. They made an error and they recognised that and so they've got that under their belt now.

As the season went on, Mark invited the C team to train with the squad and they started coming along. The biggest problem was that the C team was not party to establishing the vision, values and goals and therefore did not have ownership and struggled to become part of the team. As the boys came in from another team environment, they were basically forced to buy in to the squad systems. I believe that because they did not contribute to formulating the culture that was now firmly established for the A and B teams, they did not have ownership of it.

Plans for the Future

Mark enjoyed gaining advice from an observer in the background. He suggests that in the future he would like to have access to the same kind of advice:

> Getting advice was great. It fast-tracked the learning process. It helped having someone chipping in the odd suggestion. Even just a question like 'Why are you running this drill?' made me think about the benefits of the drill and that there may be a better way of doing it. It also meant there was another set of ideas looking for team dynamics and cohesiveness. So I

think that it is certainly beneficial to have someone who is experienced and someone who knows what they are doing to give you suggestions along the way.

Mark admits that his strength is his coaching of actual volleyball specifics. In regard to my question on the ideal way to run a team while maintaining the quality team culture, he responds:

[Ideally] I think you need the eye. If you have got someone watching the volleyball, critiquing and making comments about the volleyball, then I think it is really difficult to look at the other things. Unless you make it episodic and within the trainings, as a coach, you decide to make the focus on watching 10 minutes on their volleyball and 10 minutes on watching their interactions, cohesiveness and how they operate, but then you still might miss something that happens.

As to whether there will be a time when he thinks that he can go solo, he assures me:

Sure there will be a point where a lot of the team building strategies become second nature and I will be able to implement them on the spot when they are required. I feel I am getting a better bank of activities to promote cohesiveness and trust and am learning when to use them.

One area to work on that I identified was Mark's 'reading of people'. When I ask how he will work on that, he reflects on what he has learned from the season:

Sometimes a lot of what happens in the gym, it's hard to pick up on because I know that a lot of the time, when they are playing the game, I am commenting and giving lots of feedback, talking about decisions they are making on the court and I am often focusing on the people who are immediately in the drills or in the game … I found a number of times a couple of things that are happening out the back were highlighted. Perhaps a rude gesture or a comment that somebody else made that was perhaps not living up to the values and needs to be addressed. That's quite good because [it is] highlight[ed] for me and then we address it at the end or there at the time.

For the next season, I agreed to act as player manager again to help the team. It was so enjoyable in the year of the research that the process has motivated me to continue to be involved. Mark too has been inspired to keep up his coaching because of the success that the boys experienced, the great time that they had and their unanimous decision to come back for more.

Conclusion

Mark continues to work on his athlete-centred approach and says that he will never stop learning about it. Through the way this season developed, he can see that this approach is the way to go forward and enable athletes to reach great heights. Mark is pleased that he allowed so much input from the athletes; during the season he was often heard to say, 'Wow, these boys really have a lot of value to add to our team'.

As other coaches in this book indicate, learning the athlete-centred approach is time consuming but well worth the effort. The rewards for enhancing the athletes as individual people and watching their skill level grow are obvious from the smiles on the faces and from the comments of the athletes reported in this chapter. Given the great success of the athlete-centred approach with these adolescent boys, it is clearly an effective approach that coaches need to use for athletes at all levels.

What a fantastic opportunity this project was for me to be part of a fun, successful volleyball team. The boys were outstanding in a holistic way—cognitively, psychosocially, spiritually (wairua) and physically. I believe that we learned from each other and that, because Mark enabled the athletes to take ownership of their team, the team was successful in all domains.

> Character consists of what you do on the third and fourth tries. - James A. Michener

References

Janssen, J. (2002). *Championship Team Building*. Cary, NC: Winning the Mental Game.

Yukelson, D. (1997). Principles of effective team building, *Journal of Applied Sport Psychology*, 9(1): 73–96.

> The opponent with in one's own head is more daunting than the one on the other side of the net. -Tim Gallwey

> 'Coach', he whispered. His voice shook just a trifle. 'I found it, coach, the thing you wanted me to learn for myself.'—Schoolboy, 'Split seconds: Tales of the Cinder Track 1927', Sports Council 1991

> If only the sun-drenched celebrities are being noticed and worshiped, then our children are going to have a tough time seeing the value in the shadows, where the thinkers, probers and scientists are keeping society together. - Rita Dove, US poet, educator

Each day of our lives we make
deposits in the memory banks of
our children. - Charles Swindoll

Chapter Eleven

Don Tricker

New Zealand Black Sox (Men's Softball)
Former Coach

Don is a former coach of the New Zealand Black Sox, the national men's softball team. The Black Sox are current three-peat world champions, winning two of these titles while Don was at the helm. Although he treasures his time with the national team, Don says he is ready for the next challenge: coaching children's teams. This challenge faces him along with his role as coach manager with the New Zealand Academy of Sport. The purpose of the NZ Academy coaching team is to develop a coaching environment that delivers a quality coaching service to high performance athletes. As a volunteer international coach, Don coached as a hobby while also working in a full-time job and being a father to a young family.

Don draws on his background and experience in business, specifically information technology (IT), to deepen his understanding of human relations. He suggests that the business environment has provided him with the processes that have helped him to become a better coach. Based on his experience as an employee and manager, too, Don believes in using an athlete-centred approach to create a quality team culture, in which all team members work together towards a common goal. This chapter represents a cross-section of his coaching philosophies and approaches thus far. I interviewed Don after returning from the Athens Olympics and just before he decided to step down from coaching the Black Sox.

Don's softball career path started when he was a young lad in Porirua, growing up in a sports-oriented family and a community with plentiful opportunities. It was in Porirua that, as well as competing in rugby, rugby league, athletics, soccer and cricket, he discovered softball. It became his serious sport after injuries sustained in soccer and rugby ruled out those sports. As a softball player, he represented his community several times and played for New Zealand for a number of years. Softball became his passion. Don believes that sport, in particular softball, has played a major role in shaping him as a person. For this reason he feels indebted to sport and will be involved in it for the rest of his life.

Don's Philosophy of Coaching

Don has developed his coaching philosophy from many experiences and says it is constantly changing. As with other coaches in this book, Don's coaching philosophy is athlete-centred. He elaborates:

My philosophy on coaching is to take a holistic view as I believe that there is more to life than sport. I like to think that I have not only helped the athlete realise their athletic goals but have helped them become a more rounded person through their experience in sport. Coaching is simply about delivering a service, therefore I need to understand the requirements and expectations of each person that I coach be they five years old or a high-performance athlete. For coaching to be sustainable there must be win–win outcomes throughout the coaching experience— the win for me is that I can sit back and reflect on whatever contribution that I've made in terms of how each particular individual has grown. That's not solely limited to the athlete's athletic ability; it's more a contribution to that athlete as a person.

I have a simple test of character that I call the RSA [Returned and Services' Association] test. The test is based around the athlete walking into any RSA in New Zealand and holding a meaningful conversation with anyone in the RSA that is not about themselves and be genuinely interested in what it is that person has got to say. Again, it is not just about turning out guys in softball who can run fast and pitch the ball hard ... It's [about] people who are outstanding New Zealanders. I am delighted to say that the Black Sox are filled with athletes who pass the RSA test.

As the above discussion indicates, the individual athlete is the focus of Don's energies. He says that sport is about developing a team out of individuals who are heading together in the same direction:

... the common denominator in sport is that it is played by individuals, each with different needs and expectations. Therefore, when building teams it all comes down to ensuring that individual expectations are satisfied when developing the core components of the team culture. The components include ownership of a shared vision or common purpose, clearly defined values, standards and role definitions.

Underlining his concern with the individual athlete and his or her needs, Don relates a story about the night before the final of the 2004 World Championships, which were held in New Zealand:

Whenever a group of individuals hear the same address, or watch the same video clip, or read the same passage of text, then there will be different interpretations of what was heard, seen or read. The Black Sox are no different. I only have to look at my address to the team immediately prior to the 2004 World Championship final. To put the environment in context, it was a very emotional time for the team; it was the culmination of four years of effort. We were about to play the World Series final in front of the people who matter most to us—our families and friends, the New Zealand softball community and the New Zealand sporting public. For us, it was a once-in-a-lifetime opportunity as it will be at least another 20 years before the World Softball Championships return to New Zealand.

My final address focused on the environmental factors, how we were going to win the World Championship, and the points of difference that would separate us from the Canadians [the opposing finalists]. The address delivered the desired outcome, with 17 focused athletes who believed that in four hours they were going to be world champions. After the final I have heard a number of the athletes describe the time immediately prior to the final and the final address. What was of interest was that there were many varied interpretations of what the athletes believed the key messages were. The key messages are dependent on what the athlete is looking for. I am only grateful that under pressure I delivered one of the basics of coaching—an address that met each athlete's expectations.

An athlete-centred coach changes and adapts goals and methods based on the particular group he or she is coaching, as Don explains:

… you have different groups each with different requirements and expectations. As an example, the service that I deliver for the kids that I coach is largely about the development of their social skills, it's about being a contributor to that child gaining confidence and having a go at anything. My purpose as coach is to make sure that they have a good time, so that they want to come back week after week after week. Then we can capture them, in whatever sport they choose. This can only take place when we understand the expectations of each child. Typically kids want to be active, have heaps of turns, have some fun and play with their mates … I recruit the parents and get them involved because it is the only way that I can meet the expectations of the kids.

In another example relating to a children's team he is coaching, Don tells of athletes who, as time goes on, seem to be gaining more confidence to get involved with activities outside their comfort zone. His team of softball players became part of a school choir—an unexpected but great outcome for Don and his belief in enabling children to discover themselves:

… that is the biggest part for me. When I went to the school assembly I watched the school choir make their way up to the stage. It was a huge buzz when I realised that all of the kids in my team were part of the choir, including my son, which surprised the heck out of my wife.

As noted above, in addition to gaining an understanding about coaching through his involvement with numerous sports teams, Don acknowledges that some of his thinking about coaching came from his experience in IT work:

> ... in terms of business, I had many examples of where team culture is driven from the top down. In every instance, it didn't work as the culture was never owned by the staff; it was always someone else's ... On reflection I always considered that if I was in the same position I would find a way to obtain ownership through a bottom-up approach. Depending on the size of the organisation. one way would be to pick off the leaders or the pied pipers within the organisation and leverage off their existing relationships with their peer groups to develop and sell the culture at all stages of its development. So, again, it is not just about leveraging off the good examples only, it's about understanding each example and sitting back and reflecting on them and saying, 'If I had a similar opportunity I would do it a little bit differently'.

Don's Development as a Coach

Don had successful experiences as a softball player, which enabled him to take his passion for the game into coaching the sport. Don's coaching was influenced by many along his journey. The first was one of his coaches as a junior player:

> ... we had a coach, a guy called Neil Tuffrey, Mr Tuff we used to call him. He started coaching us as five-year-olds and finished up with us when we were about 15-year-olds. Throughout this time Mr Tuff, in addition to building a team that dominated junior softball in our area, shared many life lessons with us around working as a team: being supportive, respectful and trusting your teammates and always having a plan—do your thinking before the play.

The transition from junior to senior softball marked his next phase of development, when:

> My coach, Haggis, introduced the concept of class—whether in victory or defeat, always demonstrate class. Haggis ensured that we looked beyond every result to ensure that the lessons of each game were recognised and understood. He introduced the concept that losing is part of life—but it is how you handle yourself in defeat and how you leverage off these lessons that is the important part.

Don recognises a wide range of others who have been influential:

> ... through coaches like Mike Walsh who was very inspirational and very strong in terms of motivating ... I am a bit of everyone in the way I wanted

to do things, my mum, my dad, my school teachers, all those sorts of people … where did I pick all this up; it's just over the years and years of listening basically and asking questions.

Drawing from such influences, Don started coaching:

I coached junior teams, as an athlete … but not for an extended period. I coached a team for three or four years and that is how I got into it. It all started from there. I believed that I owe a great deal to softball so coaching was a tangible way for me to share the opportunities sport has provided me with other people, in particular children.

This induction into coaching obviously had a big effect on Don, as he then began coaching seniors before moving into the international softball arena:

Coaching to me has never been about the coach—it is about the athletes and the value the coach can add. For me it all started with the club side that I played for, Poneke Kilbirnie; I was conned into coaching really. I'd say that my ego was stroked. Some of the guys that I played with had a meeting with me and said, 'Look we are looking for a coach next year, we really want you to come and coach us, we've got no one else and you can do this' … I hadn't even considered coaching at a senior level, so it was, 'Oh yes'.

With my sporting and life experiences I always thought that I could add the value that the team was looking for. We had a very successful time and then the national coaching position became available. The national coaching role was another now-or-never type deal for me. My wife and I had two young children and the timing was right. If I had waited another four to six years, my role as a father would almost certainly have taken priority over any aspirations of coaching the national team.

This coaching job at the national level came up because, in playing for New Zealand, Don had already made a name for himself in softball circles. As a player, he was highly analytical, so taking on a coaching role seemed to be an obvious move. He reflects:

Towards the latter part of my international career, I was a spare-part player. I could hit, so therefore I would always find myself in the line-up, but not necessarily in the same position each game … I would consider myself to be, at the international level, a late developer … it took me a long time to understand how to play the game. Then, once I figured out how to play the game, I was relatively successful internationally, and it was all based around confidence and keeping things simple, which enabled me to make smart decisions under pressure.

Don started coaching seriously in the 1990s when he pooled all his experience in sport and business and applied it to coaching. Don's analytical ability made him a reflective coach, always observing and asking why certain things were done a certain way. Through his own admission, however, he did not learn his coaching trade through the 'traditional' coach education process. Instead, he learned:

> … through the ability to observe the coaches … I have picked up little bits and pieces of each of those coaches I thought were quite good and bits and pieces that I didn't think were very good … All the way through my playing career, I was always a deep thinker and listener. I often helped other players to work through and find solutions to the issues they, or we, faced. So I had all sorts of coaching roles, even when I was a player.

Another method of developing as a coach, Don suggests, is to continue to watch and analyse other coaches in his everyday life:

> I can't watch sport now without trying to break it down into understanding what happened and more importantly why it happened. Why were poor decisions being made, those sorts of thing … This is in every sport. I go to watch rugby, I go to watch netball, I am not looking in terms of the result, in terms of who won or lost, I am looking at how it happened. I am looking at particular players and attempt[ing] to understand why they chose to execute a particular play that is clearly not part of the role or skill set.

Don highlights his development of coaching the technical aspects of softball. Having technical nous about the sport is essential to athlete learning and decision making and is thus a key component of a coaching repertoire. At the same time, Don says that this component is always the easiest part of the trade for coaches to learn:

> … in softball I had the technical background through my playing it. It was my IT background that has provided me with the processes to package up my technical knowledge into a format that can be understood by each athlete.

Some of the coaches in this book describe how they began as coach-centred coaches then developed an athlete-centred approach after realising it was better for learning. When I ask Don if he fits into this category, he says:

> No, not really … when I said I was having the coaching roles when I was an athlete, it was all still about an awareness of what is happening here and why is it happening, rather than just 'do this' or 'do that'; [it was still about] always asking question[s] in a non-judgemental manner.

In Don's development as a coach, major influences have been mentors with whom he tosses ideas about and whom he listens to and observes extensively. Obviously, any coach uses these opportunities to advance his or her knowledge and pick out ideas that would suit him or her individually. Don describes the process for him personally:

> It is more from my computer background, in terms of how we have shared knowledge … whether it is a lot of transfer or you very quickly establish a relationship with whomever it is that you are working, then very quickly determine, in what part of that person you want to leverage off. It is not necessarily the whole person, or their knowledge; it is a small part that is really going to help me. So you drill down into that particular path … I have had many 'mentors' over the years, where it comes from people who really interested me and they had something of real value that has helped shaped them as a person. So I pick out a bit of each in terms of interest. Typically what happens is that you pick all that out and you find someone else who comes from a slightly different, but related [experience] and suddenly you have a different view of the same subject. That all helped.

The Process of Establishing a Quality Team Culture

A common theme across the athlete-centred coaches in this book is that they are committed to establishing a quality team culture. In this environment, athletes contribute to the direction of the team, taking responsibility for and ownership of setting and maintaining that direction. It is the same for the Black Sox.

Throughout the interview, Don refers to the significant influence from his business environment, where multi-faceted elements must combine to enable a team to function productively. To achieve this outcome, the team must have mutual goals and aim towards common ground. Don transferred this way of working to his coaching. He says that developing a quality team culture is dependent on the individuals and the groups he gets for every campaign. Don discusses the process of building a team culture:

> Part of what we do each year, particularly in our World Championship years, is that we make no assumptions in terms of culture that worked previously. For the Black Sox we could not assume that what was important to the 2000 team would still be valid for the 2004 team. Even though a number of the athletes were part of the World Championship team in 2000, [in 2004] they were four years older with greater life experiences.

> We went through a similar process to 2000 where we had an athlete-facilitated session where three questions were addressed: what do we want, what is important to the team, how are we going to deliver what is important to us? … [First,] 'What do we want?' … That is all about our values and standards. Then [we ask] 'How are we going to deliver what is important to us? How are we going to operate on a day-by-day basis to ensure that we deliver what it is that is important to us?' Then

the athletes define their roles … on an individual basis in terms of their individual roles, then by units. To put it in our context, the pitchers would get together and talk about what is the role of the pitcher and then they would draw it up with the pitchers and catchers and say, 'Well, what is the pitcher–catcher role? What is the relationship there? What is their relationship to the infield and outfield?' … The athletes then defined the role of the coach, the role of the manager, the physiotherapist, everyone in that particular campaign.

As many athlete-centred coaches acknowledge, the management team is part of the whole team. Don includes them in the process of establishing the roles of individuals:

The role of the management team is to challenge the outcomes reached by the athletes in an effort to make it better. Following this process, the outcomes are agreed, documented and implemented. This process limits the opportunity for mismatched expectations.

Establishing a team culture is initially complex and takes time. However, through forming team values and expectations and identifying the responsibilities of each team member, everyone takes individual ownership of the task of living these values, expectations and responsibilities. The process of communicating and defining meanings together, Don believes, provides individuals with a clear, shared understanding of what is expected of them. Conversely, failing to establish such mutual understanding, Don says:

… is a classic downfall in coaching and with any team that you have the coach sitting over here with certain sets of expectations of what he or she believes that the athletes require, but yet hasn't talked to the athletes about it. The athletes may have a set of very different expectations with the result being a huge disconnection. Inherently it's built into us that when things aren't going well, we will apportion blame …

In a sporting context, when things aren't going right then typically you don't want to step forward and accept responsibility. Inherently, it's like, 'Who can I drag down with me?', so you waste a lot of energy before you move forward. Again, with clearly defined role definitions … should we drop the ball in our World Championship campaign, then it will be very clear to everyone who dropped the ball. The focus is on, 'How can we pick up the ball as a group and move forward without worrying or wasting energy over all the other stuff that goes on?' That worked really well in a couple of instances through our campaign, because clearly things didn't always go right. But the pleasing part was how quickly we got back on track because in sport it's about time. Once you start trying to blame someone else then you lose time. When you lose time, you drift from game plans and then you find yourself in a situation where the game is almost over, rather than retaining your composure and belief in your game plan and just moving forward again.

Being an advocate for an athlete-centred approach, where athletes learn to make decisions for and take ownership of the team and its operation, Don gives the athletes responsibility for helping to develop roles and team expectations. His role is to facilitate this process. He gives an example of how it happens:

> … the athletes were the principal architects of our defensive patterns. The Black Sox culture encourages creativity; every idea was respected and cherished. As coaches we would facilitate discussion with the players [about] how we really want to play. The coaches' roles were more about facilitation. It was clear we had a lot of input to provide, but we were leveraging off the knowledge and experience within the side. It wasn't about saying, 'One person has got all the knowledge here, so this is the way we'd better play it'. It was like, 'No, let's respect each other; we have all got something to contribute here and we want to play out every scenario to ensure we have got it right and that we believe in it. Then we will practise it, then we will test it and if it's going to deliver what we are expecting, then we implement it in a real competition.'

As to the process of establishing the values of the team, which Don describes as 'good, classic New Zealand values', Don explains:

> It's all about respect, it's about integrity … We had three questions that we essentially asked: How are we going to deliver this? [What are] the values and how are going to live [them]? The team went through the process which included reviewing what we did in 2000, deciding what's relevant now and what's not. Some [values] survived and some were revised or adjusted. The purpose of our culture was to create an environment that is enjoyable and meets the expectations of the team … international sport, when you are playing in a world championship final, is incredibly stressful, therefore the environment must be enjoyable. When we built the team we made sure that it was an enjoyable process. We created competitive scenarios that challenged the team. The outcome was a series of shared experiences based on humour. It was these experiences that helped us get through the difficult situations.

Once these values are set up, Don believes that they need to be reinforced. Because the players chose the values, they also take responsibility for reinforcing them:

... they are policed by the athletes as well because the athletes have built and own them. The values are ours, not mine; they were not imposed on the athletes by me. The athletes ensure that the values are lived. We have a simple expectation that we all must ... be prepared to face the consequences of every decision we make. The philosophy that we have is that we will support any poor decision once. But, if the individual chooses to repeat that poor decision, then they need to be prepared to pay the consequence. That may well be non selection. That is the ultimate consequence—an athlete explaining to family and friends that they have not been selected because they could not be trusted.

Like other coaches in this book, Don believes it is important to have meaningful team-building activities to reinforce team values and enhance the team environment. An innovation in his athlete-centred approach was holding a team-building weekend for his first campaign as the Black Sox coach:

... before we went on a tour to North America in 1998, in our first training camp we spent two days building the team. That was a completely foreign concept from previous national sides that I had been involved in. We needed to build the team so we understood each other and so that when we went on tour, the focus was softball and not building a team. Previously, we tended to focus on softball, softball, softball and then we would get on tour without the team being developed with the result being teams that did not function as a cohesive unit. Then we would try and patch things up while on tour but there would be leaks all over the place. Usually the tour would start really well, but towards the back end of the tour, when the competition was at its most serious, expectations were not satisfied and performance suffered. We leveraged off these previous experiences and ensured that building the team was always the first activity completed.

Black Sox team-building exercises have even involved the army in the Southern Alps. Don tells the story:

We have used the New Zealand Army to assist us with team-building activities since we started in 1998. The main reason is that the military have been in the business of building teams for generations, [whereas] with us in sport and business we are only starting to understand the process required to build teams. Therefore, we thought it sensible to leverage off the knowledge and experience of the New Zealand Army. In addition the army facilities are conducive to building teams and not filled with anti-social devices, such as Sky TV.

For the Black Sox, practising team values in the pursuit of the team goals and vision is one of the key selection criteria for the team:

> When selecting sides, the first thing we are looking for is skill that can be executed under pressure. Then [the next question for selection] is if you've got all the other things … because we have had the opportunity to build the values, it's not like [the selectors] are coming in and saying, 'This is our core values and these are not negotiable' … we want to test that each time we bring a team together, so are these still real, are these still valid? If you've got two athletes side by side in terms of skill level and there is not much between them and someone can make another contribution somewhere else for the side, then you go with that person. It still comes down the ability to be successful. You can have all the passion and all the desire and all the belief in the world, but if you haven't got the skills that back it all up, then you are going to be dangerous, but you are not going to be effective … we want effective athletes on our side—that is athletes who have the skill set, the belief and the commitment.

So what happens if an athlete has the skill but does not live the values or take responsibility for his attitude? Don says:

> The athlete will not be part of the Black Sox. If the athlete did not live the agreed values of our culture then [he] would be cast adrift. It is all about respect. Failure to respect the contribution of each individual in the team will result in cliques or divisions within the team. This is generally the first sign of the team breaking down. Loners fall into this category. In teams, you are going to have athletes who don't enjoy socialising with other people, they prefer to be by themselves … the trick is understanding it. There were times when we first started out where athletes did not quite fit the mould, we tried to just change them so they did fit the mould, rather than actually recognising what is really important to those individuals and then ensuring that the team understands. What is important is that each individual buys into what we are trying to do and they believe that they will be a world champion and are prepared to pay a serious price … and everyone's price is different.

Achieving such success comes back to quality team culture, as Don reiterates:

> … for the athlete to succeed, then he/she needs to believe and own every aspect of our programme.

Don's Use of Questioning

The use of questioning as a coaching tool is demonstrated by Don in various aspects of his coaching, including establishing team culture. Through his verbal questions and physical questions to prompt problem solving, athletes can consider the possibilities, rationalise them and come up with the best solution—and thus become better decision makers.

When Don first started coaching the Black Sox, his use of questioning was a new tactic for many of the players. He reflects on how he has been successful with this method even when players may be hesitant at first:

> I have always believed that the solution to any issue we may face is held within the team. One of my roles is that of a facilitator. You know your team, you know your athletes, you know that there are three to four who you know are going to respond in a large group scenario, so when things are getting a little bit quiet, you go to them by asking open questions. 'Mark, what do you think?' You know that he's got an opinion, but he is waiting for someone else to say it, and then out it comes … it becomes infectious. One guy started talking and then some of the other athletes started and then it was like, 'Well what do you think?' The next thing you know, we've got everyone interacting. When I was first appointed as the Black Sox coach I ensured that the athletes understood that I did not have all the answers but, between us, we have a pretty good shot at understanding the issues and crafting the appropriate solution.

The challenge to questioning effectively is to be able to read and understand your athletes and know when to ask the question, to whom and in what situation. Don's philosophy of understanding individuals is highlighted in his method of questioning:

> Asking the right questions to the right athlete at the right time is often the most effective way of ensuring that a particular experience has been analysed and the key learnings identified. If any of these parts is missing then the communication will not be effective. Timing will always depend on the athlete and the nature of the experience. If the experience has been a pleasant one then questions may be asked immediately. If the experience has not been so pleasant then the first priority is the well-being of the athlete; questions that reflect on the experience can wait.

Questioning is a great learning tool for athletes at all levels. As well as using questioning and problem solving extensively with the Black Sox, Don achieves excellent results in using the method with children, as he relates:

I ask questions so they think it through and then we practise that and then [I ask], 'Why do you think that happened?' Even these kids at eight and nine years old are starting to capture the purpose of the game. The kids that I coach all want to understand why we are completing a particular drill.

Don and Teaching Games for Understanding

The tool of Teaching Games for Understanding (TGfU) has been shown to enable athletes to become self-aware and solve problems, which in turn develops their ability to make decisions. One of Don's strongest beliefs, on which he bases his coaching, is that:

> Sport is not black and white, there is way too much grey. One of my roles is to condition my athletes to make smart decisions under pressure.

Because so much of sport is grey, athletes must be able to understand many tactical situations that arise in the game. It follows that setting up purposeful games helps athletes to read such situations and make informed decisions. Thus when coaching the Black Sox, Don uses purposeful games to create competitive situations in which the players must operate under pressure:

> … at the elite level, the [athletes] are there because they are very driven individuals and they are very competitive at anything that they do. Therefore we ensure trainings are set in a competitive environment. All of our drills are designed to ensure that the athlete completes the 'think, recognise and execute' sequence when making a decision. The thinking takes place prior to any action; this process enables the athlete to identify the likely situations before they execute. If the athlete is surprised then typically a poor decision will be the result.

Don disagrees with those coaches who believe that playing games is just about having fun and that the athletes are not learning if the coach is not telling them what to do. As he sees TGfU:

> … it's not about always playing with your mates; it's not always about having a good time, because when we train we are at work, with the objective being quality. It's very structured; each training has a purpose. If the purpose is defending the short game (bunts and little slap hits) then, with the athletes, we design how we are going to set up our defensive patterns. We then test our patterns through structured drills that match what we would expect to experience in a game. When we have proven it in training, we then test it in competition. The purpose of the drills

is to ensure that everyone in the team recognises the situation and understands what the next action will be. At the Black Sox level, we don't try and overcomplicate things; we only ever focus on one part of a game at a time. We don't try and do a bit of everything.

In coaching both children and adult athletes, Don is always looking for the best way to get them to learn skills through game situations:

> ... when I taught kids how to throw ... rather than throw backwards and forwards, which can be pretty boring, we went off to practise at the beach, chucking rocks into the sea. [I challenged them], 'Who can make the biggest splash? Who can throw the furthest?' Then we work on the mechanics. We try to go a bit further and then we try to skim a flat rock across the sea and introducing different throwing techniques. Then you transfer that back into the game. There are, in some instances, similarities [between the two situations] and, in some instances, they're not. But at the kids' level, you have to focus on a bit of everything because otherwise they get a bit bored, they want to hit the ball, they don't want to just sit there fielding the ball and throwing the ball and things like that and running around bases, so we just set up lots and lots of games.

When TGfU is part of the coaching repertoire, a coach must be flexible in organising games or situations that need to be practised. Instead of referring to a book for specific games to learn a certain situation, the coach looks to the situation to determine the game that will be played. In keeping with this approach, Don does not necessarily have a game ready when he is coaching children; rather, he reads the situation and determines which game would suit what the children are trying to learn:

> ... you quickly recognise that they are struggling a little bit, so you introduce them with a game, such as all around ball tag [or] games inside a little wee diamond area, where it is about throwing the ball and tagging someone. It's softball-related skills, but it's all about fun and about physical activity and getting the kids running around. We [might] play a ball tag game inside a diamond with a tennis ball, where the object is that you are trying to throw the ball to try to hit someone. So, again, if you are throwing to someone and they catch it, then they can throw the ball away, so they have to go and get the ball and come back in and it builds the complexity up.

Don believes that the younger the children, the more the focus should be on providing an element of fun in games. As children get older, the games can become more competitive. At any age, however, when games are fun, athletes play intensely and learn because of the natural motivation to play. Equally, each game must be used as a learning tool and be purposeful, rather than just being included in training for the players to have fun. Don underlines this principle with reference to the Black Sox:

> Everything we do with the Black Sox has a purpose that can be aligned back to the purpose of the team (winning a world championship). To meet the athletes' competitive expectations we often break the team into smaller groups and set up drills where there is a winner and loser. At the end of each practice the session is always evaluated why teams won or lost. We never lose an opportunity to learn from our experiences. It is our belief that one of the things that separate the effective teams from the rest is their ability to leverage off their experiences whether they are poor or positive.

Implementing an Athlete-centred Approach

Implementing an athlete-centred approach requires some degree of belief in athlete-centred learning. Moreover, as Don highlights, a coach needs to be able to self-analyse and be aware of his or her own coaching:

> The process of continuous improvement is no different whether you are a coach or an athlete. Coaching is made up of activities and experiences that must be understood along with the context in which they took place. The coaching environment must be conducive to breaking down the significant points and picking up what are the real key learning points. Every campaign that you have, there would be half a dozen points of difference that have separated you from the rest of the world in terms of the competition, or a half a dozen reasons why the other team won ... so just understand, what are they? Why did that team win vs our team, or did this athlete run faster or this athlete, and try to understand that ... then create your plans to put it right, should you find yourself in a similar position in the future.

Don suggests that a coach has to understand the coaching process before beginning to use an athlete-centred approach. As Don sees it, the process is comprised of five components based on what, who, how, when and why:

> The *what* is the technical and tactical part of sport which is the area that is the easiest to learn. It is the area that is the major focus of coach education and can be found in many publications. The *who* is understanding the athletes—what are their expectations, what is important to them, why are they important, what is their background, what is their preferred learning style? The *how* is about packaging up the key messages in a format that matches the learning preference of the athlete, thereby increasing the

chance of the message being understood. The *when* is all about timing. I can know what to say, who to say it to, and how to say it but if my timing is not right it will be an ineffective message. The last part is the *why*—that is about, why are we doing this? Why are we doing anything? If the athlete doesn't believe, then the athlete will do what they believe is appropriate...

I have a simple approach—if I can't sell it, then we just don't do it. It is not necessarily about my idea, it is about how I might sell something to the athlete, or encourage the athletes to make improvements to the idea and come back with a better idea. In my experience, failure to execute a game plan can only come down to one of two reasons: the athlete does not understand, which means that it has not been communicated effectively, or the athlete does not believe in it—it has not been sold with the athlete recognising the benefits.

In an example from the business environment, Don vividly illustrates the consequences of imposing an idea on people rather than asking for their input. This particular experience is just one of many that influenced him to become an athlete-centred coach:

... one of the organisations I worked for decided to rebrand themselves ... new colours along with the purpose and core values. We knew that something was going on because the senior management team kept sneaking off. Then they launched the new brand to the staff (an organisation of about 300 people) at the same time as they did to the outside world (our major customers) ... They said 'This is our new culture'. I [was] sitting there and thinking, 'But aren't the people your culture?' They were talking about all these lovely words and all the things like that, but I had absolutely no connection to it. Given that the culture of an organisation is reflected through its staff, how did they expect it to be lived when the staff had no input into its creation?

One of the highlights of hearing Don discussing his philosophy is his great ability to analyse situations and issues, which includes an apt use of analogies. In one analogy he demonstrates how having ownership is an important aspect to being an athlete-centred coach:

I look at myself at home; I want to build a nice, white picket fence outside my house. I've got two choices. One is that I can pay someone to do it and I might admire a fantastic job but I am not emotionally attached to it. Or I can get out and do it myself. It might not be a flash job but I am emotionally attached to it. The emotional attachment is what lasts.

As with other coaches in this book, shared leadership is an important aspect to Don's coaching. Contrary to what he sees as the traditional stereotype of leaders as older, more mature people who have already paid their dues, he suggests that:

> We don't operate like that. If an athlete has leadership qualities then we leverage off them. Great things happened in this last campaign, where one of our young guys, a 21-year-old, stepped up and took ownership of an issue and its resolution during our World Series in Christchurch. I am not a believer in developing senior player groups as they are typically filled with athletes that have similar backgrounds and experiences. In short, they think alike. I have always considered that these types of groups limit creativity. We operate with an informal leadership team within the Black Sox. We don't believe that we need to formalise it as the leaders are readily identifiable to everyone in the team.

As Don practises the athlete-centred approach, the leadership role is used to enhance understanding and communication among the athletes, Don and the management team. Don describes one of his tools for ensuring two-way communication:

> I prefer to have almost all my messages delivered through the leadership team that we have within the team, not through me. The messages that I delivered needed to basically stop the team, so that we could re-group get back on task and move forward. When you are in a campaign such as our World Series, if I was the delivering all of the messages then it gets a little bit tiresome ... what can you possibly say that is different to what you have been saying all along? ... During our heavy conditioning phase, if I want to motivate a group of athletes in Auckland, I use a Wellington athlete to deliver my message. It would be in the form of a simple phone call from one athlete to another sharing how hard the Wellington guys are training. The next thing you know, there is a competition going on between the Wellington- and Auckland-based athletes.

Every coach has various strategies for implementing an athlete-centred approach in which the players understand, own and take responsibility for the mutual direction of the team. When a coach understands and shows concern for every individual athlete, trust is obtained. With mutual trust, the team goes forward and becomes the best that they can be, together. The process of gaining athletes' trust and enabling them to learn is specific to the coach's process of empowering players.

The Process of Empowering Athletes

To enable athletes to learn, coaches in this book include them in making informed decisions in all aspects of the team environment. As Don points out, a coach needs to trust in the ability of the athlete to make these decisions:

It is the athlete that makes the decision in real time; therefore you must trust the athlete to make the smart decisions under pressure. If I don't trust my athletes to make the smart decision then I would consider that I have failed them. In addition, members of the leadership team take on a mentoring role that results in a transfer of knowledge. We spend a lot of time ensuring that the athlete understands the context in which the decision is made. For example, if a decision was made at club level, we encourage the athletes to consider if the same decision would be appropriate at the international level.

As part of this process, athletes learn and recognise what they should execute to achieve the most informed type of play. Don explains how they do it:

It's part of their reflective practice. The greater lessons that you learn in life are those where you feel a little bit of pain. If you make some mistakes, then you've got to have that opportunity and the environment where you can go back and reflect on it and say, 'Okay, now that I am wiser and I have got a little bit of hindsight on my side, was that the smart play or why did I make that decision?'

Before athletes can reflect in this way, coaches need to create an environment that allows them to analyse through trial and error. At the elite level of the Black Sox, athletes should come to the team environment with some ability to think and make decisions. Unfortunately, as Don suggests, they have not necessarily had the chance to develop this ability as many athletes at the development levels are never given the opportunity to practise reflecting on decisions made:

… when I was coaching the Black Sox, we had some of the best softball players in the world. Yet their knowledge of the game and their ability to make smart decisions under pressure was our greatest weakness. That was simply because, right through their careers, they were always the best kids on the team. Therefore, whether they make a poor decision or a great decision, it didn't really matter, because they could do whatever they liked. They could typically get away with it because their skill set or their athletic ability tended to cover up poor decisions. But the higher you travel in international sport, then that all evens itself out and typically the teams that win are the teams that make the smart decisions under pressure.

In learning how to make decisions under pressure, the Black Sox were allowed to make mistakes so that they could learn and reflect on why the decisions were made. Don describes his method:

… we spent two years from '98 to 2000 encouraging our athletes to make mistakes. We spent two years with a small set of signals so that we could enable our athletes on tours of Canada (they were big tours for us) to make decisions where they would actually feel a little bit of pain in terms of making poor choices. We then go through the process to understand whether it was a smart or poor decision. We go all the way through, in terms of process, and we break the play down to understand the critical decision point through asking open questions of the athlete concerned and the rest of the team. 'What happened?' Or, 'Why did it happen?' And, 'Why didn't you think about throwing the ball to first base?' or, 'Why didn't you throw it to third base?' It is an environment where you are not necessarily challenging the athlete, saying that he made a poor choice, it is just understanding the process and improving the awareness of the athlete when making the decision.

The coach must be able to read players' level of ability to cope with taking ownership (especially if they have never been exposed to an athlete-centred approach). With this knowledge, the coach can determine how much to involve athletes in decision making and gradually move towards the ultimate goal of delegating decision making to the athletes. With reference to the Black Sox, Don elaborates on the process he uses to gradually introduce an athlete-centred approach to the players:

When building the culture of the 2000 World Champion team, I was probably a little bit [coach-centred]. This was because of the athletes' maturity level with an athlete-centred approach in developing team culture. In 2000 I met with the athlete leadership team and explained what I was looking for in terms of culture. The athlete leadership team then facilitated a meeting with the rest of the athletes. The outcome of the meeting was a perception that the athletes built the culture of the team, when in reality they delivered pretty much what I sent them away to do. In 2004 the process was very different, with the athletes taking complete ownership of developing the culture of the 2004 team. The captain of the side facilitated a meeting with the athletes; the outcome was the core components of the culture.

There was an advantage to empowering players for the 2004 campaign. Don suggests that one of the reasons for the success in 2004 was the systems that had been set up to empower players:

It depends on the team you've got … The Black Sox model is built on a solid foundation of stability. The core of the athletes will have had World Championship experience and exposure to our culture. The way we have built the 2004 Black Sox ensures that the next time we go to a World Championship, of the 17 [athletes in the team], there will be about nine or ten who will be back. So the core of the team will be back each time. We just regenerate talent, so coming out the other end is a bunch of young guys who have already been exposed to our culture and coaching style.

Don believes in using an athlete-centred approach for athletes at all levels. So is there a difference in the coaching process between the Black Sox and his son's team? Don considers:

In many ways the process is the same. The kids that I coach are now 10. At the start of this season the kids decided what the main objective is for the year. This was achieved through a series of questions. I asked the kids what they liked most about softball. They all responded that batting was the most fun. I then asked what stops us from batting. After a very little direction by me, the response was fielding—if we can't get the other team out, we never get a chance to bat. Falling out of this conversation was the decision developed by the kids that we wanted to be the best fielding team in the grade. Therefore our main objective for the year is developing our fielding capability so we can get the other team out quickly, which will mean that we will spend more time batting.

As mentioned earlier, part of empowering your athletes is to know who they are. On each Black Sox tour, Don has made a point of getting to know each player—although, as he relates, the process has not been without its challenges:

… for each tour, I spend time getting to know the athletes on a personal level, sitting on the buses with them … just talking sport and life. We have always viewed our bus trips as learning environments. However, this was tested on our first tour when some of the senior players decided that they were going to introduce a ranking system when sitting on the bus. They decided that because of their status they would sit at the back of the bus as they understood the All Blacks did. We let it go for a couple of days, then we sat down with the senior players and talked to them about it. 'Okay, why are we doing this?' 'Oh, because the All Blacks do it.' 'So, we are followers are we, we are just doing this because someone else does it? I thought we wanted to be trendsetters, why are we following everyone else?' We then asked how we could win without the younger members of the team who were sitting at the front of the bus. It was acknowledged that we couldn't. Then I asked why then were they treated differently? How were we going to leverage off each others' knowledge and experience when we did not sit together? The following day the ranking system was removed by the athletes and the bus trips returned to the required learning environment.

Don's insight on how he empowers his players will stimulate others to come up with ideas that might suit their own environment. In coaching, there is no one way that works best; what is central is the athletes. Any campaign is the athletes' campaign. But athletes need some control over their sporting lives. Don gives a personal analogy about how adults need to have faith in their children by allowing them some freedom to be innovative and acknowledging their effort:

> I am just thinking of a story of mismatched expectations. One that I always had my dad on about, when I could talk to him about these things, is when I mowed the lawns. I would do what I considered to be an absolutely fantastic job and I could pick up the lawn and take it to Wembley. I had it criss-crossed and everything. My dad wouldn't see that. He would only see that I didn't trim the edges. So that is what he'd focus on and I would get a hell of a letdown …
>
> The key learning from that was how did I feel about that? So I try look at everything in a complete and entirety and how it was done … congratulate the success and if there are some bits around the edges that you want to tidy up, then pick your timing to talk about the edges. So, role reversal, what I was looking for at that stage was my dad to pat me on the back and say 'That was a fantastic job' and then maybe the next day say, 'Hey let's come out and have a crack at these edges together' or whatever, [where] the focus is not on poor performance because I didn't do the edges, the focus is on, 'Hey, that is a fantastic performance' because of the way the lawns looked.
>
> It is so important that we deliver positive messages. Yet we typically feel more comfortable focusing on the negative parts of performance. The childhood saying, 'Sticks and stones will break my bones but names will never hurt me', is complete garbage. Broken bones mend yet emotional scaring caused by what has been said can last a lifetime.

Some Challenges of an Athlete-centred Approach

As for every innovative approach, an athlete-centred approach has its limitations. One of the challenges facing Don when he took over the World Championship team in 1996 was that the athletes had expectations of him, based on their relationship with the previous coach, that did not match his intended approach. He elaborates on the challenges of introducing his athlete-centred approach to his players:

... the relationship with the athletes was more a player–player relationship because I played with most of them. I started coaching New Zealand when I was 36, so I wasn't that far out from the players. So the first challenge for me was to actually adjust the relationship. My previous relationship with these guys gave me the opportunity to walk through the door with instant credibility. But then the challenge for me was to gain that credibility each day, to where it went without saying … it was because the relationship was completely different to the relationship Mike Walsh had with the team initially. Mine was more like a peer relationship. There were not a lot of things to handle in terms of adjusting the relationship … Because I had that relationship with a lot of those guys, and they experienced me when I was an athlete as someone who would challenge, teach and coach in the same manner as I am doing now, it wasn't a lot different to them. 'Hey, this is Don coaching us, this is not someone else.'

At this point we talked about my expectations and those of the athletes. The first thing we did was build a team as it hadn't been done in a planned way before. This approach received instant positive feedback from the athletes so straight away we had captured the imagination of the athletes. This approach enabled the athletes to contribute to the planning process that delivered a world championship. From this very first camp we gathered momentum in a structured way, ensuring that we had the right team playing our best softball at the World Championships. They saw that everything was a bit different here.

Don is a 'big picture' coach. He believes in looking to the long-term outcome and direction of his team and then encouraging his athletes to analyse what is needed to reach that outcome:

It starts with having the desired outcome clearly defined and owned by the athletes. Then it is about leveraging off the knowledge and experience of the athletes and the coaching team to develop the processes that will deliver the desired outcome. The process will include identifying the key milestones where we test our progress. At least annually after our pinnacle event for the year, I facilitate a meeting with the leadership team where we ask a simple question, 'If we continue to implement our plan, will we deliver our desired outcome?' If the answer is yes then the next question is, 'How can we improve the plan?' If the answer is no, then the question asked is, 'What do we need to do to get the programme back on track?'

Don recognises that in their development as coaches, people—in the role of athlete or coach—often experience coach-centred coaches and learn that approach to coaching as the 'correct' approach. This influence is hardly surprising given that, as human beings, we tend to copy what we have seen, based on the reasoning that it has worked in the past so it should continue to work. In this situation, the key is to inspire coaches to question the status quo, as Don says:

> … growing up in terms of my experiences I have had coaches all the way through who were very prescriptive. They tell you what to do, and you do it or you don't do it. But there is no [questioning] what is in it for me. If your style is to challenge and inspire athletes, then the athlete must recognise that there is a real value and benefit to them. If the benefits are recognised then it is easy to adjust the behaviours of an athlete.

So when training coaches it is a challenge to encourage them to take an athlete-centred approach. For the coaches being trained, it is a challenge to be confident enough to try it and believe that it is the athlete who is the most important component in sport. To gain this confidence, Don believes you need experience:

> Coaches must recognise that it is not about us. All we are doing is delivering a service to the athlete. You only have to consider how the media reacts to a win or a loss to realise that the athlete is the most important aspect in sport. On my first tour I noticed that when we won, the media focused on the athletes in terms of interviews. Yet when we lost, they bypassed the athletes and came after me. In terms of confidence in making decisions under pressure—it comes down to experience and having the discipline to reflect after each decision. I store each of these experiences away so that I can use them or a combination of them to craft solutions to issues as they confront me. There is no great mystery to sport and the issues that we are confronted with are not unique—it is only the context in which they differ.

Certainly Don can apply an athlete-centred approach confidently and effectively now. But how did he become confident enough to try it at all? He explains:

> I just believed that it was what the athlete wanted. I just believed that it is right for us in terms of our stage of development. I believe it was the right way to go in terms of coaching and hadn't been convinced otherwise through my previous experience. It was these experiences that conditioned me to realise that this is the way forward. Having said that, not all of the athletes were comfortable with this approach, so for them I delivered a coach-centred service.

The first step towards an athlete-centred approach, as coaches indicate throughout this book, is to believe that the athletes themselves will benefit from contributing to the team and making decisions. Because many coaches lack the confidence and/or the experience to implement an athlete-centred approach, I was curious to find out how Don believes we learn how to encourage athlete decision making. He says:

> I believe it is just a collection of whole heap of things. Clearly, you want to take the luck out of it, so it all depends on the environmental factors … It's not just about experiences, you can have all the experience in the world, but if you don't have the ability to take a step back and actually understand them in terms of what just happened and why it happened, then you will have to get a collection of experiences that are in no particular order or context, which will make it very difficult for them to be re-used. In short, no learning would have occurred.

Another challenge of using an athlete-centred approach is that it takes time to ask athletes and include them in decision making. Yet the focus needs to be on the outcome: athletes learn and develop more effectively when there is time to work on their learning and development. Don agrees that, if a coach is to form a quality team, it requires some time:

> As part of the Black Sox culture we believe that the big prizes in life are hard to win—for if they were easy anyone could do it. Good things typically happen when you have a plan and work incredibly hard to execute it—there are no shortcuts to sustained success. It sometimes takes time for the whole team to recognise the benefit of a particular initiative. The outcome of belief and ownership in the game plan is worth the wait, as it will not break down under pressure. Should I be the initiator of a particular idea, then I look to the team to make it better. It is through this involvement that quality solutions are developed.

Coaches are busy people and are often coaching as volunteers. To be a great coach and great at everything else in your life, it is important to have balance. It is important to not just say the right things, but to practise them. The balance comes if coaches actually live it and learn how to say 'no' in difficult circumstances. For coaches who find it challenging to achieve a balance in their life while coaching, Don offers this advice:

> … it's hard to get that balance and it is something that I constantly strive to get right. The most important part as a coach is that you need to have some space for yourself, which is why I've got to have balance. There are four main quadrants to my life that I need to balance: being a father and husband; my employment; my coaching; and my own space where I can recharge and ensure that I remain energised to deliver a quality service to the other three quadrants that they deserve.

I have not necessarily cracked the balance issue; however, what works for me is to use the coaching and family quadrants to provide me with the balance I require. It is these quadrants that I always want in my life. Therefore spending time in them is always rewarding and refreshing. I also use [both] the 30-minute commute to work and the time that I find to exercise as time to unwind and keep life in perspective. The final point about balance is that I have a close group of friends, in particular my wife, who provide advice on the load that I am carrying to ensure that I keep things in perspective

Plans for the Future

In his current employment, one of Don's roles is to develop coaches. Part of his philosophy in educating other coaches is to communicate the potential of our athletes as people. Sport is often discussed as an institution that develops character and good human citizens. However, unless we practise developing character and getting athletes to make decisions, these sport values are difficult to meet. Developing decision makers in life is important to producing a generation who are independent and informed thinkers. Coaches as educators can have a role in producing thoughtful children. Through another analogy, Don highlights the need to allow our children a bit of room to learn from their own experiences:

> ... it's all the way through life, it's about making decisions. I mean making decisions about when to cross the road and when not to cross the road. I am a parent, and I am having a debate with my wife at the moment ..., now it is time for my ten-year-old son to walk to school by himself, with his seven-year-old sister. My wife doesn't believe he is mature enough to do it. Whereas I look at it and say, 'Well we need to have confidence in him and trust him to make smart decisions.' As I see it, our role as parents is to create an environment that encourages our children to make decisions; an environment where the awareness of child is enhanced. If we continue on the current track, we are just going to create a generation of young people who haven't got the ability to make decisions because they have never had to. Sport is like that; even coaching young kids ... let the kids find out for themselves which is the best way to do something.

As a contributor to the coaching strategy for New Zealand, Don discusses how coach education can develop athletes who are decision makers as they progress though the system:

> The first step is to ensure that coach development is connected to the development requirements of whoever is coached. It then needs to

recognise that the constraints for coaches are the environmental factors in which we operate. They are never the same; therefore coaching cannot be scripted. We need to keep the development framework practical and relevant to the stage of the child/athlete who is coached. We must leverage off the knowledge and experience of coaches. We have got some fantastic coaches in New Zealand, yet we don't celebrate them. They are off doing their own thing; somehow we need to capture them and then feed them back in … it's broadly an awareness of the coaching requirement. One of the risks with coach development is that you coach by following the book, you become dependent on a development framework, and you think that there is only one solution. Coach development must move beyond the current what and when, and have a greater focus on the who, how and why.

Training future coaches, Don says, is about:

… recognising that everyone that we coach deserves a quality coaching experience. Therefore we must understand the expectations of each individual. We also need to recognise that not one group has all the answers, but together if we understand each other's roles and skill sets, then we can make a real difference. But it is like anything in sport, it starts with respect. I respect the view of science and I respect the view of the coaching academic, but I have an expectation that they respect my point of view as well. The more we enhance our awareness of the various views, the greater we are positioned to truly understand the issues and craft the required solution.

Contained within Don's insight into present coach development is the idea of networking to enhance our application and understanding of a coach's role. There is no one correct method of coaching. It is an extremely dynamic, multi-dimensional role. The coaching method always depends on the situation, and the who, when, what, how and especially why. Don emphasises the extent to which coaches can learn from each other on an ongoing basis:

… within New Zealand if you have coached a successful team, then there is a perception that you must be pretty good at what you are doing, so people tend to want to listen to you. It is as if you have the magic pill. I don't believe that at all. For every opportunity I get to talk to a group of coaches, I get just as much if not more out of the experience than the coaches I talk to. My most valued coaching development experience is talking to other coaches. It's about leveraging off each other's knowledge and experience. You won't necessarily find a perfect fit for each experience as it will always depend on the context in which the experience occurred. But you will find streams and say, 'Yes, I can identify with that.'

To reach a great height a person
needs to have great depth. - Anonymous

Conclusion

Don's refreshing goal of meeting individual needs indicates how a positive environment can be created using an athlete-centred approach. His strong emphasis on planning for long-term outcomes is another highlight in his coaching approach. In combination, these views mean that, rather than catering to outside expectations, coaches should focus first on the needs of their team and athletes and together they will establish the team direction. If the athletes own those outcomes, then the path to success is easier and more rewarding. To achieve those outcomes, certain sacrifices need to be made—like being happy using certain situations to learn, rather than focus on winning. Along the pathway to achieving a team of champions, trial-and-error learning is essential.

Although his knowledge and thinking have developed substantially already, Don believes he still has much to learn about coaching. He is a great advocate for talking with other coaches as an aid to learning, as he believes that 'answers are not found in books—books contain ideas—the answers are held with coaches. [We should] encourage coaches to talk to each other and leverage off each other's knowledge and experience.' Don also believes in constant observation and analysis of other sports and teams to provide insight and challenges as to why certain events happen in a certain way. These insights transfer well into all aspects of coaches' own sport and team.

Given the complex and multi-dimensional nature of coaching, Don favours a close analysis of any given situation in terms of who, what, when, where, how and especially why. The ability to read a situation and the people involved goes a long way to making athletes valued members of the team. As Don says, 'Coaching is not about the coach, it is about the athlete(s) and the value the coach can add.

A wise man makes his own decisions; an ignorant
man follows the public opinion. - Chinese Proverb

Too often we give children answers to remember
rather than problems to solve. - Roger Lewin, US humorist, author

The principle is competing
against yourself. It's about self
improvement, about being better
than you were the day before.
- Steve Young

Chapter Twelve

How's Your Coaching?

Guest Author: Rick Humm

International Rugby Board and USA Rugby Coach
Trainer/Educator

How do you get to a place in your coaching where you feel good about what you are doing? There are lots of modes of feedback: win–loss, player compliments, news media notices, appointments to new coaching roles, recognition of peers, and so on. Such feedback is largely outside our control and extrinsic (external). A better gauge of how we are doing is likely to involve feedback that lies within our control and that arises out of our coaching process. Such a feedback process is fundamental to answering the simple question, *'How's your coaching?'*

Coaching is about working with individuals and groups as they strive to succeed. Most peak performers and top athletic teams have coaches serving as supporters, advisers and experts. Individuals seek out coaches they trust and respect; people who express opinions for the purpose of enhancing an individual's ability to get to the next level of competition. It follows that to be a successful coach, one needs to put ego aside, be self-aware and manage self in pursuit of stronger performance in one's athletes.

This chapter provides some insight into the coaching practice along with some practical suggestions for developing standards with which we can review and reflect on our coaching. I will also discuss how we can self-manage and self-organise to enable our athletes to develop and perform—that is, how we can exercise our coaching craft. The goal is the development of intrinsic (internal) motivators and signs that, maybe, we're doing something right and that we have cause to feel good about what we are doing. The chapter also focuses on the coach's management of self in relation to athletes in the athlete-centred, humanistic coaching environment. Some questions considered include: How do you know an athlete-centred coaching approach when you see one? How does the coach conduct himself or herself? How does he or she relate to the players? How do the players interact with each other? In particular, does the coach's behaviour exhibit awareness of self and others? Do the coach and the players reflect on performance? Whose voices are most present in training sessions and meetings? Has the coach offered enough value to shift players from their comfort zones towards excellence?

Getting to Athlete-centredness

I have grown up immersed in a United States (USA) approach to sport and have played and coached a wide variety of games and sports. While experienced in coaching sports with deep traditions in the USA, professionally I have focused principally on working with rugby players and coaches.

This background is pertinent to the following discussion of two divergent sport experiences and how they have led me to embrace athlete-centredness. The divergent experiences are: first, being immersed in a USA coaching tradition and its pervasive images, icons and caricatures; and, second, coaching rugby in the United States and facing the challenges of introducing the game to older players grounded in traditional USA sports.

It is challenging to integrate understandings of coaching based in USA sport experiences with the need to accelerate game understanding in rugby athletes in the USA setting. My studies have been focused on approaches to fast-tracking development of rugby understanding and decision making among rugby players in the USA. From this perspective, an athlete-centred approach makes sense and many USA coaches are embracing it.

Sport traditions world round promote a special role for the 'coach'. Often the 'coach' is put on a pedestal and the title 'coach' is an artifice of authority. The coach's role is thought of, questionably, as a director, a 'god', a person of great expertise.

Contrary to such widespread perceptions, however, coaching is about helping athletes maximise their potential—helping them to acquire the skills and develop an understanding of the game or competition that are necessary for competitive success. A coach can assist by observing and sharing what a player may miss. It follows, then, that the authoritarian role needs to be modified; that is, coaches need to become facilitators of learning.

An athlete-centred, humanistic approach to coaching grows out of awareness of others and of self. Awareness of others is necessary to understanding an athlete's experience. We can gain that understanding by first beginning to be aware of ourselves. Self-awareness can lead us to an understanding of, for example, what motivates athletes, how they work, and how they work with others. Through understanding ourselves, we can also begin to develop empathy, an aspect missing in many coach development programmes. Self-reflection is a major tool used in developing this awareness.

Self-awareness and empathy, or an awareness of self and others, are keys to successful athlete-centred coaching. Often, as coaches, we take these perspectives for granted. A respected college-level rugby coach in California, who is pursuing an athlete-centred approach, recently related one example of how this area can be challenging. Coaching a representative rugby side, he was working on player ownership of a certain tactical approach. This task was particularly challenging as the players came from a number of programmes with a wide variety of experiences. Using questioning, he regularly checked for understanding and the players assured him that they knew their purpose and embraced the approach.

At match time, the team did not pursue the tactics on which they had been working. In exploring this outcome with the team, the coach discovered that the players had been responding with that they thought he wanted to hear and that they were not really comfortable with the approach. In the match, they fell back on the methods of the team from which several of the more assertive players came.

On reflection, the coach decided that he needed to work on increasing his awareness of the players' experience. In particular, in his previous communication he had elicited from the players judgements about the approach rather than clues to their own experience. Because the players had wanted to meet the coach's goal, asking them whether they understood had drawn the inevitable, 'Yes, coach!'

In this case, the coach determined that he could hone his questioning skills to effectively probe the players' experience and understanding. As with so many other skill-based issues, we can enhance our skills with focus, discussion and practice. In a later section, we further explore developing our self-awareness, our ability to be present and aware of others and our relationships with our players in the coaching environment.

Coaching Culture in the USA

The United States has a very strong claim to being the birthplace of coaching and certainly has a very wide and deep coaching history. Coaches there have long been associated with sporting success. The successful, focused USA coaches cover the full range of coaching approaches.

Numerous examples of successful coaches with larger than life personalities are found in both reality and popular stereotypes. The coach archetype in the USA is often a one-dimensional director figure who gets in the way of learning. The images of Bobby Knight throwing chairs or slapping players, or of Woody Hayes tackling a player from the sideline, or of the bombastic Earl Weaver cursing umpires, distract attention from the depth and breadth of coaching in the USA. Even the nearly mythical figure of Vince Lombardi is often reduced to the stereotype associated with his famous statement about winning not being everything, it's the only thing.

However, there are also strong examples of athlete-centred coaches such as basketball coaches John Wooden and Phil Jackson. Wooden is well known to have been focused on his athlete's learning from their sporting experiences, famously emphasising the need to accept mistakes as learning experiences. Jackson adopts a coaching structure that allows the players to grow as individuals as they surrender themselves to the group effort. He nurtures that environment by 'listening without judgment', by being 'truly present with impartial, open awareness' (Jackson and Delehanty, 1995, p. 67).

USA sport traditions often perpetuate an environment of hero worship of both coaches and athletes. For coaches, the honorific 'Coach' confers power and dominance and creates an implicit identity attached to the role. As noted above, that identity often entails being director, controller and external motivator—a person of unquestioned credibility.

Coaches typically embrace this implicit role in a variety of ways. Importantly many coach-centred coaches have achieved enormous success, especially as measured in wins and losses. On a personal level, too, this unspoken identity is gratifying. It is flattering to be called 'Coach'. It supports one's sense of self—one's ego.

However, if, as we have said, coaching is about unlocking a person's potential to maximise his or her own performance then the implicit identity needs to be put away. Coaching is about helping athletes '… learn rather than teaching them' (Whitmore, 2002, p. 8). Coaches need to subordinate their ego and make the athlete's learning experience the centrepiece. In stepping back and focusing on learning, coaches come to a mindful embrace of athlete-centredness. It is not necessarily a natural approach. Rather, it begins to make sense that pursuing an athlete-centred approach is a pragmatic way of fostering understanding and maximising athlete potential.

In this regard, again Phil Jackson's experience provides an example of how you can meet the desired goal of winning by establishing an athlete-centred learning culture. Pragmatically, Jackson's embrace of the triangle offence fits the bill: he calls the approach 'awareness in action' (Jackson and Delehanty, 1995, p. 87). The approach is designed to create continuous movement with the aim of causing the defence to react and then to exploit those reactions. It demands that players learn to read the defence and to react as a team. As Jackson observes, '… it empowered everybody on the team by making them more involved' (Jackson and Delehanty, 1995, p. 89).

Interestingly some in New Zealand would say the culture Wayne Smith and Robbie Deans created with the Crusaders rugby team was similar in terms of establishing playing principles based on player awareness and empowerment, embedding them through training and establishing principles-based accountability. The coach's role is focused on establishing the principles of the approach in agreement with the players, managing training and holding the players accountable for those principles.

Rugby in the USA

Until very recently, there was little or no rugby in the schools or on children's playgrounds in the USA. Athletes have typically come to rugby as young adults in high school or university. When they do so, they are often overwhelmed by the strangeness of the game. Rugby coaching in the United States demands skills that accelerate athlete learning. The great challenge for USA coaches is helping players with learning new skills (or to adapt other sport skills) and developing an understanding of the game.

Most rugby coaches in the USA are unpaid. Their education, training and experience in coaching are often minimal. There is usually little understanding of learning principles. A related challenge is that their time with the players is restricted in most programmes; a couple of hours a couple times a week is the norm.

This combination of underdeveloped coaching skills and minimal time typically leads to a highly prescriptive approach. Many coaches contemplating an athlete-centred approach assert, 'I just don't have time and "they" just don't understand so I have to be very scripted.' This assertion is conveniently nested in the cultural perspective of coaching success as arising from a directive approach.

Unless exposed to athlete-centred coaching, an individual coach is likely to use the predominantly directive techniques and methods they experienced as they learned the game. It may be more comfortable and easier for the coach, but the persistent question is, what happens to the athletes' learning and performance?

This coach-centred approach has contributed to the common occurrence of rugby as a one-dimensional game in the United States. Structure and singularity have often been the most recognisable elements of the play of the national rugby team, the Eagles. Many of the coaches of teams that have played the Eagles have identified its predictability as a weakness. In 1999, after the Eagles had fallen to the Queensland Reds (an Australian state team), Reds coach Bob Templeton commented to me that the game was easy to defend because his team could see what was coming from the Eagles.

On the other hand, although they may be in a minority, the teams of a number of USA practitioners of an athlete-centred approach have been improving significantly and achieving success. A prime example comes from the rugby programme at Penn State University. Under the stewardship of Peter Steinberg, the women's team has been in the finals for 12 of the last 14 years, has been the national champion for five of the last 10 years and currently holds the title. Players have shaped the team culture and exercised player ownership with such player-driven programme planning as creation of player behavioural norms, fund and resource development and programme goal-setting.

Importantly the players are involved in personal and team performance goal-setting and provide perspective and feedback on selection criteria, tactical approaches and training plans and execution. Steinberg conducts regular reviews of training sessions, match performances and team meetings. In sum, he works toward player responsibility for the programme individually and collectively.

For himself, Steinberg establishes his own performance goals focused on his interactions with players and development of the player-centred team culture. He regularly assesses his progress against those goals through self-reflection and a review process in partnership with coaches involved in the Penn State programme and others familiar with his work. The review process checks his own self-reflective conclusions with the impressions of those with whom he works.

The purpose of this overview of coaching systems in the USA has been to set the context of why and how we need to become aware of our own impact on our athletes. The change in coaching required to support athletes is complex and the next few sections address how coaches can change to a more athlete-centred, humanistic coaching approach that meets athletes' needs.

Picking Up New Coaching Skills

When coaches talk about a 'professional' approach to their coaching, they differ in their understanding of what this means. The most important aspect of being 'professional' is not about pay or demeanour, but about expanding one's knowledge and skills to contribute to the field in which one is engaged. It is about putting learning at the centre of activity.

Coaches working in an athlete-centred environment are certainly confronted with a number of significant challenges. We need to unlearn habits and form new ones. Often, the role is so different from what we think it should be, we wind up struggling to understand our own value to the endeavour.

Intellectually embracing learning and developing new skills may be relatively easy. Internalising a learning approach and changing one's coaching approach is more difficult. Coping with change is discussed in more detail under 'Self-motivation' below (and is also covered in Chapter Two). Seeing the outcome of new coaching skills in the behaviour and play of the team helps. That is, if you can tie your efforts to identifiable player outcomes, you can begin to identify your impact and your value to the process.

Peter Baggetta, a USA rugby staff coach, uses a clear standard for himself: 'How does my coaching process impact the player's performance?' In training, this question relates to how much the player has learned. Typically he creates high intensity games as learning activities. When he began to pursue the games approach, he found it challenging: the players struggled with understanding the point of the game, or the games were not challenging enough, or they had too little structure. Over time he learned it wasn't just about 'throwing out the ball'. As he improved his own intervention and developed better ways of modifying the rules or structure, the play (and players) improved. Baggetta's value to the team had become apparent in their play and allowed him to connect enhancement of his skills and his own learning to the coaching process.

To facilitate the implementation of these new coaching skills, we need to redefine our value and the gratification we take from the coaching experience. In a coach-centred environment, we typically seek gratification from what we see as our 'contributions. To this end, we might look for answers to questions such as:

- Was it the my game plan that led to success?
- Was it my instruction that led to the solid tackling?
- Did my attack philosophy create the opportunities?
- Was it my teaching that was responsible for our line-out success?
- Just what did I do?

In an athlete-centred environment, the gratification tends to be vicarious: it comes from the athletes' learning and successful improvement in performance. Where the athletes have played, made successful decisions, executed their skills to the best of their potential and succeeded in the heat of the moment, the coach's reward comes from knowing he or she helped with their learning and development.

It is this struggle with a changed role of the coach that ultimately will lead to our coaching success in an athlete-centred environment. It is our ability to manage our own sense of self that will lead to our success as enablers of learning. The more engaged the coach is in his or her own learning, the more the coach can enable learning. This is a truly professional approach to the coaching craft.

Developing Our Coaching Skills—Becoming Aware of Ourselves

The coaching process involves a wide range of components including traditional areas such as knowledge of the game in which the players are engaged, knowledge of biomechanics, physical conditioning, nutrition and the logistics of getting a team to a training site. Given the complexity of coaching and the dynamic nature of the sport environment, we need to focus on the development of skills involved in understanding self in relation to the athletes.

Important to the process of developing playing skills is understanding the particular requirements for successfully carrying out a particular skill. As coaches, we typically know the key factors related to successful playing skills and have developed our own systems of key factor analysis of our team's play. The focus on these playing skills is the cornerstone of the coach development programmes of both the International Rugby Board and USA rugby.

Isn't it interesting that we usually don't have a similar scheme to analyse our own coaching processes? What are the most important elements in developing our communication skills or awareness of the players' mood, learning or experience?

As we begin to develop our coaching skills in the arena of management of self and relationships, we need to create or borrow a schematic of related key factors. The concept of emotional intelligence (EQ) is such a schematic. EQ describes the skills or competencies needed to identify, assess and manage the emotions of one's self, of others and of groups. It is rooted in many sources, but was popularised in 1995 by Daniel Goleman in his book *Emotional Intelligence* which dwelt on the relationship between EQ and workplace success (Goleman, 1995; see also Goleman, 1998).

Although a number of people have described or defined EQ, Goleman's definitions apply well to our discussion here. His model proposes four emotional competencies, particularly in relation to leader performance. The EQ model reads like a skills list that can be useful in a key factors approach for successful coaching. The four main competencies are grouped in two areas: personal (managing self) and social (managing relationships). The competencies related to managing relationships align well with the skills coaches use in their work with athletes:

- In regard to the competency of *social awareness* (empathy, awareness of group or organisation), the humanistic, athlete-centred coach is tuned into team personalities, events and dynamics. Who are the natural leaders; the "cut-ups"; the quiet, hard workers? What else is going on in the players' lives? How is the intensity of a training session affecting attitude?
- *Relationship management* (inspiration, influence, catalysing change, managing conflict, collaboration, etc.) links to the humanistic, athlete-centred coach's creation of a learning environment that encourages open and honest interaction. Are the players given to expressing their feelings and opinions appropriately and openly? Is the environment free from distractions interfering with player motivation?

The skills involved in the other competencies, which are concerned with managing self, are relevant to coaching yet often missed in our coaching-related discussions:

- In regard to the competency of *self-awareness* (including accurate self-assessment and self confidence), the humanistic, athlete-centred coach uses an open system to review coaching process as well as team performance. Is there open discussion among coaches and players about training sessions? Does the coach encourage open and honest critique of the contribution of the coaches as well as players to the success of training sessions?
- *Self-management* (self control, transparency, adaptability, initiative, optimism) links to the humanistic, athlete-centred coach's upbeat outlook and reaction to events with genuine emotion. Are both coach and players able to express genuine emotion? Does the coach initiate discussion of the impact of events both good and bad? Does the coach understand his or her own behaviours and how they impact on the team? Is a coach who reacts strongly with yelling and hollering when things don't go well being genuine or out of control? The balance is the issue

here: it is important to be genuine and not hide emotion but to manage reactions appropriately. In achieving this balance one coach, who knows that he reacts strongly to events on the pitch when on the sideline, has managed his participation by observing from behind the goal area during a match.

If we embrace the effectiveness of the EQ model and development of EQ competencies as a pathway to success in coaching, we can begin to develop the skills necessary for self-management and relationship management. The next section explores how coaches relate to players and the processes involved in using these components in the context of Goleman's notion of EQ.

Managing Relationships

Managing relationships is about understanding other people: what motivates them, how they work, how they work with others—all high EQ perceptions. Coaches need a range of individual social skills to successfully manage relationships.

Probably the most important skill in managing relationships is communication. Coaches must be able to call on a variety of communication skills—verbal skills, listening skills, and the ability to interpret messages sent through body language. That is, they need to be able to read others as well as use multiple modes in communicating their understanding to the athlete.

A coach with high EQ observes the athlete's behaviour carefully (body language and actions) and interprets the meaning of what is observed. The coach needs to be aware of the physical and emotional effects of certain events. Then, drawing on empathy, he or she provides nurturing, caring feedback that is related to the athlete's needs.

The coach plays a critical role in the approach, development and effectiveness of an athlete or team in their game. To be most effective, athletes must own their own experience and be responsible for their performance. The coach's role is to provide feedback related to what the athlete needs to improve that performance. The coach enables the athlete's learning and thus enables his or her most effective performance.

A common trap for coaches lies in the moment when an athlete asks about a technical or tactical point. The coach's ability to be the expert in that moment and tell them the answer can produce real gratification about his or her knowledge and build the athlete's sense of that expertise. Often, though, such a response from the coach is counter-productive. It is likely the athlete can sort out the point without being told the answer and, by relying on the coach, the athlete loses the learning opportunity and ownership of the solution. A much more effective approach is for the coach to reflect the question back to the athlete and then both can reflexively explore solutions together.

The development of questioning skills (see Chapter Thirteen) is critical to successful communication in relationships with athletes. Skilled questioning can also serve as an antidote to the expert trap. Important to the process is being upbeat and using questioning to provide positive reinforcement as well as discover needs for improvement. Examples of helpful questions are: We had some success with our tactical kicking today; what did you see? What went well with your decisions and execution?

The coach also is key to the inter-athlete relationships that contribute to team building. Developing self-awareness and awareness of others and modelling that awareness encourage the same behaviour in athletes. Management consultant Peter Block (1993) works on building organisations that are more effective because they embrace trusting one another, to hold themselves responsible for outcomes and accountable to the larger group. This sense of responsibility for performance outcomes is key to athlete empowerment. Often development of small units within a team, where these inter-athlete relationships are practised, can serve to build overall team cohesion. Many teams use this approach and assign various tasks to the units or challenge units to develop healthy competition around particular team standards. Everyone is encouraged to take responsibility and own the team including the coaches.

Phil Jackson, in coaching professional athletes, has focused on athlete learning and the creation of team cohesion: 'My goal was to find a structure that would empower everybody on the team' (Jackson and Delehanty, 1995, p. 63). Jackson's success provides credibility to the approach that he continues to put into practice. With the aim of managing the relationships with and within the team, he seeks a clear understanding of them. He strives to develop the 'capacity to observe what's happening and act appropriately, without being distracted by self-centered thoughts' (p. 69). He works on not letting his own ego get in the way of seeing what is happening or of his own appropriate action. This work is a large part of his own process for self-management but it also is important in managing his relationships with and among his athletes.

Jackson's ability to clearly see what is happening before him allows him to understand the dynamics among the players. He is then able to effectively intervene as appropriate and determine the effectiveness of his actions.

When the coach understands his or her athletes, it is much easier to understand the quality of performance and adherence to agreed principles of play. For coaches in the field, it is easy to get so caught up impressions of the moment that important aspects of performance are lost. The heat of the battle and the coaches' impressions can obscure what actually has occurred. Video review helps here—a wonderful tool enabling dispassionate observation of performance.

Empathy—Athletes' Feelings Count

A related key skill in managing relationships is developing empathy. Empathy is about being present and aware: sensitive to the athletes' feelings and listening to what they are saying about those feelings in words, gestures and actions. Empathy enhances coaching because, when athletes feel understood, they are more likely to follow recommendations. When given the opportunity to express their emotional needs and concerns, athletes feel they can trust the coach to function in their best interests.

Empathy is an appreciation for an athlete's point of view. Again, a coach can often discover an athlete's point of view by asking open-ended questions: What did you see? What did you decide to do? How were you affected by the outcome? When listening to the athlete's response with empathy, the coach also develops an understanding of the athlete's point of view.

As Lombardo (1987, p.74) expresses it:

> ... in empathy, a coach has an understanding of underlying thoughts and feelings, internal thinking and emotional states of others. When this happens, the athlete is truly valued and intrinsic motivation (doing it for self) is enhanced. The athlete is her own best expert, and it is important that she doesn't feel judged or pushed. An athlete must be self-determining for this 'flow' in performance to occur. They can't be doing it for the coach, they have to be doing if for self.

Empathy in the coach and the athletes can be enhanced through practising at least some of the following behaviours (adapted from Lombardo, 1987):

- Give feedback, a major task for a coach, individually with the consistent intent of assisting the athlete's learning. Athlete-centred, humanistic coaches avoid public evaluations of an athlete and work with the athlete's needs and understandings. If a coach can use the athlete's words and understandings, the athlete will appreciate the choice. In short: praise in public; critique in private.
- Treat athletes as you would like to be treated if you were performing.
- Put yourself in the athlete's shoes, focusing on what it is like to be an athlete on your team.
- Attempt to understand the experience of your athletes.
- In enhancing your humanistic approach, recognise that the athlete's feelings are of utmost importance. The individual's feelings should be a topic of concern within the sport experience, rather than hidden or denied.
- Understand, without becoming overly nosey about, the athlete's interpretations, analyses, introspective thoughts and other insights regarding his or her personal feelings, as such insights are a key to performance enhancement. In other words,

by facilitating an athlete's efforts at understanding and getting in touch with his or her feelings, you will help the athlete's growth and development, which in turn helps his or her performance and motivation.

Facilitating an athlete's understanding and awareness is at the heart of athlete-centredness. Coaches enable this understanding and open players to this awareness through a variety of methods including game-like training, problem-solving opportunities, positive reinforcement, visualisation and mental rehearsal. Whatever method is used, its purpose is to help players be at a peak of confidence in the chaos of the sporting challenge.

In promoting this athlete-centredness and getting athletes to take ownership and responsibility we are asking athletes to change the way they do things in order to improve their performance. According to David Hadfield (2005, p. 36), 'All coaching can be considered as the facilitation of behavioural change'. Drawing from his extensive studies of an empowerment coaching approach based on effective questioning, he asserts that, 'becoming an *effective agent of change* is at the heart of coaching excellence' (p. 36).

Hadfield also holds that people are 'creatures of habit' who naturally resist changing those habits. Not only do people resist changing habits, they tend to revert to form when under pressure. As coaches we need to empathise with this process of change and try to understand their history of sport development. Hadfield suggests of the following strategies as ways to deal with athletes' natural resistance to change:

- Become an athlete-centred coach who understands deeply that the coach's role is to be a change and improvement facilitator.
- Learn to be a top-class Query Theory coach. Learn to ask questions that lead to self-awareness, self-discovery and change. Especially you should seek to create a clear discriminatory awareness. That is, the athlete (or you if you are seeking to change yourself) should clearly and profoundly understand the difference between the old habit and the new, improved way of doing things.
- Use a cost–benefit analysis to assist your athlete to see that change is worthwhile. Unless you can get your athlete to accept that the benefits of change outweigh the costs of change, you will struggle to make 'coaching headway'. We are all in sales; you need to be a caring salesperson of the need to change. You achieve this by being empathetic and understanding and by communicating effectively.
- Ensure that you understand your athlete's learning style. In brief, while many of your athletes can learn multi-modally, perhaps a quarter may have strong leanings towards a kinaesthetic, aural, visual or read–write

learning style. In New Zealand elite rugby, it seems many players tend to be dominant in the kinaesthetic sense. Teach using *all* learning modalities wherever possible; be creative. You can find more detail from the raft of resources on learning style; you can also apply simple tests that will indicate an athlete's dominant learning style.

- Establish a coaching or team culture in which openness, growth and change are pillars (Hadfield, 2005, p. 38).

Of course, changing to an athlete-centred approach is asking coaches to change as well, as will be discussed in the 'Self-motivation' section below.

Managing Self

In order to develop strong people skills and get the best out of others, we actually have to know ourselves first: 'EQ self management skills include motivating oneself, persisting in the face of frustrations, impulse control and gratification delay; regulation of one's moods and keeping distress from swamping ability to think' (Goleman, 1995 p. 34).

Self-awareness: Knowing Your Own Emotions

Understanding the basis of your actions and behaviours—that is, self-awareness—hinges on your ability to reflect and to know yourself. Knowing yourself is to know what you are experiencing. If you know yourself authentically and realistically, then understanding of others will be easier.

Knowing yourself is to know what you are experiencing (Whitmore, 2002). Alan Wong (2003) sums it up in this way:

> Self-awareness includes recognition of our personality, our strengths and weaknesses, our likes and dislikes. Developing self-awareness can help us to recognise when we are stressed or under pressure. It is also often a prerequisite for effective communication and interpersonal relations, as well as for developing empathy for others.

With self-awareness you can develop devices on which you can rely at times when you figure out you are stressed. Typical devices include 'personal time-outs', getting distance and managing proximity to a stressor or even checking in with your breathing. It is important in the emotional sense to know when and how emotions affect you, or distort your own perception. This ability is where the ego needs to be put on hold, controlling your emotions to suit the situation best. It is an insight into and an understanding of what makes you tick. Having this awareness enables an individual to keep the ego in tow, to question the reasons for doing particular things in certain ways.

Awareness enables you to objectively view the rationale behind your own actions, moods and words.

Self-reflection is a major tool used to understand self and emotions. There is much coaching literature (Cassidy, Jones and Potrac, 2009) on self-reflection, including on self-reflective questions in Chapter Fourteen of this book. Self-awareness and self-reflection are essential to a shift from a coach-centred to an athlete-centred approach to coaching, a topic discussed under the 'Self-motivation' section below.

Congruence and Authenticity

A basic tenet of human relationships is that they depend on the consistency of the participants' actions and intentions. Coach–athlete relationships are no less dependent on this tenet than any other kind of relationship. Given the pressures of performance, it is especially important for the coach's actions and words to be consistent. The coach's role in a coach–athlete relationship should be one of congruence, one where the coach's intentions are clear and integrated into the relationship. In short, the coach's actions should be congruent with his or her words.

Ballet dancer Mikhail Baryshnikov is adamant that what you do is more important than what you say. Action arising out of and consistent with his philosophy is what counts: 'I hate to explain what I do, it's about action' (Grey Goose Entertainment, 2007). As he sees it, ideas are nice and clarity of values is good, but you have to make them manifest with your actions. This thinking sums up congruence.

In the sporting arena, self-awareness will help athletes to respond to particular situations and emotions by managing their reactions so they are appropriate for a given situation. Responding in this way requires stress management. Examples of managing emotions congruently and authentically, as adapted from Lombardo (1987), are that a humanistic, athlete-centred coach:

- is free to express emotions as expressions of his or her real self—that is, the coach is comfortable in responding spontaneously and displaying a wide range of emotions and feelings, as well as sharing these feelings with athletes; and is open and honest and can reveal himself or herself to athletes, rather than portraying an image of a coach;
- displays verbal and non-verbal behaviours that are congruent with the situation— that is, what the coach is saying agrees with his or her gestures, posture and non-verbal expressions;
- encourages and supports athletes as they strive to be authentic, genuine and open;
- provides criticism without attacking the self-worth of the individual—which requires the coach to be truthful (rather than praising a player for a performance that has not earned that praise) but to follow the rule of thumb of praising in public

and criticising in private; in a team setting, where public criticism is a norm, focus on performance standards rather than the person is important;

- is able to express a wide range of emotions and feelings and expects athletes to respect the coach's subjectivity just as the coach respects the athletes' personal expressions;
- encourages athletes to stop 'playing a role' (usually reflecting the professional model) and start being themselves, by permitting, respecting and encouraging them to be true to themselves—for example, after competition some athletes need some quiet personal time, others are more boisterous, and others analyse their performance continually;
- encourages personal and subjective expressions and, with awareness of his or her athletes and their skill level, consistently plans practices and training regimes with the athletes, based upon their desires and needs;
- is able to reveal his or her willingness to be vulnerable, and works at being transparent;
- exhibits congruence when he or she can:
  - admit mistakes and recognise his or her shortcomings;
  - knowledge his or her deficiencies;
  - recognise that he or she is ignorant where he or she should be knowledgeable; and
- has the inner strength to permit athletes to be separate and different from him or her.

Power and Authority

To be truly effective a coach must understand the effects of power and authority in relationships with athletes. Power in this context is about control over another individual, such as an athlete, or over an organisation, such as a team. In regard to managing self and managing relationships with athletes, issues concerning the coach's power and authority permeate.

A coach's power can be constructive or destructive in this relationship. Where it is destructive, an athlete may feel valued but is actually not as the coach may be taking advantage of a weakness in the athlete and manipulating the relationship. A vulnerable athlete is susceptible to this power relationship.

Authority, or positional power, is the power placed in a position rather than power earned through relationships. The authority of a coach influences athletes in many ways. No matter what the coach says, he or she holds significant authority in selection, compensation, tactics, scheduling matches and training, game play tactics and decisions, and other areas. Earned 'power' is what the player gives. It is the power that comes with the athlete believing the coach has his or her support and has something to offer that will help the athlete achieve.

A coach has significant authority in the very nature of the job to hand. In many countries, the coach is revered, with the title 'Coach' demonstrating the status earned. The ego, or sense of self, that has been bound in such a status is difficult to overcome. If coaches rely on this socially created position, rather than the special interpersonal, humanistic qualities needed to lead people, they cannot gain true respect and trust. The position may highlight such a status, but athletes cannot be fooled and will demand the respect they deserve.

In a typical sporting experience, the coach is 'in charge'. The coach is regarded as being responsible for the success of training sessions, for the team's wins and losses and for the well-being of the players. In this context, athletes are usually accustomed to being dependent on the coach.

Early in Phil Jackson's coaching career, his authority to select and set compensation contributed to his players' scepticism about his empowerment approach. There does seem to be an inherent conflict between 'empowering' players and retaining the power to decide when and where they will play. It is not suggested that coaches dispense with the role of making selection decisions. But an effective strategy is to include players in establishing the playing principles and performance standards used for selection. Reliance on agreed principles of performance allows relaxation of power approaches. Then selection is based on principles established with the athletes. Criticism is based on principles understood by the athletes.

Ultimately in sport, athletes need to be able to perform unconsciously, intuitively; to respond to situations automatically. Performing in this way requires reaction and intuition grounded in understanding of performance principles rather than dependence on coach interventions.

A system of clear standards of performance that players have participated in establishing is liberating for players and for coaches. It is in bringing players back to such standards that the coaching and sharing of power occurs. This task is thus one of the coach's biggest challenges. A rugby coach on the East Coast of the USA develops cue words familiar to players when giving feedback during high-intensity training. Such cues are reminders of agreed standards and are meant to trigger recognition and intuitive response. In this example, the cue words come from the players; the coach just reminds them of their words, sharing the power.

Complications can arise from an approach that is meant to cue athletes rather than direct them. If a coach is not seen to be 'telling' or expounding his or her knowledge, the coach's status is often lowered in the eyes of the public. In watching a training session in which the coach is using an athlete-centred approach and sharing power, many onlookers are bemused and afterwards question what the coach did given that the players 'coached themselves'.

Athlete perception confers and moderates the coach's real power. It is this 'legitimate' (Potrac, 2004) power that develops the special relationship needed between athlete and coach. The perception of the athlete influences the power relationship and this legitimate power is what influences athlete performance. An athlete will do anything for a coach if there is respect and trust. If the power is misused, the relationship can deteriorate and athletes may choose different pathways.

Power is a constant source of athlete manipulation, where a reward can be based on an athlete doing something that the coach wants done. Often praise is given because an athlete has done what the coach wants them to do (reward power). This reward power is quite common from the traditional, coach-centred coaches, who make relatively frequent use of punishment and reward systems. Criticism can be offered based on, again, what the coach wants, rather than on an athlete's needs.

People will seek to engage and do activities if they perceive that their needs will be met. So, from a power perspective, if the athlete needs something from the coach, he or she will try to gain the praise or reward offered, regardless of what his or her actual needs are. If the coach can resist this inclination and instead focus on athlete needs and agreed performance principles, progress will be more immediate.

Self-motivation

The athlete-centred approach works because the coach subordinates his or her need for ego gratification and focuses on what the athletes need to maximise their success. That's great in principle, but what does the coach who has grown up in a coach-centred environment, and who has become used to the honorifics and other ego feedback so common to the coaching arena, actually do to change his or her approach and implement such a philosophy?

A shift to intrinsic motivation is as necessary for the coach as it is for athletes. The coach needs to learn to set and achieve goals with the athletes so that intrinsic motivation is the means to an end. Managing self, being aware of self and others, achieving successful relationships with athletes and seeing them achieve their own intrinsic goals are the legitimate measures of success.

Our motivation can reside in redefining our value and the gratification we take from the coaching experience. Peter Steinberg's experience, touched on above as an example of coaching in the USA, is useful here. His focus on his own coaching performance and EQ skill development goals provides a basis for a process of reflection and review. Such use of clear intrinsic goals and performance review has allowed Steinberg to define his value in terms of player-centredness. It also allows him to track his own progress in attaining his performance goals through open and direct reviews with peer coaches and players.

Redefining our value and redefining the sources of our gratification (which helps our motivation) go to the heart of our coaching process. Such a shift is a huge change for most of us. These issues strike directly at the question, *'How's your coaching?'*

Given that such a fundamental change is necessary to feel good about our coaching in an athlete-centred environment, how can we embrace such change? Hadfield's discussion, referenced in the previous section, can help to answer this question. 'Change is central to the coach's job' according to Hadfield (2005, p. 36). His assertion that people are 'creatures of habit' resistant to change of course applies to coaches. We have developed our methods and have found varying degrees of success in using them.

In confronting a suggestion to embrace new approaches or new sources of gratification, a coach may react in a number of ways ranging from resistance to acceptance. Hadfield suggests that we need to deal with the possibility that our own approaches may not be the most effective. Coming to grips with this idea isn't easy!

> Many coaches with whom I have worked find it difficult to become an athlete-centred coach. Why? The prescriptive coach-centred approach is how they were coached and it is how they learned how to coach; now it has become a habit and, like all habits, it is hard to change—especially under coaching pressure. When things are getting tough, prescriptive coaches who are trying to become empowering tend to revert to a 'do this, do that' approach. It is what they know, it is easier, it is quicker and it shows anyone who may be in doubt who is the boss around here and who owns the knowledge. But is it the most effective approach? I would argue that in many cases it is not. (Hadfield, 2005, p. 38)

Hadfield suggests two requirements for coaches to use to change their approach, which parallel ideas for managing self discussed in this chapter. First, coaches need to have self-awareness, or 'awareness that there is an issue and that change is needed'; and, second, they need to self-reflect so that they understand the differences between the way things are currently done and the 'new and improved way of doing things' (p. 38).

If rugby is non-democratic, then there is nothing of value in it.—Ged Glynn (twisting Baron DeCoubertan's original words)

Conclusion

We began this chapter with the question, *'How's your coaching?'* The intention has been to share a way of answering that question that is based on a conscious understanding and review of athlete-centred coaching processes. These intrinsic measures also relate to performance outcomes.

The dance icon Mikhail Baryshnikov is doing 'small things' in creating a place where dancers 'learn from each other' and where they 'experience the true color of the artistic experience'. The result in his Hell's Kitchen dance studios is the nurturing of new generations of dancers.

Phil Jackson is continually fostering a team culture that encourages the participation of all athletes and their ownership of the team performance. He manages his own participation carefully so that he is aware of his impact and of the range of team dynamics. The result has been an outstanding win–loss coaching record in the NBA.

Peter Steinberg utilises a team planning process in which the players agree on team goals and principles of performance. He and his peer coaches openly review team performance and coaching processes with the athletes. The result has been the athletes' strong sense of ownership of the team's outcomes. It has also resulted in the domination of the Penn State University rugby teams at the national championship level. The key to a coach's contribution to team success can be found in the process of setting standards of player performance—standards that are mutually agreed and appreciated by the athlete and the coach—and holding players accountable to those agreed standards.

To summarise, the following might fit well in a list of 'key factors' to use in reflecting on our performance as athlete-centred, humanistic coaches. These factors are only some possibilities. Individual coaches need to develop their own key factors that address their own coaching performance goals:

- Create a learning environment that encourages open and honest interaction.
- Develop principles of performance with the athletes.
- Create and promote a system of accountability around the agreed principles of performance.
- Create and promote an open system to review coaching process with peers and athletes.
- Assist athletes with developing game sense as well as techniques or skills.
- Use effective questioning to promote athlete understanding.
- Be tuned in to team personalities, events and dynamics.
- Create and regularly use self-reflection techniques to develop self-awareness.
- Be upbeat and react to events with genuine emotion.

Coaches can embrace standards of their own performance that are concerned with managing self and managing relationships with players and the team. They can develop their own 'key factors' similar to those listed above. Such standards then become the basis of their own accountability. Clarity about such standards and an open review process allows authentic and congruent action. Having both clarity and a review process establishes the basis on which to answer the question, 'How's your coaching?' Then self-awareness, awareness of the players and mindfulness create the genuine foundation for feeling good about your coaching.

References

Block, P. (1993). *Stewardship: Choosing service over self interest.* San Francisco: Berrett-Koehler.

Cassidy, T., Jones, R., & Potrac, P. (2009). *Understanding Sports Coaching: The social, cultural and pedagogical foundations of coaching practice* (2nd ed.). London: Routledge.

Goleman, D. (1995). *Emotional Intelligence.* New York: Bantam.

Goleman, D. (1998). *Working with Emotional Intelligence.* New York: Bantam.

Grey Goose Entertainment (2007). *Iconoclasts: Alice Waters, Mikhail Baryshnikov.* New York: Sundance Channel.

Hadfield, D. (2005). The change challenge: Facilitating self-awareness and improvement in your athletes. In L. Kidman (Ed.) *Athlete-centred Coaching: Developing inspired and inspiring people.* Christchurch: Innovative Print Communications.

Jackson, P., & Delehanty, H. (1995). *Sacred Hoops: Spiritual lessons of a hardwood warrior.* New York: Hyperion.

Potrac, P. (2004). Coaches' power. In R. Jones, K. Armour, & P. Potrac, *Sports Coaching Cultures: From practice to theory.* London: Routledge.

Whitmore, J. (2002). *Coaching for Performance* (2nd ed.). London: Nicholas Beardsley.

Wong, A. (2003). Self-awareness. *Lifeskills Web.* Retrieved 21 December 2009 from: http://www.vtaide.com/lifeskills/self_awareness.htm

I think self-awareness is probably the most important thing towards being a champion. - Billie Jean King

Take the attitude of a student, Never be too big to ask questions, Never know too much to learn something new. - Og Mandino

Do not let what you cannot do interfere with what you can do. - John Wooden

Millions saw the apple fall,
but Newton asked why.
- Bernard Baruch

Chapter Thirteen

Asking Meaningful Questions

From all the coaches and athletes interviewed for this book, a clear message about an athlete-centred approach to coaching emerges: to use it effectively, ask meaningful questions. When the coach asks questions, athletes must find answers, which in turn increases their knowledge and understanding of the purpose of particular skill performances and tactical plays in the context of competition. As John Dewey said, 'Thinking in itself is questioning'. Questioning stimulates athletes' thinking, providing them with a chance to be creative and make decisions. It is also an extremely powerful means to inspire in athletes an intrinsic motivation to learn.

An athlete-centred coaching approach is ineffectual without a high level of questioning and clarifying to generate answers from the athletes. It is known that athletes learn well and have higher retention rates if they are given the opportunity to work out for themselves what to do and how to do it. As part of becoming athlete-centred coaches, we need to learn to apply an effective questioning technique at training sessions, to enhance athlete learning.

As David Hadfield (2005) suggests, implementing an athlete-centred, humanistic approach and using questioning may be uncommon and, to some, feel unnatural. Athletes may initially be surprised that they can have input into solving problems and thus their immediate response may not be favourable. However, if questioning becomes part of a coach's repertoire and the coach focuses on questioning well, then athletes will enjoy solving problems and be successful.

To create situations where athletes learn best, by listening to their responses, then redirecting, prompting or probing for better or more complete answers, coaches must have an in-depth understanding of the material they are asking about and the context in which it will be applied. As Lyn Gunson suggests:

> What I find interesting is that [in England] they are taking the pieces of activity in isolation without that integrated approach. It doesn't work. People are saying they want more athlete decision making and taking responsibility, [therefore] we have to use more questioning. I have been asked to take sessions about this a lot. Some of the coaches have really attempted this approach and I have seen them struggling with it.

Solving problems in simulated situations enhances athletes' decision making and in-depth understanding.

When the coach poses questions and gives athletes the opportunity to solve a problem, the athletes will try hard to solve it. The solution they generate is theirs; thus they will take ownership of it and remember, understand and apply the content more effectively than if they were told what to do, when to do it and how to do it. Solving problems through coach questioning enables athletes to explore, discover, create and generally experiment with a variety of moving and tactical processes of a specific sport. On this enhancing decision making, Mike Ruddock says:

> … Now, there are all sorts of processes involved, that I feel you need to do with the players and coaches, i.e. decision making with input from the group, getting an understanding of what they think about the input, what is right, what is not right for this particular group and there's the questioning approach about boundaries that need to be implemented. Some players and groups find it confusing and others relish the fact that there are little or no rigid boundaries and that they are free to have or make decisions or set their own standards. Every group is slightly different and I think what I'd like to do is try to adapt a little to the changing times and changing groups, as well as [develop] key principles of how I want my teams to play.

Lyn suggests that the major consideration in formulating a question is what outcome is required:

> What is the question that is going to open up the outcome possibilities? It's being conscious of the situations all the time. We constrain [players] by our inability [to ask questions] and focus their attention … How do you know that person you are dealing with doesn't have the next revolutionary idea about sport? [For example,] who started two-handed backhands? Who starts wearing their cap on back-to-front and sets the trend? Where is the one who has the confidence to do that? So are you going to be a follower or somebody who keeps ahead of the game? Coaches have to allow [innovation] to happen, otherwise the game doesn't develop and champions do not emerge.

Questions to Promote Low-order and High-order Thinking

The goals of effective questioning include actively involving athletes in the learning process, and enhancing their task mastery and conceptual understanding. Another goal is to promote both simple (low-order) and complex (high-order) thinking. These two forms of thinking require different types of questions.

When athletes need to remember specific ideas or concepts, *simple* or *low-order questions* are appropriate. These questions serve as reminder cues that might be important to a learning sequence. Low-order questions are often *what?* or *where?* questions asked during drills. Low-order questions are factual, generally with only one possible answer. Examples of low-order questions used in coaching are:

- 'What part of the hand should you contact the ball when you spike it?'
- 'Where should you aim when shooting in netball?'
- 'How many points do you receive for a goal in lacrosse?'
- 'Who is the captain of the New Zealand women's hockey team?'

Research indicates that coaches tend to use low-order questions and certainly in some instances low-order questions are appropriate. However, coaches should strive to ask more *high-order questions* to extend athletes' opportunities to self-evaluate.

High-order questions require abstract or higher-level thinking processes. These questions challenge athletes to apply, analyse, synthesise, evaluate and create knowledge. They are generally more appropriate for analysing tactics and complex skills. Although both children and élite athletes respond well to high-order questions, it is advantageous for coaches to create the questions according to the athletes' developmental needs. Designing high-order questions and questioning sequence is more appropriate when encouraging independent learning, where athletes are required to think in greater depth about the subject matter or context and can search for multiple answers. Examples of high-order questions in sport settings include:

- 'How can we get the ball down the court quickly?'
- 'In how many different ways can you balance on the balance beam?'
- 'How can you get around the defence?'
- 'Why should we push the defence to the sideline?'
- 'Why do we need to tuck when doing a somersault?'

Why? and *how?* questions enhance athletes' ability to make decisions, one of the central goals of an athlete-centred approach emphasised in earlier chapters. It is important for coaches to allow athletes to think about questions and help and encourage them to answer. If athletes are having difficulty with the answer, a coach can redirect or rephrase a high-order question so they can think carefully about what has been asked. However, the coach should never give the answer itself, as it takes ownership of the problem-solving process away from the athletes.

With high-order questions, there are no 'wrong' answers as the athletes generally interpret the questions at their own level of understanding. Coaches need to listen closely to the answers, interpret the significance and respond accordingly. Often athletes come up with answers that coaches may find useful to elaborate and apply within their game plan. By listening, in other words, coaches can learn much from their athletes.

Tactical questioning and technique questioning are two specific kinds of high-order questions that can be very helpful to the athlete-centred coach. Both strategies are detailed below, before consideration is given to a third strategy that forms a useful part of high-order questioning: movement response.

Tactical Questioning

Questions that call for decision making and problem solving with respect to the strategies of the competition are tactical questions. Prescriptive coaches often direct and decide on the competition plan. Yet unless athletes understand why the game plan exists and take ownership of it, coaches will find the athletes have difficulty accepting and understanding it. To increase tactical awareness and decision making, coaches should use many high-order questions that allow athletes to create and develop their ideas.

In an athlete-centred approach, coaches set up tactical situations as problem-solving exercises. They then ask *how?* and *why?* questions to solve tactical problems and enhance understanding. Examples of some useful questions might be 'Given a three-on-two situation, where is the space? Why?' or 'How would you finish the race in the last 100 metres?' It is important for the athletes to perform the actual movement so they solve problems, seek solutions through practice and try various alternatives, and thus build a better understanding of variable situations.

Technique Questioning

Formulating questions for athletes to become aware of their technique helps to provide them with purposeful feedback. Through this mechanism, coaches prompt athletes and compare their actions to an ideal model of performance. David Hadfield (2005) discusses this method as the 'query theory', which Kidman and Hadfield (2000, p. 14) summarise as follows:

> While words are different to bodily feelings and are associated with different parts of the brain, athletes must answer questions (such as 'what happened to your hips when you played that shot?') based on knowledge and understanding passed to their brain by their proprioceptive sensors. The basis of this approach is to increase kinaesthetic (body and sensory) awareness of appropriate skill execution and be able to make decisions about what strengths to keep and what weaknesses to fix (and how to fix it). In plain language, if athletes cannot feel it, they cannot change it.

To help the athletes gain kinaesthetic awareness, a coach uses demonstrations that provide them with mental images. The athletes then execute the skill based on their own knowledge and existing motor programme. In the process of skill execution, the coach observes and analyses the athletes and identifies strengths and weaknesses.

To aid the athletes in comparing their action with the ideal model, the coach asks *what?*, *where?*, *why?* and *how?* questions (e.g. 'What did your arms do when you released the ball?', 'Where was your head when the hockey stick contacted the ball?',

'Why is it important to have a follow through?', 'How did your legs move to complete the handspring?'). These types of questions should help athletes become aware of their own body movements in executing a skill. If athletes are still unaware of what their bodies are doing, the coach can use 'shaping' questions (e.g. 'What did the demonstration show you about using your legs?', 'How did you use your legs?').

Next the athletes execute the technique using their knowledge and kinaesthetic awareness. At this stage, the coach should allow the athletes to experience the technique several times before asking another question. The purpose of such sequences is to enable the athletes to become self-aware in using the technique and to take responsibility for making decisions. In this way, when they are performing the technique in a competition, the athletes can understand how to perform it and when it feels right.

Movement Responses

Although questioning has always been considered a mental strategy, athletes can learn much through problem solving and questioning using movement responses. A movement response requires an answer that involves a physical demonstration.

A typical example of a problem that requires movement response is 'Show us how to control the ball most effectively' or 'Show me how to grip the racquet'. Even though the coach does not express either of these statements as a question, the athletes must provide answers by showing the coach how they understand.

Posing movement questions is an effective tool to enhance physical skill learning. In providing movement responses, athletes can identify faults or determine correct skill technique. Consistent with the query theory, if athletes have input into correcting skill performance, along with appropriate self-awareness, they tend to retain the information they have discovered. Through this mechanism, some athletes may determine the correction they need for a technique that their coach has been trying to correct in them for years.

A Note on Rhetorical Questions

Coaches should avoid using *rhetorical questions*. A rhetorical question is one that coaches do not expect athletes to answer or that coaches answer themselves. An example is 'Can you please pick up that baton?' The response might be 'No, I can't ...' Other examples are when the coach asks, 'Will you please sit down?' but is actually giving a direction, or asks, 'What is the best way to pass to another player?' then gives the answer, encouraging the athletes to be passive.

Techniques for Effective Questioning

Questions are only as good as the answers they extract. What follows are some useful tips to enhance coaches' questioning skills.

Planning Questions

Formulating meaningful questions is a key element in establishing a great questioning environment. Planning the questions for the training session ahead is the most important step, especially if questioning is a very new part of the coaching repertoire. As noted in the previous edition Wayne Smith (International rugby coach) and Ian Rutledge (former New Zealand Black Sticks hockey coach) encourage such planning. Wayne explains:

> On my practice plan, I have questions, general questions that I would be asking them. Like the decision, where I saw [someone] in an attacking situation that didn't pass the ball, 'What did you do, what did you see, why didn't you pass it?'—basically to get feedback and ensure they were developing self-awareness about skill execution and tactical understanding.

For his part, Ian is strongly committed to planning questions:

> … If you have got purpose to a subject, you have to have a plan for questions. I think if you have no plan for questioning, you won't know what the problem is. You have a coaching plan, a training plan; you have to have a questioning plan. I think having an awareness of the coaching points [is important]. I still [see other coaches] who don't use training plans … Even if you are working with a mentor coach, you need to have training plans. I ask my students, 'Out of this drill, what are the coaching points that you are trying to achieve?' You need to plan that. Somebody had a simple drill set up the other day and asked the mentor coach to give them an example of each of the coaching points. He couldn't answer what they were … you have to understand coaching points to ask the right questions.

To plan meaningful, clear and coherent questions, an athlete-centred coach will:
* consider the nature of the content to be mastered and the athletes' readiness to contribute;
* practise the questions for the next training session by writing them down;
* ensure there is a variety of high and low-order questions;
* ensure there is an answer to work towards (and know the answer), with the questions planned to lead systematically to the planned answer; and

- formulate the questions appropriate to the athletes' level of learning by reading the questions aloud (e.g. 'What flight angle will be most appropriate to get the ball through the goal post?' may not suit athletes under the age of six).

For example, a coach's goal may be for the athletes to learn the footwork involved in a bowl in tenpin bowling. The coach would like the athletes to find out what the steps might be. Before starting to question, the coach determines the steps up the bowling lane to where the ball is released. Then he or she begins to create the questions. The first question might be 'If you were to release the ball at the boundary line, which foot would have to be in the front?' Once the athletes have worked out the answer, the coach might ask, 'How many steps would it take to get to the line where you release the ball?' The next question might be 'So if it takes three steps to the release line, what should your foot position be at the start?' The athletes will give many different answers, but each of them will work out the answer in his or her own way. By the end of the set of questions, athletes will have solved the problem about their footwork, with no instruction from the coach.

In planning questions, it is also important to be flexible in both developing the questions and timing them. Among coaches who are new to questioning, it is common to ask the planned questions but not to move beyond those questions in the training session. However, the real art of questioning is to read the athletes, look at what is happening and ask relevant questions *when* the athletes are ready or need to solve a problem. For example, Wayne Smith plans general questions, then in training he formulates further meaningful questions based on the situation as he reads it.

After implementing the questioning strategy, coaches should evaluate the session to improve their questioning skills. To this end, they may write down questions used and determine their relevance, or get someone on the sideline to evaluate these questions.

Gain the Athletes' Attention

An important management strategy in questioning is to ensure that all athletes are quiet and listening to the questioning sequence. To this end, a coach may create rules to encourage attention. Useful examples of rules include 'When one person is talking, everyone else listens' or 'Raise your hand and wait to be called on'. Notice that to contribute to a supportive environment, both rules contain positive words, rather than negative words like 'Don't'.

Once the coach has the attention of all athletes, everyone can hear the questions, while the coach can make appropriate eye contact and look for nonverbal signs of misunderstanding or excitement among the athletes. At this stage, the coach can begin the planned segment using questioning strategies.

When Is It Appropriate to Ask Questions?

An issue that Don Tricker raises is the need to choose the right moment for athletes to solve problems. The ability to pick this moment is considered part of the art of coaching. When Wayne Smith first implemented his empowering approach, he noted that he often overquestioned in his enthusiasm to get athletes to take responsibility. Don suggests that understanding the individual athlete is one key to knowing when to question:

> Asking the right questions to the right athlete at the right time is often the most effective way of ensuring that a particular experience has been analysed and the key learnings identified. If any of these parts is missing then the communication will not be effective. Timing will always depend on the athlete and the nature of the experience. If the experience has been a pleasant one then questions may be asked immediately. If the experience has not been so pleasant then the first priority is the well-being of the athlete; questions that reflect on the experience can wait.

There is no formula for the right time to ask questions. The answer is 'It depends'. It depends on fatigue, it depends on 'teachable moments', it depends—as Don noted above—on individual differences such as intrinsic motivation and it depends on whether the athlete has managed to solve the problem by himself or herself. A coach should read or analyse each situation to determine if the athletes need to solve a problem at that time and in that situation. Often coaches jump in because they feel like they are not doing anything and need to advise. More often athletes can determine their own mistakes and fix them because of their own decision-making ability and self-awareness. When an athlete makes a mistake and obviously knows it, there is nothing so stressful as being reminded of it by some significant other.

Athletes are bright; coaches should allow them to determine their needs and have faith in their ability to solve problems. As Rene Deleplace says, 'There is no point in coaching unless the teaching you do helps the student to overtake you.'

Wait Time

One of the reasons for gaining and maintaining athletes' attention is to provide wait time for athletes to consider their responses to the question. Increasing wait time enables athletes to formulate better responses and encourages them to give longer answers because they have had the opportunity to think. When given this 'thinking time', athletes tend to volunteer more appropriate answers and are less likely to fail to respond. They are more able to respond to high-order questions because they tend to speculate more. With longer wait time, athletes tend to ask more questions in return.

If they do not understand or they need to find out more information, athletes also feel they have been given an opportunity to clarify the question. With longer wait time, athletes exhibit more confidence in their comments and those athletes whom coaches rate as relatively slow learners offer more questions and more responses.

Ian Rutledge highlights the need to deal with those moments of 'uncomfortable' silence for coaches using wait time to enhance athletes' answers:

> ... you have to feel comfortable during those uncomfortable times of silences. I reckon it is a true bit of advice because I think that when I ask questions, the thinking takes time and as a coach, you want thinking activity ... As a naive coach, I used to feel uncomfortable by those silences and I would give the answers. Now, I just sit tight and allow players valuable thinking time and then get the players to answer.

Wait time is quite difficult for coaches when they are first learning how to question. Research on teaching suggests that teachers tend to answer their own questions when a wrong answer is given or tend to become impatient. As in teaching, an appropriate wait time in coaching is three to five seconds. Once they have mastered wait time, coaches will find that athletes benefit more from questioning than they do if the coach calls on them for an immediate response.

To increase wait time, an athlete-centred coach will:

- listen to athletes' responses without repeating what they have said (*coach echo*) and give them time to think in silence while they are formulating their thoughts;
- be careful not to call an athlete's name immediately after posing the question. Once the coach identifies an athlete to answer the question, the other athletes tend to relax and discontinue their thinking process;
- show he or she is listening by limiting comments and being aware of using 'uh-huh' and 'okay';
- avoid a 'Yes but ...' reaction to an athlete's response, which signals that coach rejects the athlete's idea; and
- allow the athletes to provide the answers.

Reinforcement

As athletes offer solutions, either verbally or through a movement response, a coach should encourage their innovative ideas—no matter how silly or inadequate the coach may perceive those ideas to be. If they find no sincere support for answers (either verbal or nonverbal), the athletes will be less likely to respond next time they are questioned. If the response to an athlete's answer was 'What a stupid answer', how would the athlete feel? Would the athlete feel respected by the coach? Thus part of the process of questioning is to encourage athletes to continue to try for a solution, even though they may appear to be a long way from it.

All of the coaches in this book highlight the importance of establishing an environment in which athletes feel confident to volunteer responses. The difficulty here, when a coach is deciding how to handle an inadequate answer, is to determine whether the athlete is off task or deliberately trying to be silly. If the response is off task, the coach should refocus or ignore it, then reinforce the athlete's next attempt to respond. Sincere positive reinforcement will be more likely to motivate athletes to respond enthusiastically to later questions. It is also noted that different individuals respond to different types of reinforcement.

For effective reinforcement, an athlete-centred coach will:

- praise based on the athlete's answer—for example, 'That's an interesting answer, can you tell us why you said that?';
- praise with the focus on reinforcing the athlete's response;
- praise honestly and sincerely; and
- give nonverbal reinforcement such as eye contact, thumbs up, smiling, nodding, and clapping hands—all extremely useful as forms of praise.

Prompting

With prompting, a coach uses cues to 'remind' athletes of something that they have learned and help them to answer a question. Examples are 'What did you determine about using a fake on offence?' or 'How have you been putting the shuttlecock on the floor? Think about the racquet swing.'

It is important that in giving cues, a coach does not give athletes the whole answer. The purpose of prompting is to encourage athletes to provide a response. Prompting can help them gain the confidence to answer the question.

Probing

Probing is a questioning strategy in which a coach asks follow-up questions so that athletes can extend, amplify or refine their answers. Here the coach should avoid using 'uh-huh's or 'okay's as these comments show a lack of interest in athletes' responses.

The following is an example of an effective probing sequence.

Coach:	'How can we get the ball down the court?'
Athlete:	'Dribble it.'
Coach:	'Is there a way you can get it down faster?' *(probe)*
Athlete:	'You could run faster.'

Coach:	'That is a good answer. What other skill have we been learning to move the ball around?' *(probe)*
Athlete:	'Passing.'
Coach:	'Great. Now what is it about passing the ball that gets the ball down the court faster?' *(probe)*
Athlete:	'When you pass the ball to a person, the speed of the ball is faster than when you dribble.'
Coach:	'Now you are getting the idea. If the ball is faster when passing, what does that mean when you are being defended?' *(probe)*
Athlete:	'The defender has less time to recover when you pass the ball to someone else. When you dribble, the ball is moved more slowly and therefore the defender has more time to catch up.'

Probing and reinforcing promote learning through extending current thought processes and encouraging athletes' responses.

Equity of Directing and Distributing Questions

Coaches will notice that some athletes cannot wait to answer the questions while others prefer to remain anonymous in the background. The athletes who volunteer readily are probably the most confident in their skills and their cognitive abilities. Research in teaching suggests that the teacher tends to neglect the students in the back. This same tendency will be found in sport settings as well. A coach must make a conscious effort to include all members of the team or squad in problem solving.

A coach should allow equal time for all athletes to contribute to the discussion. Through skilfully directing and distributing discussion, he or she will provide a fair environment where athletes can contribute equally. Directing questions to athletes in a nonthreatening way can encourage those who still may prefer not to participate. If a reluctant participant responds to a question, the coach should praise this answer and use the content of the response in further discussion.

Guided Discovery of a New Skill

Many coaches believe that they must tell and show their athletes exactly how to perform a correct technique. In contrast, through Teaching Games for Understanding (TGfU; see Chapter Eight) athletes learn technique through guided discovery (and through self-awareness). The coach gives guidance with a series of meaningful questions about the athletes' technique (while recognising that athletes are capable of participating in sport without being taught the perfect technique). Athletes then learn by discovering how to do the technique themselves, in a process similar to the query theory, but learning is a result of self-discovery rather than of watching a demonstration.

Techniques do not have to be taught explicitly as athletes at all levels can often figure out the approach needed. A good example is found by observing children in action in the playground, where they are highly capable of discovering how to perform the 'game' without being told by someone else.

To use guided discovery as a coaching tool, it is useful to plan the line of inquiry. The coach should first decide and plan the answer or ultimate technique, then arrange the questions for the athletes to discover the answer. Athletes then provide demonstrations of the techniques as they discover the solution.

This process may be illustrated through the following example, in which athletes discover how to find the open space after a dribble in soccer.

Coach: 'In a three-on-three situation, what is the best way to get the ball to your teammate? Let's try it.'

Athletes pass all kinds of different ways.

Coach: 'What happens if you pass the ball behind your teammate? Let's try it.'

Athletes pass to partners and aim everywhere. Some athletes have to turn around and run for the ball, some are going forward nicely.

Coach: 'Now, if you want to make sure that your teammate goes forward (towards the goal), where do you want the pass to go?'

Johnny: 'They should go behind the person.'

Coach: 'Great, let's see how that works, Johnny. All go out in your threes and try to pass behind the person'.

The athletes try this approach.

Coach: 'Did that work?'

Athletes: (In unison) 'No!'

Coach: 'Why didn't it work?'

Athletes: 'Because we had to keep coming backwards.'

Coach: 'So how shall we do it this time?'

Kirsten: 'We should pass it to the front of the player.'

Coach: 'Great, let's try what Kirsten said.'

From this step the coach might get the athletes to practise in a game, concentrating on passing forward or passing to the place where the athletes are headed. After the athletes have mastered the concept, the coach might call them in again and try the same sort of discovery for passing and running to a space. An example might be 'Now that we can pass it well, what do you think the player who just passed the ball should do?'

Notice that in the above example, the coach never provides an explanation or demonstration. Instead, the athletes figure out for themselves how to pass forward. With any method where athletes have to figure out how a technique is performed, they will not only retain and understand that technique more fully, but also get more practice opportunities and take control of their own technique experience. Athletes tend to remember more because they are doing it, rather than watching a coach explain and demonstrate.

Conclusion

Asking meaningful questions can give coaches a huge advantage in applying an athlete-centred approach. This chapter has highlighted some useful techniques to ensure their questions are meaningful. It is important for coaches to realise that it takes plenty of practice to use meaningful questions in a purposeful way. Moreover, coaches who use questioning well will enjoy it for the rewards it brings. While they need to be aware of the considerations that should shape the way they use meaningful questions, they can also be aware of how athletes will benefit from being able to work out problems, discover their own abilities and make informed decisions. The use of effective questioning will further enhance a coach's repertoire and promote the learning of his or her athletes.

References

Hadfield, D. (2005). The change challenge: Facilitating self-awareness and improvement in your athletes, In L. Kidman (Ed) *Athlete-centred Coaching: Developing inspired and inspiring people,* Christchurch: Innovative Print Communications.

Kidman, L., & Hadfield, D. (2000). Athlete empowerment. *New Zealand Coach, 8*(4), 14–15.

Questions provide the key to unlocking
our unlimited potential. Anthony Robbins

All the world is a laboratory to
the inquiring mind. - Martin H. Fischer

We learn more by looking for the answer to
a question and not finding it than we do from
learning the answer itself. - Lloyd Alexander

Chapter Fourteen

The Future (Quo Vadis):

Where Do We Go from Here?

The future of sport is bright as we move deeper into the 21st century. Quite possibly the brightest light on the horizon comes from the major changes to sport that are clearly on the way; specifically, changes to coaching behaviour, coaching leadership and the profession of sport coaching. More and more discussions, both professional and otherwise, are focusing on related questions such as how to improve the sport experience for all performers, how to attend to the educational outcomes of the sport experience, and how to enable athletes.

Another aspect of these discussions and the intense scrutiny to which current practice is being subjected relates to efforts to 'give the games back to the athletes'. The concern here is to reorganise sporting experiences, especially youth and other development programmes, so that they more closely replicate the 'true' play experience (also see Chapter Seven). That is, how can we redesign sport programmes so that each participant develops in all of the many dimensions that make up a person— social, emotional, physical and intellectual? Many professionals are reassessing the value of early motor experiences supervised and constructed by adults for our young athletes. Many professionals are suggesting that formal, organised and adult-led sport experiences should not be encouraged for youth until the age of eight or nine years (Farrey, 2008). The value of 'free' play (i.e. organised and conducted by children) in the early years is being carefully re-evaluated as we write this chapter. This kind of reassessment is a move in a positive direction.

A major reason why the play elements and the organisation of sport have become such a focus of conversation is that the number of drop-outs in sport at about the age athletes enter high school continues to grow. This is a trend of major concern around the world. How can the profession of coaching respond to this significant reduction in the number of participants? How can we encourage the lifelong activity of our young participants?

These issues are critical given the small number of competitors who win scholarships. Those who go on to experience the financial rewards of a professional career realise how short these careers are (at an average three to four years across most professional sports in the USA). In short, if the goals of the athlete experience include fun, affective attachment to movement and activity and—dare we say it— education, then sport must be refocused and reorganised to those ends. The importance of achieving these goals needs to be promulgated to all parties. A particular target for this information must be parents, especially those parents who are intensely involved in the lives of their children ('hover' parents; helicopter parents, etc.)—those parents who apparently feel that their children need to do everything earlier, longer, harder, to gain competitive advantages over other children. These mislaid beliefs often result in early burn-out, physical breakdown and 'overuse' injuries, the development of one-dimensional athletes, a lack of creativity and limited focus on the educational intent. Often the children experiencing this style of parenting crash and burn and quit their sport prematurely to the detriment of their affective experience (a reason for playing) in the thrill of competing. Inevitably their desire for movement experiences decreases. No wonder there is a large drop-out rate.

However, we have reason to be optimistic for we perceive some interesting turns in, at the very least, perceptions and philosophical aspects of the profession. We see a stronger desire to enable the children and older athletes to have input and to own their experiences.

First among these critical turning points is the realisation, at long last, among professionals that outstanding athletic performance must include high-quality cognitions and decision-making capabilities. Professionally prepared coaches have begun to include such arguments in discussions of how to select and/or create excellent athletes. Superior athletes more often than not are superior thinkers. (Often, such superior athletic intellect emerges from the 'free play' experience—that is, among athletes who have a wealth of experience playing without adult supervision (see Chapter Seven.)

How Does a Coach Prepare a Superior Thinker and Decision Maker?

Sport today is faced with the problem of the walk-on mum and/or dad coach who, with good intentions, volunteers to coach a group of motivated youngsters, yet does not have any preparation or understanding of athletes' needs. These individuals tend to coach in the manner portrayed in the media, as general or commander, without providing the athletes opportunities to manifest or demonstrate their intellectual prowess.

Such novice coaches, without formal preparation, are often overly ego-invested, to the extent that they cannot empower their athletes without feeling that they have 'lost face'. If they share the power with the athletes, they feel that they have less control, less knowledge and less importance. In contrast, the more experienced and possibly more developed coach, who has studied (formally or informally) empowering, athlete-centred, humanistic coaching approach, can empower the athlete without losing face or a sense of diminished ego, and does not care about the public persona of a coach as depicted in the media. An athlete-centred coach cares about the full development of the athlete and about winning, probably in that order.

Another cause of optimism is the fast-growing and increasing number of coach development programmes across the world. Although the USA is lagging far behind the rest of the world, excellent professional development opportunities currently exist in France, Canada, Australia and New Zealand and other countries enhancing theirs. Coach preparation programmes are becoming more visible, if not dominant in many professional meetings and organisations. At the very least the development and education of sport coaches has been, and should remain, on the agenda of many diverse professional meetings related to sport and physical activity.

The advent and significant effect of the Teaching Games for Understanding (TGfU) and the Tactical Approach (also see Chapter Eight) have made major inroads, at least at the philosophical level of coach development. The indirect aspect of such approaches is congruent with the athlete-centred approach presented in this book. Coaches who have embraced the TGfU/games approach are well on their way to implementing the athlete-centred approach.

Putting Athlete-centred Coaching into Practice

In looking at how to get started with an athlete-centred, humanistic approach, we pick up on crucial tips from the various coaches who have related their experiences and insights in this book. Every one of them has suggested that it is important to at least 'give an athlete-centred approach a go'. You will probably not feel accomplished the first time you try it but, as you develop it, an athlete-centred approach becomes a powerful way to enable athletes to learn, to be motivated to put in huge effort, and to enjoy their sporting experience. As a result, their performance will naturally improve.

If you have never tried this approach, you need to implement it in small steps. One of the real hurdles to overcome is a lack of confidence to try an athlete-centred approach. It is important to accept that you may not be successful the first time; remember that a big step towards success in your use of the approach is just getting in and learning it, applying it and seeing how the athletes respond. High school coach Mark Norton (see Chapter Ten) says that, although he had been using an athlete-centred approach in some form for a while, he needed more confidence to extend his coaching to incorporate other parts of the athlete-centred approach:

> **Mark:** … it's more involved, there is more to it. It's the approach I wanted to do but I didn't know enough about it. So, now that I have learned these things, it is the way I want to coach, so I'll continue to do it. No doubt, I won't get it perfect, there are still lots of things that [have been] pointed

out to me that I had to do … There are always going to be things that you don't get, and you don't get it all together perfect every time. It's like anything. So, if you let those things worry you, then you will never do anything. You have to be confident with what you do know and what you are going to do.

Mike Ruddock, Director of Rugby for the Worcester Warriors (see Chapter Three), highlights where he obtained his confidence to use an athlete-centred approach:

> **Mike:** Ultimately you are who you are … but you can take many different roles … as a coach sometimes you can don your different hats e.g. sometimes go authoritarian and sometimes go with a more relaxed approach and sometimes in the middle. Sometimes you might get into the players for poor performance, sometimes you have to pick players up. Sometimes you have got to hire people and sometimes you have to fire people. The guy you might have had a very good working relationship with might have dropped his playing and he has come to the end of his career and you have to let him go. So you have many different guises in terms of the roles that you do and the job part of a coach … I don't know all the answers either. Also I believe that by using everyone's expertise and knowledge we can find those extra couple of answers that make a difference.

Former international softball coach Don Tricker says he personally obtained the confidence to try this approach because:

> **Don:** I just believed that it was what the athletes wanted. I just believed that it is right for us in terms of our stage of development. I believe it was the right way to go in terms of coaching and hadn't been convinced otherwise through my previous experience. It was these experiences that conditioned me to realise that this is the way forward.

The athlete-centred approach does not succeed simply because the coach applies it. It is important for you as a coach to continually develop and practise your empowering strategies (just as in any skill learning). In addition, your athletes (if they have never been coached in this way) must buy in to the approach before it can be successful. Gaining the support of some athletes may take time, along with effort in facilitating and nurturing.

Because the entire team may not catch on to the athlete-centred approach at the same time, the coach must cater for individual needs and nurture each athlete. In a sense, the coach has to continue to 'sell' the approach and enable athletes to understand the benefits they may gain through it. Lyn Gunson, international netball coach, and Don Tricker both tell of their experiences in winning athletes over:

Lyn: … the players, when they first experience how you are doing this, they think you are soft and confusing. It is a whole change of behaviour for them. At times, they don't cope with that very well. Sometimes you have to be autocratic, e.g. 'Stop doing that and do this', and then they feel comfortable. If you are really, genuinely trying to help them get into this whole scene, you do have to assist them through that process of change.

Don: When building the culture of the 2000 World Champion team I was probably a little bit [coach-centred]. This was because of the athletes' maturity level with an athlete-centred approach in developing team culture. In 2000 I met with the athlete leadership team and explained what I was looking for in terms of culture. The athlete leadership team then facilitated a meeting with the rest of the athletes. The outcome of the meeting was a perception that the athletes built the culture of the team, when in reality they delivered pretty much what I sent them away to do. In 2004 the process was very different, with the athletes taking complete ownership of developing the culture of the 2004 team. The captain of the side facilitated a meeting with the athletes; the outcome was the core components of the culture.

One of the most challenging yet rewarding aspects of this coaching approach lies in drawing on the art of coaching. This art includes the ability to read and understand your athletes, then help them by using great communication and coaching strategies that are suitable for the athlete in that particular situation. Lyn Gunson and Mark Norton elaborate on what it means for a coach to successfully apply the art of coaching through an athlete-centred approach:

Lyn: It is such an intertwining of observing what's happening, looking at the contextual relationships and then deciding is this the time and is this the way forward? Does this intervention need this type of information, process, experience, support … not just what to do but when to do it. That timing is incredibly difficult to teach. I experienced this when lecturing teachers in training. I have seen people [who'll] react to [a situation] or they'll get a piece of information and they'll react to it. Two days before or two days later they might react completely different to the same piece of information or activity, so it's matching up when that person is ready to take on that experience or information; in other words, are they ready to learn?

Mark: Sometimes a lot of what happens in the gym, it's hard to pick up on because I know that a lot of the time, when they are playing the game,

I am commenting and giving lots of feedback, talking about decisions they are making on the court and I am often focusing on the people who are immediately in the drills or in the game … I found a number of times a couple of things that are happening out the back were highlighted. Perhaps a rude gesture or a comment that somebody else made that was perhaps not living up to the values and needs to be addressed. That's quite good because [it is] highlight[ed] for me and then we address it at the end or there at the time.

Determining when to jump in and when to leave the athletes to make their own decisions is another important facet to the art of coaching. Judging the situation correctly takes time while the coach tries it out in different contexts, and it is not uncommon to make mistakes along the way. We learn best through trial and error.

As Ian Renshaw (see Chapter Eight) and Rick Humm (see Chapter Twelve) point out, one notably 'different' aspect of the athlete-centred approach is that the coach stands back and observes for longer, enabling the athletes to make decisions and organise themselves. If we, as coaches, jump in and try to take over, athletes learn very little. So, when observing and analysing your athletes, you might try counting for 5 to 10 seconds, or allowing several trials of the game, before providing feedback. Then, when providing feedback, jump in with a meaningful, open-ended question that enables athletes to think and become self-aware.

Clearly, then, when the coach interjects, it is important to ask the right question (see Chapter Thirteen). As most contributors to this book point out, it can be tempting to tell people what you know. That is certainly a temptation for a lot of coaches who have never tried an athlete-centred, humanistic approach. On many occasions, even when posing a question, they also answer it for the athletes. With reference to the ideas from this book, what outcomes are likely from this kind of coaching approach? How do athletes feel when their knowledge is undermined? Questioning is not easy but it is thoroughly worthwhile when athletes make informed decisions because of what they learn. Therefore, planning and practising are critical. In discussing their own processes of learning how to question in previous chapters, the athlete-centred coaches offer ideas that will be helpful to someone new to the approach.

As coaches, we continually look for better ways to enhance the performance of our athletes. Our search is for a process of learning and practising that will give that edge to us and our teams. So allow your athletes to interact and question. It will enhance your coaching approach and athlete performance even further, once they understand it, value it and become more self-aware and better decision makers.

In summary, the following are some key points for putting an athlete-centred approach into practice:

- Go for it. An athlete-centred, humanistic approach is fantastic, enhancing learning and the sport environment.
- Take small steps. You cannot be proficient immediately; it takes practice.
- Tell your athletes about the approach so they can begin to understand why you are using it.
- Add the approach to your current practice as another part of your coaching repertoire.
- Cater for athletes. Remember patience is a virtue.
- Observe your athletes for a period before interrupting. Often athletes are already self-aware and can fix errors on their own.
- Ask meaningful questions. Remember that learning this technique takes time, so practise it.
- Evaluate:
  - how your approach is working;
  - how athletes are responding to it; and
  - your questioning repertoire.
- Be careful not to overquestion and not to answer your own questions.
- Most of all, enjoy using the athlete-centred, humansitic approach—your athletes sure will.

Self-reflection: A Key to Developing and Improving Your Coaching

An important part of learning any approach is to reflect on your own coaching. Self-reflection is a particularly significant part of an athlete-centred approach (see Chapter Twelve), in which a core component is that coaches themselves take ownership of their own learning and decision making. Each coach should take responsibility for evaluating the way he or she coaches, the way the athletes respond and the general team environment.

Just as they expect athletes to practise to improve their performance (socially, emotionally, physically and intellectually), coaches need to practise their coaching performance. Extending this principle, we would expect that if coaches do not evaluate what they do, it is difficult for them to achieve a high standard of performance. A successful athlete-centred, humanistic coach should practise and understand the theoretical elements of sport and coaching as well as technical fundamentals of instruction. After gaining feedback and advice about their coaching, Mark Norton and Guy Evans report that they enjoyed the experience and that it helped with their self-analysis:

> **Mark:** Getting advice was great. It fast-tracked the learning process. It helped having someone chipping in the odd suggestion. Even just a

question like 'Why are you running this drill?' made me think about the benefits of the drill and that there may be a better way of doing it. It also meant there was another set of ideas looking for team dynamics and cohesiveness. So I think that it is certainly beneficial to have someone who is experienced and someone who knows what they are doing to give you suggestions along the way.

Guy: I think any coach would benefit from having an objective observer cast a critical eye on their coaching process. It's interesting to look back to the time of the study and reflect on how some things have changed. However, if there wasn't the opportunity for someone to come in, it wouldn't be possible for that type of retrospection.

Mike Ruddock also suggests that self-analysis is a way to continue improving and learning about coaching at both elite and junior levels:

Mike: I would say that personal reflection on what I am doing is good and bad, but we have started doing some work at [Worcester], where we give feedback to each other as a group and try to work with a buddy on that, although I [personally] haven't been that successful with that. The timing is a problem, it is the kind of thing that I should be putting in my diary and saying, 'Well, come and tell me about how you perceive my coaching and I will tell you how I perceive a job that you are doing.'

As part of his self-reflection, Guy Evans asked players to evaluate how things are going with the team, including their coaching. The feedback he received included the following:
- I learned fundamentals, identified weaknesses, coaches push us to develop.
- I have developed under [Guy] more mentally and emotionally than physically.
- I enjoy having [Guy] as our coach, sessions are of a high intensity and are enjoyable.
- We feel we are achieving our goals and we are on track.
- I have matured mentally, emotionally and physically.
- He dictates, but if someone has an idea he will listen and may take it in to consideration.

Don Tricker constantly analyses other coaches, which helps his self-reflective process:

Don: I can't watch sport now without trying to break it down into understanding what happened and more importantly why it happened.

Why were poor decisions being made, those sorts of thing ... This is in every sport. I go to watch rugby, I go to watch netball, I am not looking in terms of the result, in terms of who won or lost, I am looking at how it happened. I am looking at particular players and attempt[ing] to understand why they chose to execute a particular play that is clearly not part of the role or skill set.

Self-reflection empowers coaches to accept the challenge to become the best coaches they can be. Visual recording, a useful tool for self-reflection in teacher education, has gained great status in coach education as a means of self-training. As Christian Edwards comments on Guy's coaching:

> **Christian:** I also observed that Guy's perceived leadership behaviour and his actual leadership behaviour was different. It is common that coaches often fail to self-reflect on their coaching behaviour and the effect that these behaviours have on their athletes. A beneficial method to aid self-reflection is for the coach's match and training behaviour to be videoed, then the coach may self-reflect on adopted behaviours and the athlete's responses.

Many coaches already use visual recordings of their training sessions as an insightful means of observing their own coaching. Trying it for the first time can be daunting as many people, when confronting themselves on DVD, are surprised at their physical image. This confrontation is a barrier that you overcome by getting accustomed to and accepting mannerisms that only you notice. Thereafter you can objectively and realistically look at your coaching, how your athletes are empowered, and what impact your philosophy and methods are having. Figure 14.1 illustrates a model of how self-reflection works, whether or not you are using a DVD of your coaching to assist you in the process.

The five-step model shown in Figure 14.1 is designed for coaches to self-reflect by analysing, evaluating and modifying their coaching skills. In reflecting on what they do, coaches observe certain elements of the training session in a process of:

- collecting pertinent information;
- analysing the information;
- using the information to formulate goals and directions;
- designing a plan of action;
- implementing the plan of action;
- reassessing the outcome of the plan; and
- continually repeating the cycle.

The cycle continues for every aspect of coaching that a coach may wish to improve.

Figure 14.1: The Coaching Process—A Five-step Model for Self-reflection

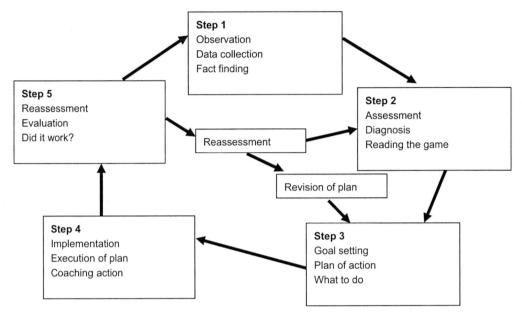

Source: J.R. Fairs (1987). The coaching process: Essence of coaching. *Sports Coach*, *11*(1), 19. Copyright 1987 by Australian Coaching Council. Reprinted with permission.

As highlighted consistently in this book, to enhance an athlete-centred , humanistic approach coaches frequently use questioning and problem solving as tools to develop their athletes. Coaches should also ask themselves reflective questions as an important element of their ongoing self-analysis. Reflective questions provide guidelines and information about your coaching. They can also be designed to suit your own development needs. You may find it useful to ask sport-specific personnel or another respected person to help develop reflective questions about a particular strategy that you wish to analyse or change. This person would also be a good source for advice about your coaching (provided he or she has nothing to do with your coaching career, as that person's objectivity may be lost, while you may find your coaching becomes unrealistic and unnatural).

Sample Questions: A Starting Point for Self-analysis

Below are some examples of very general reflective questions about coaching. Although not specific to individual needs, they may be a starting point for your self-analysis (using your DVD recording to answer each question):

1. What did you learn about your coaching? and about your management?
2. What did you learn about the athletes?
3. What did athletes learn about themselves?

4. What effects did your coaching have on the athletes? Discuss benefits and barriers.
5. How can the athletes rectify any barriers discussed? How can you rectify any barriers discussed?
6. How do you think the session could be improved?
7. Do you think you can solve any identified coaching difficulties by yourself?
8. How do you plan to follow up in the next sessions?
9. How was this session relevant or transferable to other aspects of the athletes' lives?
10. What did you learn about yourself?
11. Describe in detail one significant event that happened during your lesson. It may be significant because it was something that excited you, bothered you, made you rethink your intentions/beliefs, or made you realise that your intentions/beliefs were sound.

Sample Questions: A Starting Point for Reflecting on Your Athlete-centred Approach

The next set of general reflective questions may help to get you started in looking at how you focus on being athlete-centred (again, while referring to the DVD from the training session):
1. How was the session designed to gain input from the athletes? Analyse your planned questions.
2. Did athletes have input to training? If so, how; if not, why not?
3. Reflect on your session by answering these questions:
    (a) What did you like best about the session?
    (b) What did you like least about the session?
    (c) How would you improve the session plan?
    (d) What did the athlete(s) learn?
4. Analyse your line of questioning. Did it encourage athletes' learning? Were the questions clear? Were you flexible in your ability to ask purposeful questions?
5. Explain the general motivational climate of the session.
6. How well did you plan for different ability levels?
7. How well did you cater to athlete-centred learning? Explain.
8. How did athletes respond to being able to have input? Give examples.
9. Explain how this training session nurtured the holistic needs of the athletes.
10. Are athletes' needs identified and how do you encourage independent development?

Sample Questions: A Starting Point for Reflecting on Your Use of Teaching Games for Understanding

As Chapter Eight discusses, many athlete-centred coaches make use of TGfU. The following reflective questions may help you to analyse how you use TGfU in your training session:

1. Discuss how this session was designed to cater for TGfU.
2. Analyse the games you provided. How can they be improved?
3. Analyse the purposefulness of the games.
4. How did athletes respond to the TGfU session?
5. Explain the social benefits and/or challenges of applying TGfU in this session.
6. Analyse the enjoyment and motivation of the athletes participating in this session.
7. Were you happy with the amount of time that the athletes were able to practise for the session? Why or why not?
8. Comment on how the learning environment was designed for athletes to explore the task constraints and find solutions to match their needs.
9. Explain how the learning environment was realistic or authentic.

Sample Questions: A Starting Point for Reflecting on Your Questioning

Chapter Thirteen focuses on asking meaningful questions. Here are some questions that will help you reflect on your questioning of your athletes (together with your DVD recording):

1. How clear and coherent were the questions that you asked your athletes?
2. When asking questions, did you have the attention of all the athletes?
3. Analyse the responses to the questions. Who answered them? Did they give the answers that you expected? How well did you probe?
4. How well did you listen and accept athlete responses?
5. Did learning occur? Explain your answer.
6. List the questions that you asked during the session. How many were high-order questions and how many were low-order questions? Was the ratio effective? Why or why not?
7. Discuss any thinking that occurred (or did not occur) after you asked high-order questions.
8. Were the questions meaningful to the purpose of the training session? Explain.
9. Were you flexible in accepting and exploring athletes' responses?
10. How well did you encourage your athletes to reflect and process what they learned? Explain.

To enhance your use of visual recordings to analyse coaching, show the DVD to a colleague, coach, teacher or any other respected person and ask for feedback. It is an advantage if this person comes from a similar philosophical belief so that he or she can help to analyse how you are using a particular empowering approach. The feedback enhances your learning, verifying what areas you need to develop, and is ultimately beneficial to the athletes. Your colleagues will also gain a lot from observing and analysing you; in this way, the learning process spreads throughout the coaching world. Finally, coaches should obtain positive feedback both from other people and from themselves. Identify your positive strategies and pat yourself on the back as much as you try to improve yourself.

Team Culture

After discussing the ways to put an athlete-centred approach into action, we believe that it is important to reiterate that, as each coach has pointed out in this book, without any focus on team culture, the athletes have little chance for real success. Team culture is basically the environment that the athletes, coach and manager create. It defines the purpose of the team, establishing a mutual direction so that everyone is on the same wavelength. Team culture is based on standards and values that direct how things are done. The way a team behaves on and off the field or court is a reflection on the team culture (Hadfield, 2002).

Don Tricker emphasises that each individual is important. From this principle, it follows that coaches need to understand each individual and draw all the individuals in the team together to establish a quality team environment:

> **Don:** ... the common denominator in sport is that it is played by individuals, each with different needs and expectations. Therefore, when building teams, it all comes down to ensuring that individual expectations are satisfied when developing the core components of the team culture. The components include ownership of a shared vision or common purpose, clearly defined values, standards and role definitions.

While recognising individual differences, we usually have the added challenge of finding a way to encourage these individuals to form a team. Bringing a group of athletes together does not automatically create a harmonious team (Kidman and Hanrahan, 2004). In a quality team culture, the athletes work together in pursuit of the group's goals or objectives. Creating this team culture is a process; it does not just happen. Coaches must focus on it and prepare the athletes for it.

Gareth Jones (see Chapter Six) advocates that every person on the team needs individual roles and responsibilities as a way of helping the team to run smoothly. If a quality team culture is to be created, athletes need to feel that they have ownership of the team. If they feel they have nothing to contribute to the team, then they will not feel they are a part of it, which in turn will detract from team culture. Additionally each member of the team should be acquainted with the roles and responsibilities of other members and appreciate their importance.

One of the roles that each athlete should have is that of a leader. Shared leadership has been a theme with every coach profiled in this book. Mark Norton puts his beliefs about shared leadership into practice in this way:

> **Mark:** Within the overall squad, we created smaller groups, which were responsible for different aspects that we were trying to do. I empowered each student to have some leadership or have some responsibility. Without responsibility, you can't learn how to use it, learn how to develop.

In team sports, role rotation during training has been cited as a key way to develop empathy towards teammates and understanding of their individual responsibilities to the team. Playing other positions in this way can help athletes understand the demands on their teammates. Alternatively, athletes may be given the task of performing team drills with one position removed, which highlights the importance of that position (Kidman and Hanrahan, 2004).

One very important aspect of a quality team culture is trust. Individuals who trust each other are more likely to be open with their feelings, ideas and information, which will enhance communication. The day-to-day behaviour of athletes has a powerful impact on the establishment of trust. Coaches can also enhance trust by allowing and encouraging athletes to become involved in decisions that affect the team and them personally, such as decisions about team direction, training times, drills and/or tactics, and thus giving athletes a sense of ownership of the team. Another way of strengthening a sense of ownership is to encourage them to choose how they will be distinct from other teams (Kidman and Hanrahan, 2004).

With this trust come the seven components of team culture through developing and maintaining a quality team environment that Gareth Jones (see Chapter Six) formulated: developing and maintaining a quality team environment: team vision; shared values and behaviours; clear roles and responsibilities; team cohesion; respect and integrity; effective communication; and social support. Guy Evans found great benefit for his team arising from the values and process of setting values and strategies to live them by:

> **Guy:** ... values are required to underpin the behaviour necessary to achieve the goals. The importance of establishing values, in my eyes, is for the purpose of underpinning and supporting the team's goals with a collective, shared point of reference for what our team hopes to incarnate.

What makes a mere group of people a team is both a shared vision and interdependency, but establishing goals alone is not enough. Constructing a list of values acts almost as an informal morals and beliefs system, with the hope that the behaviour exhibited in our particular social world of basketball has a domino effect on how we conduct ourselves when not directly in the presence of the team. It is desired that their basketball experience is simply a microcosm for their actions in wider society.

Using team-building activities is a practice mentioned by a couple of coaches in this book. The lesson from their comments is that it is important to carefully think through the purpose and nature of those activities. It is easy to organise a ropes course, run by someone else, or to go through an obstacle course at the local army base. However, any effective team-building activity will also have a clear purpose. Sometimes the purpose is to get to know each other better; sometimes it is to perform an activity in which each team member has a responsibility. Fundamentally, each team should evaluate their vision statement and gear any team-building activity towards teaching or promoting that vision.

A Process of Developing a Team Culture

A step-by-step method of creating a quality team culture is presented here as a useful guide for coaches interested in putting an athlete-centred approach into practice. It focuses on establishing the team's overall mission, in which the athletes are involved in making decisions about and developing the vision and values, and the coach's role is to facilitate the process. Once created, the values and strategies that are established must be taught, nurtured and practised for the team culture to work. Many companies and teams have been caught out because they hang up the poster or sign announcing their vision and key values and then forget about it.

The following steps, then, represent one approach to creating a quality team culture, which was successful with Mark Norton's volleyball team. (For the full story of the process, see Chapter Ten.) It is important to note that many other different strategies could be used for the same purpose; this is just one way that worked:

Step 1: Establish the goals and dream goals for the season. As Mike Chu (c. 2004) says, 'A team without a vision or team goals is like a team without a rudder.' It is useful to establish these goals by asking athletes meaningful questions. Mark's approach was to ask, 'If you were at the end-of-season dinner and had to make a speech and talk to everyone about the sort of team that we are, what would be the things that you would liked to be able to say?' An example of such a dream goal might be to win the local championships or place in top 10 at Nationals.

Step 2: Establish the strategy to meet the goals. Once goals are established, ask, 'How do we do these things?' This step is the start to developing the actual values. But, first, it is important to have an idea of what the team needs to do to be able to meet the vision. For example, as a way to achieve the dream goal of winning a local championship, the team might choose to be the most exciting team to watch.

Step 3: Formulate the values. Values are non-negotiable rules with which the team will live. Some examples are respect, unity and honesty. In this step, Mark gave a list of values to the athletes, and then had them pick six and define each one. The meaning of the values must be interpreted in the same way by everyone. A good place to start the process of choosing values is with the 30 values listed by Jeff Janssen (2002).

Step 4: Develop strategies to meet the values. The purpose of these strategies is to set up some action so that the team can live by the values. An example might be, 'Take care of things outside the sport so we can enjoy our sport more'.

Step 5: Create a single mission statement. This statement serves as a reminder to the athletes of their campaign—it is what they decide as a team to follow. For example, 'Brothers in Arms' might refer to the unity and respect for each other, the commitment to the team.

Step 6: Find a symbol to represent the whole mission. An example from the volleyball team was a gluestick, which symbolised 'Binding together to be better' (their mission statement). The New Zealand women's hockey team carried around laminated cards emblazoned with the team values.

Step 7: Practise and reinforce the values.

After formulating the vision, values and strategies, some teams confirm their commitment to the team's mission through some formal method of agreement, such as a poster, a card, a song or even a certain handshake. The form of agreement can also continue to remind athletes of their commitment and strengthen the team bond.

There are many other examples of ways to set up the vision and values for a team. The Internet is one useful source (see, for example, Mike Chu at www.nzrugby.com). Whatever process you choose to follow, it is important to revisit and practise the vision and values regularly once they are established, rather than leaving them to hide in the cupboard. As Mark Norton has shown, the process of establishing the team mission and then monitoring it is a key to developing a quality team culture and creating that team spirit (wairua) in your team.

Continuing Coach Development

As presented above, self-reflective analysis is a means of learning about and improving an athlete-centred, humansitic approach in coaching. An advantage of using visual recording as a tool in this process is that it is easy to apply. It does take time to sit down and analyse these DVDs, but once coaches become accustomed to using DVDs, they can participate in a self-directed training approach when it suits to their own needs and time.

An Example of Self-reflective Analysis

The following outline of a self-reflective analysis process can aid in reviewing your coaching and targeting parts of your coaching you might want to improve.

> **Step 1**: Visually record a training session and conduct a self-reflective analysis of your coaching. Identify one or two parts of your coaching you want to change or improve. Give the DVD to a critical friend and gather feedback about your coaching. Tell the friend your philosophy and what you are intending to focus on. It is important that this critical friend acts as a sounding board rather than an adviser. You need to feel empowered with the process, meaning that it is you who decides what to change, for your reasons.

> **Step 2**: Develop a plan of action for changing or improving the parts you have identified. Ask yourself, 'How can I design a method to change/improve this part of my coaching?' You can get relevant reflective questions from a critical friend, another respected individual, or written resources (like this book or others that are in the library).

> **Step 3**: You will need several training sessions to work on improving each of the parts you identified. Use the first few training sessions to practise these parts. After practising, visually record another training session. Ensure you have prepared some reflective questions to help in the self-reflective analysis of this DVD.

> **Step 4**: Repeat the above process to focus on other parts of your coaching or to revisit parts you may have identified in the first process. Remember you can only work on one or two matters at a time, and it takes a long time master or get where you want it to be with some strategies (Kidman and Hanrahan, 2004).

Self-reflective analysis is one method that will help you to continue developing as a coach. Another way to continue developing as a coach is to do research. Research does not mean having to understand academic language and gobbledegook. What it does mean is read books, search the Internet, network with coaches, observe other coaches who use an athlete-centred approach and attend conferences. Asking athletes can also help in your research.

Gathering Information and Continuing to Learn

In some countries and some sport cultures, people do not communicate with the 'enemy' for fear of giving away secrets about team strategies. This attitude seems absurd, given that one of the main reasons we coach (at least from an athlete-centred, humanistic perspective) is to develop athletes. To develop philosophical beliefs, we need to talk with other people, including coaches, parents, administrators, athletes and educators.

By talking with other people who have insights from their own experience of what has and has not worked, we may gather ideas that may help individuals and teams. Perhaps you have a specific problem in designing a game that enhances an old drill in a particular sport, so ask another coach for advice. You are not admitting defeat; you are demonstrating a desire to search for knowledge or new methods and to help athletes learn. It cannot hurt to ask. The worst that can happen is for someone to say, 'No'. All coaches profiled in this book are always looking for advice to improve their coaching. A commonality of an athlete-centred, humanistic approach seems to be that such coaches admit to still needing to learn, so they continually search for better ways. Other coaches, parents and administrators have some great ideas. Ask anyone; everyone has an opinion, especially in sport.

Most athletes may have experienced several different coaches. Ask them for their opinion—and in the process apply a key element of an athlete-centred, humanistic approach. Mike Ruddock found that gaining a written evaluation from players is extremely useful to his coaching development. The player evaluations pointed out positives and negatives of the season, information the coaches can use to better their coaching for the next season. Through an athlete-centred approach, coaches are constantly asking for player feedback, reading them and interpreting their ideas and values. Through an athlete-centred approach, you can make a natural evaluation from the players when they answer questions and you read them, which is useful to everything that occurs in the sporting environment.

Educators (teachers, university lecturers, coach educators) can offer great advice and information. Although some coaches may see educators as too academic or out of their league, there are many educators who understand coaching as they have been there. Educators are able to benefit from keeping up to date with current research and many put these new strategies into practice. This perspective is where empowerment came from: coaches who have achieved great success, but realised that through an empowerment approach they can enable greater success and fulfilment among their athletes. Coaches should be empowered to enhance their coaching by having the 'nous' to search for better approaches.

Some speak of a gap between educators and coaches but, in reality, many of us are trying to get rid of this perceived gap. Educators and coaches learn from each other; educators and coaches learn from athletes (and students). The athletes are the ones to benefit from this sharing of ideas. Through this sharing, coaches can provide terrific learning experiences that enhance athletes' lifestyles, in which sport is a means to an end, rather than the end. No one has all the answers, but through conversations and observations we can learn from each other. Among the coaches interviewed for this book, a common characteristic is their belief that they are still learning. Their ego does not get in the way; rather, the athletes are truly more important than the sport.

Recommendations for the Future

The following questions are posed to guide the future study and development of an athlete-centred, humanistic coaching approach, and should help formulate an agenda for the future.

1. How do we develop 'artful' coaches—as decision makers themselves—in establishing the essence of the coaching act/responsibility/task?
2. Should coaching behaviour/leadership concern itself with full development (i.e. intellectual, physical, mental, social, emotional) of all athletes, regardless of level of competition (recreational, developmental, youth league, high school, collegiate or professional)?
3. How do we refocus the institution of sport to further emphasise the growth and development (both personal and professional) of all who are involved in sport (coach, athletes and administrators)?
4. How do we reframe/redesign coach development to create an 'athlete-centred coach development programme'? Specifically, coach development programmes must be redesigned to model those leadership/coaching behaviours that the programme would like coaches to demonstrate. (How will we design programmes that include instructors who, in their developmental programmes, treat the coaches as they would have the coaches treat their athletes—in a humanistic, individualised manner?)
5. How do we ensure that induction/development programmes for novice coaches at all levels include humanistic, athlete-centred strategies?
6. How do we continue to disseminate the benefits of TGfU in theory and practice, and encourage a constraints-led approach to skill acquisition-like approaches (e.g. games) as they relate to athlete-centred approaches and its desired outcomes?

7. How do we prepare coaches to be more aware of the potential physical and mental dangers of specialisation, year-round, 12 month training and/or competitive programmes (e.g. travel teams, all-stars)?

8. How do we address the issues related to parental involvement in the sport experiences of their children?

9. A major issue is how do we educate parents regarding the need for children to experience play without parental/adult supervision? How do we keep parents informed of the miniscule odds of their child obtaining a scholarship or developing into a professional athlete or the brevity of the length of a professional athlete's professional career? How do sincere coaches and other professionals disseminate such information without discouraging both athletes and parents?

10. How do we re-centre the sport experience on fun? On free play? On sport organised and directed by the athletes themselves? (i.e. without adult intervention). The Internet site Give Us Back Our Game (www.giveusbackourgame.co.uk) (also see Chapter Seven) has begun to address this.

11. We need to continue and increase our study ethnographically (i.e. in a non-behavioural fashion) into the micro-political aspects of the coaching endeavour. How do coaches respond to the various publics that they serve and yet maintain good relationships with their athletes? How do coaches become aware of political issues that harm children and have the ability to overcome those issues for the betterment of their athletes? How does a coach share power with athletes and yet maintain their respect, without a feeling of loss of face and respect?

12. How can the coaching profession respond to the increasing number of athletes who drop out of the sport experience at an early age? Not only does this drop-out rate reduce the quality of the athletes who continue on in the sport experience, but it also strongly relates to the world wide increase in the levels of obesity among our youth.

13. How can coaches be trained to have empathy, to be able to read their athletes, and those around them to communicate more effectively to meet their needs?

As you can see from the listed questions, there is much research to be done, much educating and reminding the public of the main reasons why athletes participate in sport. There is still much to be done and accepted to return to the educational intent of sport and focus on the development of athletes, both as people and as performers. One of the highlights of producing this second edition has been discovering the number of authors who want to deliver a message and continue on the pathway to make sport more humanistic and athlete-centred. However, the authors in this book don't have the answers; they simply offer some suggestions. The real answers depend on the athletes' stage of development, their interest, the environment that is given and the ability for society in general to consider the original intent of sport.

Conclusion

It has been an intention of this book to inform and teach coaches about an athlete-centred approach, including how athletes learn and enjoy their sport. Another goal has been to empower coaches themselves to increase their knowledge, practise more, reflect and analyse, and continue to improve in their own time and using their own methods. Coaches should provide athletes with choice and control, both of which are offered through this book. Take bits from it that you think will work, and skip the bits that you have trouble with. The previous chapters have illustrated some successes, but this book does not have all the answers. It simply shares ideas so that coaches can take the ones that suit their philosophy and purpose and apply them to their sport.

In this chapter, you have been encouraged to obtain feedback. You should also provide feedback to other coaches. Based on your thinking and understanding and all the research that you have completed by reading through this book and other resources, you can offer valuable information to aid other coaches in their development. Coaches should serve as critical friends who can provide sound advice and at the same time identify the positive aspects of others' coaching.

Those who endeavour to be a thinking, proactive coach, and who take advantages of opportunities to improve their athletes' performance, enjoyment and lifestyle, will be the most successful coaches. These coaches will make a difference to sport and athlete development. An athlete-centred, humanistic coaching approach encourages a holistic learning environment in which athletes can learn about life and about sport.

Treat people as if they were what they ought to be and you help them to become what they are capable of being. - Johann Wolfgang Von Goethe

References

Chu, M. (c. 2004). *High performance with Mike Chu*. Retrieved on 11 October 2004 from www.nzrugbynet.com/NZRFU/Coaching+Info/gameplanRUGBY/gameplan+Rugby

Fairs, J.R. (1987). The coaching process: essence of coaching. *Sports Coach, 11*(1), 19.

Farrey, T. (2008). *Game On: The all-American race to make champions of our children*. USA: ESPN.

Hadfield, D.C. (2002). Developing team leaders in rugby. *Rugby Football Union Technical Journal*. Retrieved on 7 October 2002 from http://www.rfu.com/pdfs/technical-journal/Developing_leaders_captains.pdf

Janssen, J. (2002). *Championship Team Building*. Cary, NC: Winning the Mental Game.

Kidman, L. & Hanrahan, S. (2004). *The Coaching Process: A practical guide to improving your effectiveness* (2nd ed.). Palmerston North: Dunmore.

About the Contributing Authors

Lynn Kidman is a coach educator. She currently works at Auckland University of Technology (AUT) in New Zealand as a lecturer in Sports Coaching. Lynn has been a Senior Advisor to Sport Recreation New Zealand (SPARC) to coordinate the writing and implementation of a coach development system where an athlete-centred coaching is the underpinning philosophy. Lynn is the author/editor of *Athlete-centred Coaching: Developing inspired and inspiring people, Developing Decision Makers: An empowerment approach to coaching* and co-author of *The Coaching Process*. Lynn has coached many teams, mostly secondary school age, in the sports of basketball, swimming, softball, and volleyball. Lynn and Bob have two children, Matthew and Simon and a new grandchild Isabelle.

Bennett J. Lombardo is a professor of Health and Physical Education at Rhode Island College. He was a three sport athlete at Queens College in New York City and has coached several sports at several levels of competition. After completing his doctoral studies at Boston University with Dr. John Cheffers, he has focused his professional endeavours on the specific leadership and interactive behaviours of both teachers and coaches. The father of John and Susan, he currently resides in Warwick, Rhode Island with his wife Angela.

Gareth Jones is a Principal Lecturer in the Institute of Sport and Exercise Science at the University of Worcester, England. His research interests include team cohesion, group dynamics and performance analysis. Specific projects include 'The role of perceived social loafing in collective efficacy and performance in sports teams'. Gareth has coached many sport teams and his main areas of expertise are in coaching football and rugby union. Any correspondence with Gareth, please contact g.jones@ worc.ac.uk

Paul Cooper is a grassroots football coach who founded the children's football initiative *Give Us Back Our Game* with Rick Fenoglio in 2006. He has written two books, 'Learning Through Play (small sided games) 2008' and a humorous book on growing up playing football in the street called 'Chapped Legs and Punctured Balls' 2009. He writes a regular column for Soccer Coaching International and holds coaching workshops across the UK and other countries. Paul also works part time at a school as an Inclusion Support Worker and has used football as a way to engage teenagers there. He is married to Gill and has two children, both now in their twenties. He lives in Gloucestershire, England where he drinks copious amounts of tea and eats far too many biscuits.

> Good character is more to be praised than outstanding talent. Most talents are, to some extent, a gift. Good character, by contrast, is not given to us. We have to build it piece by piece-by thought, choice, courage and determination.
> - John Luther

Ian Renshaw is a Senior Lecturer in the School of Human Movement Studies at Queensland University of Technology; Brisbane, Australia and is currently working as a skill acquisition consultant with Cricket Australia. His research interest is in the coordination and control of human movement, and skill acquisition, in particular viewing human movement systems as belonging to a class of nonlinear dynamical systems. His research examines how the fundamental relationship between perception and action supports elite and developing sport performance. In recent years this research effort has been directed towards establishing a Constraints-based framework for motor learning. The development of a theory of Nonlinear Pedagogy for coaching and teaching is a natural consequence of these efforts. Ian's passion is cricket and he has coached junior teams for over 20 years. Any correspondence with Ian, please contact i.renshaw@qut.edu.au

Christian Edwards is a lecturer in Sports Coaching Science at the University of Worcester. His teaching, research and coaching interest focuses on interlinking mental skills into the coaching process. Christian is particularly interested in the methods coaches can use to incorporate the use of mental skills. He started to forge this link between mental skills and coaching practice during his undergraduate studies at Aberystywth University which he then progressed to research during his postgraduate studies at the University of Worcester. In 2009 he graduated from the University of Worcester with a MSc in Sports Coaching Science, and a Post graduate Teaching Certificate in Higher Education. He is a rugby union player and currently competes at club level. Christian has coached many youth teams in the sports of rugby union and field hockey.

Rick Humm is an avid student of athlete learning. He continues to be an active coach with rugby players and draws on his experience with a variety of sport in the USA including baseball, basketball, football, golf, sailing, swimming and volleyball. His rugby coaching focus began with collegiate rugby working with both men's and women's teams. Humm has coached representative teams in the United States at local, regional and national levels. In addition, Humm led USA Rugby's coach development programs for 10 years aligning its approach with the International Rugby Board and UK Sport licensing programs. He is a licensed trainer and educator with the iRB, USA Rugby and the Positive Coaching Alliance. Rick lives in California with his wife Veronica Ferguson and holds an advanced degree in physical education.

Cowardice asks the question, is it safe? Expediency asks the question, is it politic? Vanity asks the question, is it popular? But conscience asks the question, Is it right? And there comes a time when one must take a position that is neither safe, nor politic, nor popular, but he must take it because his conscience tells him it is right... - Martin Luther